100 Years of Nobel Prizes

$18.95

100 Years of Nobel Prizes

Baruch Aba Shalev

THE AMERICAS GROUP
9200 Sunset Blvd., Suite 404
Los Angeles, CA 90069 USA

© Baruch Aba Shalev
All rights reserved. 2002

FIRST EDITION
1st Printing—August 2002
2nd Printing—November 2002
SECOND EDITION
1st Printing—June 2003
THIRD EDITION
1st Printing—May 2005
2nd Printing— October 2007

No part of this book may be transmitted, reproduced, or utilized in any form or by any means, electronic or mechanical, including photocopying, recording, or by any information storage and retrieval system, without the written permission of the author who may be contacted through the publishers at the street or EMail address and/or telephone/fax numbers below.

The Americas Group
654 N. Sepulveda Blvd., Suite 1
Los Angeles, California 90049-2070
U.S.A.
☎   + (1) 310 476 6374
FX   + (1) 310 471 3276
EM   hrmg@aol.com
WWW   AMERICASGROUP.COM

ISBN:
0-935047-37-9
Library of Congress Cataloging-in-Publication Data

Shalev, Baruch Aba, 1936-

   100 years of Nobel prizes / Baruch Aba Shalev.--1st ed.
     p. cm.
   ISBN 0-935047-37-9 (alk. paper)
   Includes bibliographical references and index.
   1. Nobel Prizes--History. 2. Nobel Prizes--Evaluation. 3. Nobel Prizes--Statistics.
   I. Title: One hundred years of Nobel prizes. II. Title

AS911 .N9 S47 2002
001.4'4--dc21   2002038538

Printed in the United States of America by
Fidlar Doubleday, Portage, Michigan 49002

TABLE OF CONTENTS

Foreword to Third Edition (with Listing of 2001-2004 Laureates)	i-viii
Introduction	7
Statistical Analysis	10
Number of Nobel Prize Winners by Category and Gender	11
Nationality of Nobel Prize Winners	12
Nationality of Nobel Prize Winners—Population and Index	15
Table of Total Number of Nobel Prize Winners—By Nationality	17
Nationality of Nobel Prize Winners—Major Democratic Countries	20
Distribution of Nobel Prizes—By Country, Categories and Years	22
Leading Institutions Where Nobel Prize Winners were Educated	37
Universities/Institutes Whose Researchers Have Received Nobel Prizes	39
Age at Publication and the Interval to Winning the Nobel Prize	41
Age of Nobel Prize Winners	44
Women As Winners of the Nobel Prize During the First 100 Years	46
Collaboration and Simultaneous Work Leading to Nobel Prizes	50
Other Awards Earned by Nobel Prize Winners Between 1901 and 2000	53
Academic Degrees of Nobel Prize Winners Between 1900 and 2000	55
Religion of Nobel Prize Winners	57
Birth Dates of Laureates by Seasons and Astrological Signs	62
Commentary	65
Luck, Genius, and Environment	66
Major Innovations of Nobel Prize Laureates Between 1901 and 2000	73
Nobel Prizes Within Families	77
Winners of More than One Nobel Prize—or Rejecting It	78
Brain Migration	81
Marriages, Divorces, and Childless Instances of Laureates	90
Nobel Laureates Imprisoned or Killed	91
Have the Goals of Alfred Nobel Been Fulfilled in the Past 100 Years?	94
Summary and Conclusions	99
Appendix	107
List of Nobel Prize Winners in Chemistry	108
List of Nobel Prize Winners in Physiology or Medicine	114
List of Nobel Prize Winners in Physics	120
List of Nobel Prize Winners in Economics	126
List of Nobel Prize Winners in Literature	128
List of Nobel Prize Winners in Peace	133
Selected Bibliography	138
Index	139
About Author/Note on CD Rom	148

Imagination is more important than knowledge. Knowledge is limited, imagination embraces the world, stimulating progress, giving birth to evolution.

Albert Einstein

ACKNOWLEDGEMENTS

While the work of a writer or researcher is often a solitary undertaking, the publication of his effort is clearly a collaborative enterprise. No one has become more aware of this fact than I. It took at team of editorial and administrative talent at The Americas Group in the United States to turn my statistical analysis of the first 100 years of Nobel prize-winners into a commercially-attractive book. The team was led by Godfrey Harris, an author of some 30 books in his own right, who designed, edited, and supervised this project at every stage of its development; he was assisted by Desiree Vidal, who oversaw the layout and typography, and Penelope Morensen, who managed the administrative details. In Israel, Dr. Hanoch Pasternak, a dear friend, offered valuable comments, and my wife, Rina Shalev, provided the encouragement that made every question answerable and every obstacle manageable.

Baruch Aba Shalev

FOREWORD TO THE THIRD EDITION

This Third Edition of *100 Years of Nobel Prizes* not only brings the list of recipients of the world's most famous prize up-to-date, but it incorporates their particular contributions into our statistical compilations. This book now represents the single most current information on the world's most prestigious intellectual award. Equally important, we have again looked at the same key question of previous editions: Have the patterns in Nobel awards discerned between 1901 and 2000 manifested themselves in the awards given over the last four years? It appears that they indeed follow previous trends with a few changes noted below.

1. During the 2001 to 2004 period, a total of 51 individuals received Nobel Prizes: 12 in Physics; 11 in Chemistry; 10 in Medicine; 9 in Economics; 5 in Peace; and 4 in Literature. This distribution is similar to the ratios found in previous years, as the science categories always require more collaborative effort than the others. (For further discussion of this point, see pages vii-viii, 11, and 50-52).

2. The total number of Nobel Prize laureates between 1901 and 2004 is now 770. Medicine (Physiology or Medicine)—182 awards; Physics—174; Chemistry—146; Peace—112; Literature—101. Because Nobel Prizes in Economics were initiated in 1969, the number of laureates now totals only 55 (see page 11).

3. In the 2001 to 2004 period, the share of prizes those awarded to U.S. residents increased to about 55%, while Europe's share decreased—partly due to emigration. Perhaps American Laureate Eric Cornell (Physics 2001) expressed the reason most movingly: "I have been fortunate to live in a society that values [and supports] scientific research." The United Kingdom remained in second place with nearly 16% of the laureates—a drop, nevertheless, of some 5% from previous years. Together, however, the old World War II Atlantic Alliance earned more than 71% of the Nobel Prizes awarded in the 2001-2004 period. (See pages vii-viii, 12-36).

4. Only one woman (E. Shirin) was awarded a Nobel Prize in the 2001 to 2003 period—a statistically insignificant 2.6% of the awards. The woeful trend of the previous 100 years—where only 4% of the awards have gone to women —continued. But in 2004 there was a change. Three women won Nobel Prizes (B. Linda in Medicine, W. Maathai in Peace, and E. Jelinek in Literature)— nearly 25% of the 2004 awards. "This is a change in the right direction," admitted Bengt Samuelsson, chairman of the board of the Nobel Foundation. As an example of the trend, Nobel Peace prizes for the last two years were awarded to women: Ebadi Shirin in 2003, the first Muslim woman to win a Nobel Prize, for advancing human rights and promoting nonviolent reform in Islamic countries and Wangari Maathai, the first black woman from Africa to win a Nobel Prize (2004) for promoting

FORWORD TO THIRD EDITION

ecology, democracy, women's rights and peace. (For further discussion of women and Nobel prizes, see pages vii-viii, 11, and 46-49).

5. Again, luck or destiny seems to have played an important roll in the Nobel Prize awards. Eric A. Cornell (Physics, 2001) was uncertain whether to continue with physics at college: "I began to worry that my future is choosing me instead of the other way around." Jimmy Carter (Peace, 2002) may have had destiny on his side as well. His father's death forced him to give up his naval career to manage the family business. This led him into local politics, eventually rising to become the governor of Georgia, and then president of the United States. Chance events have been reported by many laureates during the Nobel's first 100 years. (Please see pages 66-70).

6. Just as in the first 100 years, most laureates selected during the 2001 to 2004 period received their Nobel Prize many years after their major contributions had been recognized. Note the case of Jimmy Carter. As the architect of the successful peace treaty between Israel and Egypt, he was ignored while Menachem Begin of Israel and Anwar El-Sadat of Egypt were awarded the Nobel Peace Prize in 1978. Geir Lundestad, secretary of the Nobel Peace committee, explained: "Nobody nominated him in time." Perhaps, but subsequent nominations did not lead to a prize either. Then in 2002—24 years after his historic contribution—he won over 156 nominees for the totality of his work as a global peacemaker and humanitarian. Similar time gaps appear in other Nobel prizes. The scientific contributions of the Chemistry laureates of 2004 occurred between 1976 and 1981, some 23 years before the importance of their contribution was acknowledged by the Nobel committee. Israeli-born Daniel Kahaneman and the late Amos Tversky wrote a paper for *Science* in 1981 showing how psychological insights affected economic behavior. That work eventually led to the 2002 Nobel Prize in Economics. Although the committee cited Tversky for his contribution, his death in 1996 prevented him from having his name attached to the award. (For cases of previous delays during first 100 years, see pages 41-43, 102.)

7. During the first 100 years of Nobel prizes, many laureates suffered from various stressful conditions during the early years of their lives. This, in turn, led to their early maturation. The winner of the Literature award for 2002, Imre Kert'sz, is a typical example. He was sent from Hungary to Auschwitz and then Buchenwald at the age of 13. His writings have been rooted in his Holocaust experiences. Koichi Tanaka (Chemistry, 2002) lost his mother when he was a baby and his father was unable to raise him; Aaron Ciechanover (Chemistry, 2004) also lost his parents when he was a young boy. (See also page 103.)

8. The past 100 years have shown that about 50% of Nobel Prizes were awarded to research associated with just 18 universities, a tiny fraction of the institutions of higher learning in the world. In general, the same trend held true during the 2001 to 2004 period. Yet, Harvard University—the top

of the list of Nobel institutions during the first 100 years—was unable to add a single award during the last four years. (See pages vii-viii, 39-40).

9. Just one totalitarian country out of 39 winning nations—a tiny 2.6%—could claim a Nobel Prize during 2001- 2004. In fact, Ebadi Shirin's win in 2003 could only have come *because* she was trying to improve human rights in Iran. The dominance of democratic societies in the last four years continues the previous 100-year trend: from winning 65% of the Literature awards to about 90% in the scientific categories. Free societies clearly offer the kind of intellectual atmosphere that seems an important contributor to Nobel-level work. (See pages vii-viii, 20-21).

10. The relatively high ratio of Jewish laureates continued during the years 2001 to 2004. Eleven out of 51 laureates (22%) were Jewish: S. Brenner, R. Horvitz, I. Kerts'z, D. Kahaneman, V. Ginzburg, A. Ciechanover, A. Hershko, I. Rose. D. Gross, D. Politizer, and E. Jelinek. This continues the historic trend that more than 20% of laureates are Jewish. This statistic continues to be particularly striking given the fact that the Jewish population comprises only 13 million people, a mere 0.2% of the world's population. To make the point even more relevant, in 2004 Jews received as many Nobel Prizes as Muslims had in the entire 104-year-history of Nobel Prizes despite the fact that Muslims comprise 20% (1.4 billion) of the world's population. Moreover, the state of Israel has been credited with more Nobel Prize awards than all the Islamic states put together. Do Jews have a special gene pool that leads toward intellectual success? Or is it fair to say that their intellectual endeavors are supported by favorable traditions and environments? (See pages vii-viii and more information on pages 57-61.)

11. All living laureates were invited to Stockholm in 2001 to commemorate the 100th anniversary of the death of Alfred Nobel on December 10th. Amazingly, about 20% of them (150 out of about 700) were able to attend. It seems that the life expectancy of laureates is significantly longer than that of the population at large. This extended longevity can also be observed in the laureates who died during the 2001 to 2004 period. For example, Edward Lewis (Medicine, 1995), who studied the DNA of flies, died at the age of 86; Czelaw Milosz, Poland's poet laureate (Literature, 1980) died at the age of 93, still actively writing until the end. Francis Crick (Medicine, 1962), who with James Watson discovered the structure of DNA, died at the age of 88 and on his deathbed was still editing a manuscript. Can their long lives be attributed to the love of interesting work that keeps their minds active, and their physical health more robust? (See also pages 16, 105).

12. As in the first 100 years, new important findings have finally been acknowledged by the Nobel committees during the 2001-2004 period. First is the recognition of M.R.I. diagnostic technology, developed by P. Lauterbur and P. Mansfield (1973, 1974). They were awarded the Nobel Prize in Medicine in

FORWORD TO THIRD EDITION

2003. Not less important are findings obtained by joint biochemistry teams, headed by laureates A. Hershko and A. Ciechanover from Israel and I. Rose from the USA (Chemistry, 2004). They identified how the human body kills faulty proteins in cells to defend itself against diseases. This breakthrough in understanding is now involved in treating cancer, cystic fibrosis and other disorders. While Hershko and Ciechanover are physicians who received their prize in Chemistry, the benefit they developed is to medicine. As Professor Hershko noted: It shows how "the boundaries among biology, physics and medicine are quickly disappearing." The 2004 Economic award was presented to Norwegian F. Kydland and American E. Prescott for research into business cycles. They concluded that governments should not interfere with market fluctuations in fighting inflation. Their research has resulted in more robust models that have been widely adopted by many countries.

13. Nobel Prizes are also about taking new approaches. In Physics 2004, three Americans (D. Gross, D. Politzer, and F. Wilczek) won for exploring the force that binds particles inside an atomic nucleus, "fulfilling the grand dream to formulate a unified theory...for everything" as the Royal Swedish Academy explained. Their breakthrough came with a completely new mathematical theory, including a minus sign where previously tested theories gave an incorrect positive sign. "Seldom has a negative result had such a positive effect", said Lars Brink, a member of the Royal Academy of Sciences. As for the 2004 Nobel Peace Prize, it is the first time that the Nobel committee put emphasis on ecology and preservation, noting that "peace on earth depends on our ability to secure our environment." Wangari Maathai, founded the Green Belt Movement in Kenya, which has planted 30 million trees and fights for preservation of natural resources, advocates democracy and supports women's rights. This movement has also spread to other countries. (See pages 73-76 for major innovations in the first 100 years.)

14. As before, there were protests for failing to be included in the award of a Nobel Prize. Raymond V. Damadian published full-page advertisements concerning the 2003 award for Medicine under a headline that read: "The Shameful Wrong That Must Be Righted". He claimed that he was the first to discover the benefits of magnetic resonance imaging (M.R.I.) and that the two who received credit for the technology had merely *refined* his work. Another such claim was presented by Dr. David Michaeli of Israel. Although it is true that Dr. Damadian took an early step in 1970 in developing M.R.I. technology, many other scientists—including the members of the Nobel committee—maintain that the two chosen for the award were directly responsible for the current technology. In making past awards, however, the Nobel committee has behaved differently. In the case of the Nobel Prize for penicillin (Medicine, 1945), Ernest B. Chain and Sir Howard Florey were credited with making the product work, saving million of lives. Nevertheless, they shared the prize with Sir Alexander Flemming, who first observed the antibiotic properties of mold, but never developed it. An even more bizarre

case involved Maurice Wilkins, who shared the Nobel Prize for Medicine in 1962. His award seems to be based on showing the crucial X-ray diffraction photograph of a DNA molecule to Dr. Watson. But Dr. Wilkins did not take the crucial photograph! The actual image was made by Dr. Rosalind Franklin. She however had died long before the award was decided. In the case of Dr. Damadian of the M.R.I. controversy, he was given the Bower Award in March 2004 by the Franklin Institute of Philadelphia in what might be seen as a consolation prize. The Bower recognized Dr. Damadian for "taking amazing technology that he has a legitimate claim for inventing and taking that technology to market successfully." In an even more relevant twist to his claim as the father of M.R.I, the U.S. Supreme Court found in 1997 that General Electric had infringed on Dr. Damadian's 1974 patent. GE paid Dr. Damadian $129 million in damages.

15. Rather than protests over exclusion, the 2004 class of laureates had claims of unworthiness, particularly against Literature laureate Elfriede Jelinek. Many suggested that far more qualified nominees were ignored. As for the 2004 Nobel Peace Prize, Carl Hagen, the leader of the Progress Party of Norway, said "I thought the intention of Alfred Nobel's Will was to focus on a person or organization who had worked actively to promote peace not to an environmental activist." Be that as it may, the Norwegian Nobel Peace committee had already extended the concept of the Nobel Peace Prize several times before: Carl von Ossietzky (1935), tried to warn the world against Hitler and died for it; Norman Borlaug (1970) developed the "green revolution" which reduced famine; and Mother Tereza (1979) sponsored charities. None of their work seemed to promote the cessation of war or limit its possibility *per se*, but all of them encouraged more peaceful social environments. In fact, many claimed that the late Pope John Paul II had been the most worthy nominee for the 2004 Nobel Peace Prize. (See also pages 79-80 and 95-98).

16. On August 2003, Chung Mong-hun, heir of the vast Hyundai conglomerate, committed suicide over revelations that he had been secretly involved in the delivery of some $500 million to North Korea, $100 million of which were from government funds. The payment was said to ensure that Kim Jong Il, the North Korean leader, would receive the president of South Korea, Kim Dae Jung. Indeed, the Korean summit of both leaders took place as planned in June 2000 and shortly thereafter, the South Korean president received the 2000 Nobel Peace Prize for promoting the reconciliation of the two Koreas. No reconciliation, however, resulted—just a single meeting for which one of the participants was well compensated. It looks now as if this award can be added to the list of peace prizes that failed to achieve their goal in several other areas: Vietnam, Central America, and Israel to name a few. Unlike the long-delayed scientific prizes, the Nobel Peace Prize tends to be given in the hope of encouraging a beneficial result. (See page 98).

FORWORD TO THIRD EDITION

17. Some laureates have donated their prize money for public benefit. Wangary Maathai (Peace, 2004) stated she will donate her prize money to her "Green Belt Movement." Shirin Ebadi (Peace, 2003) did the same when she gave her award to her foundation of human rights in Iran. Jimmy Carter donated his award to the Carter Center, a human rights organization. In the case of the three Prime Ministers of Israel to win the Nobel Peace Prize—Menachem Begin (1978), Yitzhak Rabin (1994), and Shimon Peres (1994)—all donated their prize money for public benefit. Such cases have not only been in the Peace category. Take Günter Blobel (Medicine, 1999). He was born in East Germany and as a boy of 8-years-old he saw the ruins of Dresden at the end of World War II. He said "if there ever be a chance I can do something to resurrect this whole thing, I will do so." When he got the prize money of about $1 million, he donated it to the city of Dresden.

18. The year of 2005 will commemorate 100 years of Albert Einstein's revolutionizing papers. These led to his Nobel Prize in Physics in 1921. He was awarded the Nobel Prize for the law of photoelectric effect, first published in 1905, and not for his most important theory of relativity. At that time many physicists did not understand his theory and even some very famous ones called it "Jewish physics." His theory was confirmed in 1919, however. When asked how he came to such hypothesis when no proof was yet available, he answered: "I was thinking if I were God how would I construct the universe." Similarly, Günter Blobel hypothesized in 1980 that there are different "ZIP codes" in a cell so that proteins can move to their exact spot. It was only in 1991 that he got the proof he was looking for. When asked how he came to such an idea, his answer was: "I kept asking myself, if I were to design a system, how would I do it". To this day quite a number of laureates have been awarded their Nobel Prizes on the basis of the same system of thought.

Herzliya, Israel   Baruch A. Shalev
March 2005

100 YEARS OF NOBEL PRIZES

NOBEL PRIZE WINNERS: 2001-2004

Cat/Year	Name/Contribution	Born	Place	Prize Age	National	Country Credit	Univ. Credit	Postion	Degree
Chem. 2001	Knowles, William S.	1917	USA	84	American	USA	St. Louis	Researcher	Ph.D.
	Noyori, Ryoji	1938	Japan	63	Japanese	Japan	Nagoya	Professor	Dr. Eng.
	For chirally catalyzed hydrogenation reactions								
	Sharpless, Barry K.	1941	USA	60	American	USA	Scripps Inst.	Researcher	Ph.D.
	For chirally catalyzed oxidation reactions								
Chem. 2002	Fenn, John B.	1917	USA	85	American	USA	Virginia Com.	Professor	Ph.D.
	Tanaka, Koichi	1959	Japan	43	Japanese	Japan	Shimadzu Co.	Researcher	Eng.
	Wüthrich, Kurt	1938	Switz.	64	Swiss	Switz.	Scripps Inst.	Prof/Res.	Ph.D.
	Methods for identification and structure analysis of biological macromolecules								
Chem. 2003	Agre, Peter	1949	USA	54	American	USA	Johns Hopkins	Prof.	M.D.,
	Discoveries concerning water channels in cell membranes								
	MacKinnon, Roderick	1956	USA	47	American	USA	Rockefeller U.	Prof.	M.D.
	Discoveries concerning ion channels in cell membranes								
Chem. 2004	Ciechanover, Aaron	1947	Israel	57	Israeli	Israel	Technion	Prof./Dir.	M.D.,Ph.D.
	Hershko, Avram	1937	Hung	67	Israeli	Israel	Technion	Prof.	M.D.,Ph.D.
	Rose, Irvin	1926	USA	78	American	USA	UC Irvine	Prof.	Ph. D.
	Discovery of uniquitin protein degradation in immune defense function								
Med. 2001	Hartwell, Leland H.	1939	USA	62	American	USA	Hutch. Cancer	Prof./Dir.	Ph.D.
	Hunt, Thimothy R.	1943	UK	58	English	UK	Imp. Cancer	Researcher	Ph.D.
	Nurse, Sir Paul	1949	UK	52	English	UK	Imp. Cancer	Director	Ph.D.
	Discoveries of key regulators of the cell cycle								
Med. 2002	Brenner, Sydney	1927	S. Africa	75	So. African	UK	Mol Sci. Inst.	Researcher	Ph.D.
	Horvitz, Robert H.	1947	USA	55	American	USA	M.I.T.	Professor	Ph.D.
	Sulston, Sir John E.	1942	UK	60	English	UK	Sanger Instit.,	Director	Ph.D.
	Discoveries concerning genetic regulation of organ development and programmed cell death								
Med 2003	Lauterbur, Paul C.	1929	USA	74	American	USA	U. of Illinois	Prof.	Ph.D.
	Mansfield, Sir Peter	1933	UK	70	English	UK	U. Nottingham	Prof.	Ph. D.
	Discoveries concerning magnetic resonance imaging (M.R.I.)								
Med. 2004	Axel, Richard	1946	USA	58	American	USA	Columbia U.	Prof.	Ph.D.
	Buck, Linda B. (Female)	1947	USA	57	American	USA	Hutch. Cancer	Prof.	Ph.D.
	Organization of the alfactory system in the sense of smell								
Phy. 2001	Cornell, Eric A.	1961	USA	40	American	USA	JLA, USA	Researcher	Ph.D.
	Ketterle, Wolfgang	1957	Germany	44	German	German	M.I.T.	Researcher	Ph.D.
	Wieman, Carl E.	1951	USA	50	American	USA	JLA, USA	Researcher	Ph.D.
	Studies of condensates and for Bose-Einstein condensation								
Phy. 2002	Davis, Raymond Jr.	1914	USA	88	American	USA	Penn. Univ.	Researcher	Ph.D.
	Koshiba, Masatoshi	1926	Japan	76	Japanese	Japan	Univ. of Tokyo	Prof.	Ph.D.
	For detection of cosmic neutrinos and contributions to astrophysics								
	Giacconi, Riccardo	1931	Italy	71	American	USA	Assoc. U. Inc.	Prof.	Ph.D.
	Contributions toward discovery of cosmic X-ray sources								
Phy. 2003	Abrikosov, Alexei A.	1928	Russia	75	Russian	Rus.,USA	Argonne Lab.	Researcher	Ph.D..
	Ginzburg, Vitaly L.	1916	Russia	87	Russian	Russia	Lebedev Instit.	Director	Ph.D.
	Leggett, Anthony J.	1938	UK	65	American	UK, USA	U. of Illinois	Prof.	Ph.D.
	Contributions to theory of superconductors								

FORWORD TO THIRD EDITION

Cat/ Year	Name/ Contribution	Born	Place	Prize Age	National.	Country Credit	Univ. Credit	Postion	Degree
Phy. 2004	Gross, David J.	1941	USA	63	American	USA	UCSB	Prof.	Ph.D.
	Politzer, David H.	1949	USA	55	American	USA	Cal. Tech	Prof.	Ph.D.
	Wilczek, Frank	1951	USA	53	American	USA	M.I.T., USA	Prof.	Ph.D.
	Discovery of asymtotic freedom in the theory of strong interaction								
E2001	Akerlof, George A.	1940	USA	61	American	USA	UC Berk.	Prof.	Ph.D.
	Spence, Michael A.	1943	USA	58	American	USA	Stanford U.	Prof.	Ph.D.
	Stiglitz, Joseph E.	1943	USA	63	American	USA	Columbia U..	Chairman	Ph.D.
	For their analyses of markets with asymmetric information								
E2002	Kahneman, Daniel	1934	Israel	68	Israeli, Am.	Israel, USA	Princeton/Heb.	Prof.	Ph.D..
	Combining psychological factors with economic judgements.								
	Smith, Vernon L.	1927	USA	75	American	USA	G. Mason U	Prof.	Ph.D.
	Created experiments economic analysis and market mechanisms								
E2003	Engle, Robert E. III	1942	USA	61	American	USA	NewYork U	Prof.	Ph.D.
	Granger, Clive W.J.	1934	UK	69	English	UK	UCSD	Prof.	Ph.D.
	Analysis of economic time series with time-varying volatility, or trends.								
E2004	Kydland, Finn E.	1943	Norway	61	American	Norway	Carneg./UCSB	Prof.	Ph.D.
	Prescott, Edward C.	1940	USA	64	American	USA	UCSB	Prof.	Ph.D..
	Contribution to macroeconomics: economic policy/ business cycle								
L2001	Naipaul, Sir Surajprasad V.	1932	Trinidad	69	British	UK	--	Journalist Writer	--
	For works that compel us to see suppressed histories								
L2002	Kert'sz, Imre	1929	Hungary	73	Hungarian	Hungary	--	Translator Writer	--
	For writing of the individual against the barbaric arbitrariness of history								
L2003	Coetzee, Maxwell John	1940	S. Africa	63	S. African	S. Africa		Writer	Ph.D.
	Portrays the surprising involvement of the outsider								
L2004	Jelinek, Elfriede (Female)	1946	Austria	58	Austrian	Austria		Writer, poet	--
	For voices in novels and plays revealing the absurdity of society's cliches								
P2001	Annan, Kofi United Nations	1938	Ghana	63	Ghanan	Ghana		Sec. Gen.	M. Sc.
	For work in seeking a better organized and more peaceful world								
P2002	Carter, James E (Jimmy)	1924	USA	78	American	USA	Naval Acad.	President	BA
	For efforts to find peaceful solutions and advance democracy, human rights and economics								
P2003	Shirin, Ebadi (Female)	1947	Iran	56	Iranian	Iran	--	Lawyer	LL.B.
	For her efforts for democracy and human rights								
P2004	Maathai, Wangari (Female)	1940	Kenya	64	Kenyan	Kenya	--	Ecologist	Ph.D.
	For her contribution to sustainable development, democracy and peace								

Abbreviations: Cat=Category; Nat= Nationality; Chem=Chemistry; Med=Physiology or Medicine; Phy=Physics; E=Economics; L=Literature; P=Peace; Res.=Research

viii

INTRODUCTION

Alfred Bernhard Nobel (1833-1896) wrote plays, poetry, and loved peace; he held 355 patents and his invention of dynamite in 1886 made him one of the wealthiest men in the world. He believed that his invention would be used for peaceful purposes only and was disappointed when dynamite actually became a powerful instrument of war. Although this invention already earned him a place in the world, his subsequent establishment of the Nobel Prize Foundation bought him another century of fame, and brought benefits to the world through remarkable achievements. As it turned out, this was Nobel's way of compensating for the harm his invention caused.

It was in Sweden in 1895, a year before his death, that Alfred Nobel signed the famous Will establishing the Nobel Prize Foundation. In the Will he created a fund "…the interest of which shall be annually distributed in the form of prizes to those who, during the preceding year shall have conferred the greatest benefit on mankind. The said interest shall be divided into five equal parts..." in the fields of physics, chemistry, physiology or medicine, literature, and peace. Nobel believed that these five areas served the most immediate needs of mankind.

Nobel specified that Swedish institutes would select the winners in the first four fields, while the Norwegians would nominate the Peace Prize winner. In his will, Alfred Nobel expressed the wish that only "the most worthy shall receive the prize," regardless of nationality. However, he also specified that the winner had to be alive to receive an award. The first Nobel Prizes were presented in 1901 and the year 2000 marked the 100th presentations.

In 1968, the Bank of Sweden created a Prize in Economic Sciences in memory of Alfred Nobel. The Bank undertook to put an annual amount at the disposal of the Nobel Foundation. The first prize in Economic Sciences was presented in 1969, which means that by the year 2000 there had been only 32 years (but 46 winners) in this category.

Activities of the Nobel Foundation are carried out by four organizations:
1. The Swedish Academy—for prizes in literature.
2. The Karolinska Institute—for prizes in medicine and physiology.
3. The Royal Swedish Academy of Sciences—for prizes in physics, chemistry and economics.
4. The Nobel committee of the Norwegian Storting (parliament)—for the peace prize.

Each year the Nobel committees send invitations to hundreds of specialists all over the world, asking for nominations for the Nobel Prizes. As a result, the Nobel Prize has come to be regarded as the best-known and most prestigious award available in the fields of literature, medicine, physics, chemistry, peace, and economics

The Nobel Foundation now has a worth of more than $400 million. In its first year (1901) the prize value was about $40,000; this year's prizes will be worth about $960,000 each. Nevertheless, after taking inflation into account over the years, these sums are not that far apart. In addition, winners gain such additional benefits as new attractive professional opportunities, worldwide fame, and increased funding for their work.

In preparing this book, records of over 700 Nobel Prize winners of the past 100 years were carefully examined. The examination resulted in an exploration of such questions as:
- What is the role of creativity and genius versus luck in the achievements of Laureates? Or is it a combination of these two?
- Are there differences between the sexes in obtaining Nobel prizes?
- Are there countries and universities which have excelled

through the years in producing Nobel Prize winners?
- What is the effect of brain migration?
- Can dictatorship (avoiding freedom of press, etc.) suppress development of science and literature as seen in terms of the winners in these countries?
- Are there common denominators among the bulk of the Nobel Prize winners in each field (nationality, education, age, gender, degree, career, religion, date of birth, etc.)?
- In these last 100 years have the goals set by Alfred Nobel been achieved.

Because of the immense attention paid to the Nobel Prizes everywhere, the answers to these questions are of interest not only to policy makers, scientists, writers, and students, but also to the general public as well.

100 YEARS OF NOBEL PRIZES

STATISTICAL ANALYSIS

NUMBER OF NOBEL PRIZE WINNERS BY CATEGORY AND GENDER: 1901-2000

The total number of Nobel Prize winners between 1901 and 2000 has been 719. There have been more winners in the scientific categories—Medicine, Physics, Chemistry—than Peace and Literature. The reason is simple: In the latter categories, there is usually only one Nobel Prize recipient each year; whereas in such fields as Medicine and Physics, the prize has often been shared among several winners who have either collaborated or achieved similar results independently. The smallest number of winners has been in Economics, simply because these prizes were initiated in 1969 (see Table 1, below).

Please note that the number of winners listed in Table 1 below is not identical to the number of winning countries. Some winners are affiliated with more than one country (see Table 2, p. 13).

Note also the contrast between the numbers of awards to men and to women: Less than 5% of the Nobel Prizes awarded have gone to women, compared to more than 93% to men. In the scientific categories, women have won less than 3% of the prizes and no woman has yet to win the Nobel Prize in Economics. In the Peace and Literature categories, on the other hand, women have won about 10% of the prizes. Although this is an improvement over the other categories, it still must be considered very low.

Table 1
NOBEL PRIZE WINNERS BY CATEGORY AND GENDER

Category	Winners	Men	%	Women	%
Medicine	172	167	97.1	5	2.9
Physics	162	160	98.8	2	1.2
Chemistry	135	132	97.8	3	2.2
Peace*	107	78	72.9	10	9.3
Literature	97	88	90.7	9	9.3
Economics**	46	46	100.0	0	0.0
Totals	**719**	**671**	**93.3**	**29**	**4.0**

*   19 Nobel Peace Prizes have been awarded to international organizations.
** Nobel Prizes for Economics were initiated in 1969.

NATIONALITY OF NOBEL PRIZE WINNERS

The United States leads in the total number of Nobel Prizes awarded, with 258 or 36.4% of the total. Far behind in second position is the United Kingdom with 92 (13%) winners, followed by Germany with 74 (10.5%), France with 49 (6.9%), Sweden with 29 (4.1%), Switzerland with 21 (3.0%), and Russia with 18 (2.5%).

The lead of the United States is even greater in the scientific categories, where it accounts for about half of all prizes awarded (see Table 2, Figs.1 and 2). This one statistic suggests why the United States is the world's most powerful country, a position which, in turn, stimulates migration, leading to still greater potential progress.

In the scientific categories, four countries cover more than three quarters of the Nobel Prizes:
- the United States—43.8%
- the United Kingdom—14.0%;
- Germany—12.1%;
- France—5.2%.

As for Literature and Peace, the above four countries together with Sweden comprise half of the Nobel Prizes that have been awarded.

When considering the number of Nobel Laureates by category, Medicine (24.7%) and Physics (22.9%), have produced nearly twice as many winners as Peace (12.6%) and Literature (13.8%). The Chemistry category is in third place in number of winners (19.5%). The Economic category has accounted for the smallest number of winners (6.5%), again since this category was first established some 65 years after the others (see Table 2).

It should be pointed out that there is a very high correlation (of 0.9 or more) among countries' achievements in the four scientific categories. In other words, the scientific categories are interrelated and excellence tends to be achieved in all of them together. The correlation between the scientific categories and Peace is also quite high ($r = 0.8$). But the correlation is much lower ($r = 0.6$) between the scientific categories and the Literature awards.

Table 2
NATIONALITY OF NOBEL PRIZE WINNERS: 1901-2000

Country	Chem.	Med.	Physics	Peace*	Lit.	Econ.	Total	%
Argentina	1	2	0	2	0	0	5	0.7
Australia	1	3	0	0	1	0	5	0.7
Austria	1	5	3	2	0	0	11	1.6
Belgium	1	4	0	3	1	0	9	1.3
Burma	0	0	0	1	0	0	1	0.1
Canada	4	2	2	1	0	1	10	1.4
Chile	0	0	0	0	2	0	2	0.3
China	0	0	2	0	0	0	2	0.3
Colombia	0	0	0	0	1	0	1	0.1
Costa Rica	0	0	0	1	0	0	1	0.1
Czechoslovakia	1	0	0	0	1	0	2	0.3
Denmark	1	5	3	1	3	0	13	1.8
East Timor	0	0	0	2	0	0	2	0.3
Egypt	1	0	0	1	1	0	3	0.4
Finland	1	0	0	0	1	0	2	0.3
France	7	8	11	9	13	1	49	6.9
Germany	28	15	19	4	7	1	74	10.5
Greece	0	0	0	0	2	0	2	0.3
Guatemala	0	0	0	1	1	0	2	0.3
Hungary	1	1	0	0	0	0	2	0.3
Iceland	0	0	0	0	1	0	1	0.1
India	0	0	1	1	1	1	4	0.6
Ireland	0	0	1	1	4	0	6	0.8
Israel	0	0	0	3	1	0	4	0.6
Italy	1	3	3	1	6	0	14	2.0
Japan	2	1	3	1	2	0	9	1.3
Mexico	0	0	0	1	1	0	2	0.3
Netherlands	2	2	8	1	0	1	14	2.0
Nigeria	0	0	0	0	1	0	1	0.1
No. Ireland	0	0	0	2	0	0	2	0.3
No. Vietnam	0	0	0	1	0	0	1	0.1
Norway	1	0	0	2	3	2	8	1.1
Pakistan	0	0	1	0	0	0	1	0.1
Palestine	0	0	0	1	0	0	1	0.1
Poland	0	0	0	1	4	0	5	0.7
Portugal	0	1	0	0	1	0	2	0.3
Russia	1	2	8	2	4	1	18	2.5
South Africa	0	1	0	5	1	0	7	1.0
South Korea	0	0	0	1	0	0	1	0.1
Spain	0	1	0	0	5	0	6	0.8
St. Lucia	0	0	0	0	1	0	1	0.1
Sweden	4	7	4	5	7	2	29	4.1
Switzerland	5	7	4	3	2	0	21	3.0
Tibet	0	0	0	1	0	0	1	0.1
United Kingdom	26	23	20	10	6	7	92	13.0
United States	48	82	69	18	12	29	258	36.4
Yugoslavia	0	0	0	0	1	0	1	0.1
Total	138	175	162	88	98	46	708	100.0
% of total	19.5	24.7	22.9	12.6	13.8	6.5	100.0	--

* An additional 19 Peace Nobel Prizes were awarded to various international organizations.
NOTE Some of the Nobel Prize winners were of more than one nationality.

Fig 1. NUMBER OF NOBEL PRIZE WINNERS OF TEN LEADING COUNTRIES (1901-2000)

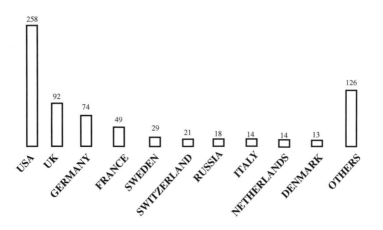

Fig 2. NOBEL PRIZE WINNERS IN THE SCIENTIFIC CATEGORIES (1901-2000)

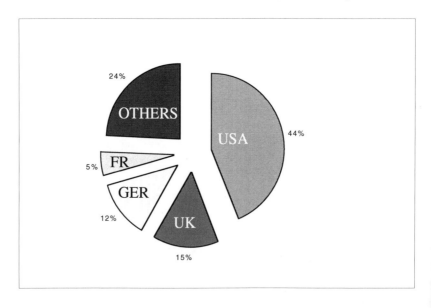

NATIONALITY OF NOBEL PRIZE WINNERS—POPULATION AND INDEX

The top 20 countries in Per Capital Gross National Product (GNPC), or listed on the United Nations' Index (based on the "Human Development Index" constructed by Nobel Laureate Amartya Sen), are also the countries that have the highest longevity and the greatest number of Nobel Prizes. This is probably because the poorer countries are those preoccupied with basic problems of providing sufficient food and maintaining security for their people and lack the resources needed to carry out expensive basic research. Their problems are those of survival and the research they need is of a more practical sort.

The number of Nobel Prizes per nation may indicate its scientific and cultural level, and may also suggest better health care exemplified by modern hospitals and equipment. For example, the four leading countries in terms of the number of Noble Laureates (the United States, United Kingdom, Germany, and France) also have a very high life expectancy (77 to 79 years of age). Russia (or the former USSR), on the other hand, has only 18 Nobel Laureates with a national life expectancy of 67.5 years of age; India has four Nobel Prize winners and the country's life expectancy is only 62.8 years of age (see Table 3).

The correlation between the GNPC and the United Nations' Index is only more than moderate ($r = 0.75$), indicating that this Index also encompasses other equal criteria, such as life expectancy and level of education. Indeed, the correlation between the Index and longevity is very high ($r = -0.92$). On the other hand, there is no correlation between the size of the population and the number of Nobel Prize winners ($r = 0.07$). For example, China with a population of 1.27 billion people has produced only two Nobel Laureates, while Switzerland, with a population of 7.4 million, has 21 Laureates. Likewise, India with about one billion people has only four Laureates; the United States, by contrast, with 275.6 million people has nearly a Laureate for each million in population (258).

Table 3
NATIONALITY OF NOBEL PRIZE WINNERS—POPULATION AND INDEX

Country	Science[1]	Peace+ Liter.[2]	Total	Pop. (mil.)[3]	Life Expt.[4]	Index[5]	GNPC$[6]	%GNPC$[7]
Argentina	3	2	5	37.0	75.5	36	10,200	75.3
Australia	4	1	5	19.4	78.7	5	20,130	148.7
Austria	9	2	11	8.1	78	15	22,740	167.9
Belgium	5	4	9	10.2	78.5	4	23,480	173.4
Burma	0	1	1	49.3	60.3	131	1,199	8.9
Canada	9	1	10	30.7	78.5	3	24,050	177.6
Chile	0	2	2	15.2	75.5	31	12,890	95.2
China	2	0	2	1265.3	71.5	55	3,220	23.8
Colombia	0	1	1	42.3	70.5	53	7,500	55.4
Costa Rica	0	1	1	3.8	75.8	34	6,620	48.9
Czechoslovakia	1	1	2	15.9	74.5	41	10,510	77.6
Denmark	9	4	13	5.3	77	14	23,830	176.0
East Timor	0	2	2	----	----	----	----	----
Egypt	1	2	3	68.1	66.5	112	3,130	23.1
Finland	1	1	2	5.2	76.8	10	20,270	149.7
France	27	22	49	59.1	78.3	12	22,320	164.8
Germany	63	11	74	82.8	77	17	20,810	153.7
Greece	0	2	2	10.6	78.2	24	13,010	96.1
Guatemala	0	2	2	12.2	64.3	111	4,070	30.1
Hungary	2	0	2	9.8	71	47	7,200	53.2
Iceland	0	1	1	0.3	78.9	7	22,830	168.6
India	2	2	4	1006.8	62.8	139	1,700	12.6
Ireland	1	5	6	3.7	77	18	18,340	135.4
Israel	0	4	4	6.5	78.3	22	17,310	127.8
Italy	7	7	14	57.4	78.2	20	20,200	149.2
Japan	6	3	9	127.1	80.5	9	23,180	171.2
Mexico	0	2	2	98.9	71.8	49	8,190	60.5
No. Vietnam	0	1	1	80.6	67.5	122	1,690	12.5
Netherlands	13	1	14	15.6	77	8	21,620	159.7
Nigeria	0	1	1	128.8	50.3	142	820	6.1
No. Ireland	0	2	2	1.8	----	----	----	----
Norway	3	5	8	4.4	78.3	1	24,290	179.4
Pakistan	1	0	1	156.0	61	138	1,560	11.5
Palestine	0	1	1	----	----	----	----	----
Poland	0	5	5	38.7	72.8	52	6,740	49.8
Portugal	1	1	2	9.8	75.5	28	14,380	106.2
Russia	12	6	18	146.2	67.5	72	3,950	29.2
South Africa	1	6	7	46.3	51.3	89	6,990	51.6
South Korea	0	1	1	46.9	74.8	27	12,270	90.6
Spain	1	5	6	39.8	79	21	16,060	118.6
St. Lucia	0	1	1	0.2	73.2	58	4,610	34.0
Sweden	17	12	29	8.9	79.3	2	19,480	143.9
Switzerland	16	5	21	7.4	78.6	11	26,620	196.6
Tibet	0	1	1	2.6	----	----	----	----
UK	76	16	92	59.4	77.3	13	20,640	152.4
USA	228	30	258	275.6	77	6	29,340	216.7
Yugoslavia	0	1	1	10.6	72.3	----	2,280	16.8
Total/Average	**521**	**187**	**708**	----	**73.2**	----	**13,541**	**100.0**

1. Scientific categories
2. Peace & Literature
3. Population in millions
4. Life expectancy
5. "Human Development Index," designated by the United Nations in 1998, measures life expectancy, amount of education, and income levels equally.
6. GNPC$= Per Capita Gross National Product in US dollars
7. %GNPC$$=Percentage of average of Per Capita Gross National Product in US dollars. Countries under the average (100) have trouble providing the resources required for Nobel prize level research.
NOTE Some of the Laureates credited the Nobel Prize to more than one country.

Table 4A
TOTAL NUMBER OF NOBEL PRIZE WINNERS— BY NATIONALITY

Country	Science[1]	Peace+ Liter.[2]	Total	Pop. (mil.)[3]	Life Expt.[4]	Index[5]	GNPC$[6]
Denmark	9	4	13	5.3	77	14	23,830
France	27	22	49	59.1	78.3	12	22,320
Germany	63	11	74	82.8	77	17	20,810
Italy	7	7	14	57.4	78.2	20	20,200
Netherlands	13	1	14	15.6	77	8	21,600
Russia	12	6	18	146.2	67.5	72	3,950
Sweden	17	12	29	8.9	79.3	2	19,480
Switzerland	16	5	21	7.4	78.6	11	26,620
United Kingdom	76	16	92	59.4	77.3	13	20,640
United States	228	30	258	275.6	77	6	29,340
Sub Total	468	114	582	717.7	----	----	----
Others	54	72	126	5782.3	----	----	----
Total	**522**	**186**	**708**	**6500.0**	----	----	----

1 Scientific categories
2 Peace & Literature
3 Population in millions
4 Life expectancy
5 "Human Development Index" designated by the United Nations (1998)
6 GNPC$= Per Capita Gross National Product in US dollars

Table 4B
PERCENTAGE OF NOBEL PRIZE WINNERS—BY NATIONALITY

Country	Science[1]	Peace+ Liter.[2]	Total	% Pop. (mil.)[3]
Denmark	1.7	2.2	1.8	0.08
France	5.2	11.8	6.9	0.90
Germany	12.1	5.9	10.5	1.27
Italy	1.3	3.8	2.0	0.88
Netherlands	2.5	0.5	2.0	0.24
Russia	2.3	3.2	2.5	2.26
Sweden	3.3	6.5	4.1	0.14
Switzerland	3.1	2.7	3.0	0.11
United Kingdom	14.6	8.6	13.0	0.90
United States	43.8	16.1	36.5	4.16
Sub Total	**89.8**	**61.3**	**82.3**	**10.95**
Others	10.2	38.7	17.7	88.89
Total	100.0	100.0	100.0	100.0

1 Scientific categories
2 Peace & Literature
3 Population in millions

NOTE:
- Ten countries hold about 90% of Nobel Prizes in the 4 scientific categories (Chemistry, Medicine, Physics and Economics), 60% of the Nobel Prizes in Peace and Literature, and more than 80% of total Nobel Prizes.
- However, these ten countries have only 11% of the world's population. Nine out of ten of these countries have very high per capita gross national products, are high on the UN Index, and have extended life expectancies.

The graph below and Table 6 on page 23 show that Germany was a leading Nobel country during the years 1901 to 1940, but during and after World War II, the United States became the leading recipient of Nobel prizes. In fact, during the 1981 to 2000 period, citizens and residents of the United States won *half* of all the Nobel prizes awarded.

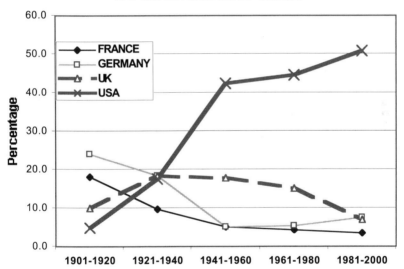

Fig 3. NOBEL PRIZES IN ALL 6 CATEGORIES BY COUNTRY AND YEAR

NATIONALITY OF NOBEL PRIZE WINNERS CREDITED TO MAJOR DEMOCRATIC COUNTRIES

The 17 principal democratic countries won 84.4% of the total Nobel Prizes awarded during the years 1901 to 2000, and they earned more than 90% of the Chemistry, Medicine, and Economic prizes.

Moreover, these 17 countries rate among the top 20 countries out of 174 in terms of the United Nation's Human Development Index which measures such indicators as standard of living, life expectancy, and education level. Looked at another way, 11% of the world's population holds over 90% of the prizes in the scientific categories and about 65% to 70% in the Literature and Peace categories (see Table 5).

Piotr Kapista, the Soviet Laureate in Physics in 1978 and a Ph.D. graduate of Cambridge University in the United Kingdom, was in a unique position to see the difference between democratic and autocratic systems. According to him, open scientific debates lead to "collective creativity." Such meetings were possible in the democratic countries, impossible under the Communist regimes.

Table 5
NUMBER OF NOBEL PRIZES CREDITED TO MAIN DEMOCRATIC COUNTRIES BETWEEN 1901 AND 2000

Country*	Chem.	Med.	Physics	Peace**	Lit.	Econ.	Total	%Total
Australia (5)	1	3	0	0	1	0	5	0.7
Belgium (4)	1	4	0	3	1	0	9	1.3
Canada (3)	4	2	2	1	0	1	10	1.4
Denmark (14)	1	5	3	1	3	0	13	1.8
Finland (10)	1	0	0	0	1	0	2	0.3
France (12)	7	8	11	9	13	1	49	6.9
Germany (17)	28	15	19	4	7	1	74	10.5
Greece (24)	0	0	0	0	2	0	2	0.3
Iceland (7)	0	0	0	0	1	0	1	0.1
Ireland (18)	0	0	1	1	4	0	6	0.8
Israel (22)	0	0	0	3	1	0	4	0.6
Netherlands (8)	2	2	8	1	0	1	14	2.0
Norway (1)	1	0	0	2	3	2	8	1.1
Sweden (2)	4	7	4	5	7	2	29	4.1
Switzerland (11)	5	7	4	3	2	0	21	3.0
UK (13)	26	23	20	10	6	7	92	13.0
USA (6)	48	82	69	18	12	29	258	36.5
Total	**129**	**158**	**141**	**61**	**64**	**44**	**597**	**84.4**
% of total	93.5	90.3	87.0	69.3	65.3	95.7	84.4	---

* The numbers in parenthesis represent the "Human Development Index" as designated by the United Nations. It is based on standard of living, life expectancy, and level of education. Some of the winners preferred to be recorded as citizens of two countries.

** An additional 19 Peace Nobel Prizes were awarded to international organizations.

DISTRIBUTION OF NOBEL PRIZES— BY COUNTRY, CATEGORIES, AND YEARS

The 582 Nobel Prizes were awarded over the first 100 years of their existence, to individuals in the 10 countries with the greatest number of prizes. These countries were analyzed in this section according to category and grouped into five 20-year-periods: 1901-1920, 1921-1940, 1941-1960, 1961-1980 and 1981-2000. It appears that over the years the total number of Nobel Prizes was reduced for most contries and especially for France (from 18% to 3.5%) and Germany (from 24% to 7.5%), while that of the United States was increased enormously (from 5% to about 50%). (See Table 6).

Table 6
NUMBER OF NOBEL PRIZE WINNERS IN ALL CATEGORIES BY COUNTRY AND YEARS

	1901-1920	1921-1940	1941-1960	1961-1980	1981-2000	TOT
Denmark	5	2	2	2	2	13
France	18	10	6	8	7	49
Germany	24	19	6	10	15	74
Italy	4	3	2	2	3	14
Netherlands	5	3	1	1	4	14
Russia	2	1	5	8	2	18
Sweden	7	5	3	9	5	29
Switzerland	7	3	4	2	5	21
United Kingdom	10	19	21	28	14	92
United States	5	18	50	83	102	258
Others	13	20	18	33	42	126
Total	**100**	**103**	**118**	**186**	**201**	**708**

PERCENTAGE OF NOBEL PRIZE WINNERS IN ALL CATEGORIES BY COUNTRY AND YEARS

	1901-1920	1921-1940	1941-1960	1961-1980	1981-2000	% TOT
Denmark	5.0	1.9	1.7	1.1	1.0	1.8
France	18.0	9.7	5.1	4.3	3.5	6.9
Germany	24.0	18.4	5.1	5.4	7.5	10.5
Italy	4.0	2.9	1.7	1.1	1.5	2.0
Netherlands	5.0	2.9	0.8	0.5	2.0	2.0
Russia	2.0	1.0	4.2	4.3	1.0	2.5
Sweden	7.0	4.9	2.5	4.8	2.5	4.1
Switzerland	7.0	2.9	3.4	1.1	2.5	3.0
United Kingdom	10.0	18.4	17.8	15.1	7.0	13.0
United States	5.0	17.5	42.4	44.6	50.7	36.4
Others	13.0	19.4	15.3	17.7	20.9	17.8
% of Total	100.0	100.0	100.0	100.0	100.0	100.0

NOTE The top ten countries earned 582, or 82.2% of total Nobel Prizes.

Chemistry

In the category of Chemistry, 10 countries are credited with 123 or 89.1% of the Nobel Prizes awarded: The United States with 48 of the prizes awarded (34.8%), Germany with 28 (20.3%) and the United Kingdom with 26 (18.8%) are far in the lead of all other countries (see Table 7).

It is interesting to note that during the 1901 to 1940 period, Germany was the leading country with 17 of the Chemistry prizes, or nearly 50% of those awarded. The United States, on the other hand, was credited with only three prizes. Since 1941 there has been a sharp drop in Germany's tally of Nobel Prizes, while at the same time there was dramatic increase in the number of awards won by scientists in the United States and, to a lesser extent, by those of the United Kingdom. This can be explained by the fact that during the Nazi dominance of Europe, scientists (mostly Jews such as George de Hevesy) fled to the West from Germany, Italy, and the occupied countries. They brought with them well-established European knowledge and expertise, and were able to establish high quality research facilities in their new countries in the years that followed.

About 12% (16) prize-winning works in Chemistry were involved with genetics and 3% (4) with vitamins.

Table 7
NOBEL PRIZE WINNERS IN CHEMISTRY BY COUNTRY AND YEARS

	1901-1920	1921-1940	1941-1960	1961-1980	1981-2000	TOT
Denmark	0	0	0	0	1	1
France	4	2	0	0	1	7
Germany	9	8	4	4	3	28
Italy	0	0	0	1	0	1
Netherlands	0	1	0	0	1	2
Russia	0	0	1	0	0	1
Sweden	1	2	1	0	0	4
Switzerland	1	2	0	1	1	5
United Kingdom	2	4	7	9	4	26
United States	1	2	9	12	24	48
Others	0	1	3	5	6	15
Total	18	22	25	32	41	138

PERCENTAGE OF NOBEL PRIZE WINNERS IN CHEMISTRY BY COUNTRY AND YEARS

	1901-1920	1921-1940	1941-1960	1961-1980	1981-2000	% TOT
Denmark	0	0	0	0	2.4	0.7
France	22.2	9.1	0.0	0.0	2.4	5.1
Germany	50.0	36.4	16.0	12.5	7.3	20.3
Italy	0.0	0.0	0.0	3.1	0.0	0.7
Netherlands	0.0	4.5	0.0	0.0	2.4	1.4
Russia	0.0	0.0	4.0	0.0	0.0	0.7
Sweden	5.6	9.1	4.0	0.0	0.0	2.9
Switzerland	5.6	9.1	0.0	3.1	2.4	3.6
United Kingdom	11.1	18.2	28.0	28.1	9.8	18.8
United States	5.6	9.1	36.0	37.5	58.5	34.8
Others	0.0	4.5	12.0	15.6	14.6	10.9
% of Total	13.0	15.9	18.1	23.2	29.7	100.0

NOTE: The Top Ten countries earned 123, or 89.1% of the Nobel Chemistry prizes awarded.

Physiology or Medicine

Ten countries were credited with 154 Nobel Prizes in Medicine, or 88% of the total number awarded in the first 100 years. Of the 154 prizes, the United States earned by far the most, with 82 (46.9%), followed by the United Kingdom with 13.1% and Germany with 8.6%. Table 8 indicates that during the years 1901 to 1920 the United States failed to capture *any* Nobel Prize in Medicine, while Germany was the leading winner with four (22.2%).

During and after World War II, the United States moved into the lead. In the 1981 to 2000 period, it had 28 of the prizes (60.9%). The reason for this dramatic change is the same as for the Chemistry Prizes—brain migration from Germany, Italy, and the occupied countries. The most up-to-date knowledge of Europe was transferred mainly to the United States. This had an impact for years afterwards.

During the first fifty years of Nobel Prizes, the main prize-winning works were in physiology (10%) and bacteriology (10%); however, in the next fifty years biochemistry became the dominant area of interest. DNA was involved in about one-third of the prize-winning works in Medicine (59); about 10% (17) were in physiology and about the same percentage in bacteriology. While some 3.5% involved vitamins (6), only two Nobel Prizes were awarded in psychiatry.

100 YEARS OF NOBEL PRIZES

Table 8
NOBEL PRIZE WINNERS IN MEDICINE BY COUNTRY AND YEARS

	1901-1920	1921-1940	1941-1960	1961-1980	1981-2000	TOT
Denmark	2	1	1	0	1	5
France	3	1	0	4	0	8
Germany	4	4	1	2	4	15
Italy	1	0	1	0	1	3
Netherlands	0	2	0	0	0	2
Russia	2	0	0	0	0	2
Sweden	1	0	1	2	3	7
Switzerland	1	0	3	1	2	7
United Kingdom	1	5	5	8	4	23
United States	0	4	20	30	28	82
Others	3	7	4	4	3	21
Total	**18**	**24**	**36**	**51**	**46**	**175**

PERCENTAGE OF NOBEL PRIZE WINNERS IN MEDICINE BY COUNTRY AND YEARS

	1901-1920	1921-1940	1941-1960	1961-1980	1981-2000	% TOT
Denmark	11.1	4.2	2.8	0.0	2.2	2.9
France	16.7	4.2	0.0	7.8	0.0	4.6
Germany	22.2	16.7	2.8	3.9	8.7	8.6
Italy	5.6	0.0	2.8	0.0	2.2	1.7
Netherlands	0.0	8.3	0.0	0.0	0.0	1.1
Russia	11.1	0.0	0.0	0.0	0.0	1.1
Sweden	5.6	0.0	2.8	3.9	6.5	4.0
Switzerland	5.6	0.0	8.3	2.0	4.3	4.0
United Kingdom	5.6	20.8	13.9	15.7	8.7	13.1
United States	0.0	16.7	55.6	58.8	60.9	46.9
Others	16.7	29.2	11.1	7.8	6.5	12.0
% of Total	**13.0**	**17.4**	**26.1**	**37.0**	**33.3**	**100.0**

NOTE: The Top Ten countries earned 154, or 88.0% of the Nobel Medicine prizes awarded.

Physics

Ten countries were credited with 149, or 92% of the Nobel Prizes in Physics. The United States again leads strongly with 69 (42.6%) of these, followed by the United Kingdom with 20 (12.3%) and Germany with 19 (11.7%) (see Table 9). During the years 1901-1920 Germany was the leading country with seven prizes (29.2%), whereas the United States earned only one (4.2%). Again, brain migration before and during World War II, gave the advantage to the United States and the West. Such immigrants as Albert Einstein, Max Born, Emilio Gino Segre (all Jewish) and Enrico Fermi (with a Jewish wife) were among the best physicists in the world and were awarded many prizes including the Nobel Prize.

Table 9
NOBEL PRIZE WINNERS IN PHYSICS BY COUNTRY AND YEARS

	1901-1920	1921-1940	1941-1960	1961-1980	1981-2000	TOT
Denmark	0	1	0	2	0	3
France	4	2	0	2	3	11
Germany	7	3	1	2	6	19
Italy	1	1	0	0	1	3
Netherlands	4	0	1	0	3	8
Russia	0	0	3	4	1	8
Sweden	1	1	0	1	1	4
Switzerland	1	1	0	0	2	4
United Kingdom	5	5	5	5	0	20
United States	1	5	13	24	26	69
Others	0	3	5	3	2	13
Total	24	22	28	43	45	162

PERCENTAGE OF NOBEL PRIZE WINNERS IN PHYSICS BY COUNTRY AND YEARS

	1901-1920	1921-1940	1941-1960	1961-1980	1981-2000	% TOT
Denmark	0.0	4.5	0.0	4.7	0.0	1.9
France	16.7	9.1	0.0	4.7	6.7	6.8
Germany	29.2	13.6	3.6	4.7	13.3	11.7
Italy	4.2	4.5	0.0	0.0	2.2	1.9
Netherlands	16.7	0.0	3.6	0.0	6.7	4.9
Russia	0.0	0.0	10.7	9.3	2.2	4.9
Sweden	4.2	4.5	0.0	2.3	2.2	2.5
Switzerland	4.2	4.5	0.0	0.0	4.4	2.5
United Kingdom	20.8	22.7	17.9	11.6	0.0	12.3
United States	4.2	22.7	46.4	55.8	57.8	42.6
Others	0.0	13.6	17.9	7.0	4.4	8.0
% of Total	14.8	13.6	17.3	26.5	27.8	100.0

NOTE: The Top Ten countries earned 149, or 92.0% of the Nobel Medicine prizes awarded.

Economics

The Nobel Prize for Economics was established in 1968; the first prizes in this category were awarded in 1969. Seven out of the top ten countries gained 42 Nobel economic awards, which comprise 91.3% of all the prizes in this category (see Table 10). In fact, the United States holds 63% of the economic awards and the United Kingdom another 15.2%; together these two countries share nearly 80% of the Nobel Prizes in Economics. Yet not one woman has won a Nobel Prize in Economics.

Table 10
NOBEL PRIZE WINNERS IN ECONOMICS BY COUNTRY AND YEARS

	1969-1980	1981-2000	TOTAL
Denmark	0	0	0
France	0	1	1
Germany	0	1	1
Italy	0	0	0
Netherlands	1	0	1
Russia	1	0	1
Sweden	2	0	2
Switzerland	0	0	0
United Kingdom	4	3	7
United States	9	20	29
Others	1	3	4
Total	**18**	**28**	**46**

PERCENTAGE OF NOBEL PRIZE WINNERS IN ECONOMICS BY COUNTRY AND YEARS

	1969-1980	1981-2000	TOTAL
Denmark	0.0	0.0	0.0
France	0.0	3.6	2.2
Germany	0.0	3.6	2.2
Italy	0.0	0.0	0.0
Netherlands	5.6	0.0	2.2
Russia	5.6	0.0	2.2
Sweden	11.1	0.0	4.3
Switzerland	0.0	0.0	0.0
United Kingdom	22.2	10.7	15.2
United States	50.0	71.4	63.0
Others	5.6	10.7	8.7
Total	**39.1**	**60.9**	**100.0**

NOTE: The Top Ten countries earned 42, or 91.3% of the Nobel Economic prizes awarded.

Literature

The same 10 prominent countries were credited with only 60, or 61.2% of all the Nobel Prizes awarded for Literature (see Table 11). This means, of course, that many more countries were involved in this category. As would be expected, there have been only a few migrations of authors (e.g., Thomas Mann who left Germany because of the Nazi regime, or Gao Xingjian who fled from China). The evident conclusion is that most are at their prolific best on their home soil.

France has been the leading country in Nobel Prizes for Literature (13.3%) and the United States second (12.2%). There was relatively little change in the *number* of prizes awarded during each of the 20-year periods, which indicates that usually one individual was recognized each year. During the 1901 to 1920 period, the leading country in Nobel Prizes for Literature was Germany; the United States received none during this period.

In later years there was a sharp drop in German prizes, partly because some authors had left Nazi Germany. The greatest relative prominence in the Literature category was achieved by France. It won four awards (23.5%) in this category during the 1941 to 1960 period.

About 40% of the winners did not have an academic degree. Four of the Literature Laureates were awarded for philosophical writing. Two of the prizes were awarded for historical studies: Winston Churchill for his memoirs of World War II and other historical works, as well as for his speeches; and Christian Mommsen for his *History of Rome*. In terms of the type of writing honored, note the following:

- Fiction writers—52 Nobel Prizes
- Poets—28 Nobel Prizes
- Dramatists—11 Nobel Prizes.

In short, fiction writers have won about five times more Nobel Prizes than drama writers and nearly twice as many as poets.

Table 11
NOBEL PRIZE WINNERS IN LITERATURE BY COUNTRY AND YEARS

	1901-1920	1921-1940	1941-1960	1961-1980	1981-2000	TOT
Denmark	2	0	1	0	0	3
France	3	3	4	1	2	13
Germany	4	1	0	1	1	7
Italy	1	2	1	1	1	6
Netherlands	0	0	0	0	0	0
Russia	0	1	1	2	0	4
Sweden	3	0	1	3	0	7
Switzerland	1	0	1	0	0	2
United Kingdom	1	1	2	0	2	6
United States	0	3	3	4	2	12
Others	6	6	3	11	12	38
Total	21	17	17	23	20	98

PERCENTAGE OF NOBEL PRIZE WINNERS IN LITERATURE BY COUNTRY AND YEARS

	1901-1920	1921-1940	1941-1960	1961-1980	1981-2000	% TOT
Denmark	9.5	0.0	5.9	0.0	0.0	3.1
France	14.3	17.6	23.5	4.3	10.0	13.3
Germany	19.0	5.9	0.0	4.3	5.0	7.1
Italy	4.8	11.8	5.9	4.3	5.0	6.1
Netherlands	0.0	0.0	0.0	0.0	0.0	0.0
Russia	0.0	5.9	5.9	8.7	0.0	4.1
Sweden	14.3	0.0	5.9	13.0	0.0	7.1
Switzerland	4.8	0.0	5.9	0.0	0.0	2.0
United Kingdom	4.8	5.9	11.8	0.0	10.0	6.1
United States	0.0	17.6	17.6	17.4	10.0	12.2
Others	28.6	35.3	17.6	47.8	60.0	38.8
% of Total	21.4	17.3	17.3	23.5	20.4	100.0

NOTE: The Top Ten countries earned 60, or 61.2% of the Nobel Literature prizes awarded.

Peace

The 10 countries that dominate the scientific prizes were credited with only 61.4% of the total Nobel Prizes in the Peace category (see Table 12). This prize is generally awarded for achieving peace agreements between countries or communities in a state of war or conflict. Vietnam, Israel, Egypt, Northern Ireland, East Timor, Tibet, South Africa, and other countries have been in this situation. By the same token, the 10 top scientific countries have generally served as mediators in these conflicts and have been awarded Nobel Prizes for the effort they expended on behalf of peace.

There have been, of course, other reasons for a Peace award. Peace-promotion organizations have been honored as have individuals who contributed to peace or resisted war. Two American presidents (Teddy Roosevelt and Woodrow Wilson) and several other heads of states have won the Nobel Peace Prize for their efforts to end conflicts. General George Catlett Marshall was the first-ever military leader to win the Nobel Peace Prize (1953) for his plan to help Europe recover from the devastation of World War II. Linus Pauling won for the United States in 1962 for his campaign against the dangers of radioactive fallout. Norman Borlaug of the United States won in 1970 for initiating the "green revolution," which tripled wheat production and went on to develop "miracle" strains of rice and other grains.

The leading country in the Nobel Peace prize category is the United States, with 18 (20.5%) of the 54 awarded to the top 10 scientific countries. The United Kingdom is second with 10 (11.4%) and France is third with nine (10.2%). There was relatively little change over time in the number of Nobel Prizes in each of the 20-year periods. However, this prize has not been awarded in every year. During the years 1901-1920, the leading country in Nobel Prizes for Peace was France. In percentage terms, the United States was most prominent during the years 1941-1960 with 41.7% of prizes, but in later years its relative importance has fallen sharply (see Table 12).

Two final notes: There have been only few migrant winners (intellectual or otherwise) in this category, and most of the winners have not had academic degrees.

Table 12
NOBEL PEACE PRIZE WINNERS BY COUNTRY AND YEARS

	1901-1920	1921-1940	1941-1960	1961-1980	1981-2000	TOT
Denmark	1	0	0	0	0	1
France	4	2	2	1	0	9
Germany	0	3	0	1	0	4
Italy	1	0	0	0	0	1
Netherlands	1	0	0	0	0	1
Russia	0	0	0	1	1	2
Sweden	1	2	0	1	1	5
Switzerland	3	0	0	0	0	3
United Kingdom	1	4	2	2	1	10
United States	3	4	5	4	2	18
Others	4	3	3	9	15	34
Total	**19**	**18**	**12**	**19**	**20**	**88**

PERCENTAGE OF NOBEL PEACE PRIZE WINNERS BY COUNTRY AND YEARS

	1901-1920	1921-1940	1941-1960	1961-1980	1981-2000	% TOT
Denmark	5.3	0.0	0.0	0.0	0.0	1.1
France	21.1	11.1	16.7	5.3	0.0	10.2
Germany	0.0	16.7	0.0	5.3	0.0	4.5
Italy	5.3	0.0	0.0	0.0	0.0	1.1
Netherlands	5.3	0.0	0.0	0.0	0.0	1.1
Russia	0.0	0.0	0.0	5.3	5.0	2.3
Sweden	5.3	11.1	0.0	5.3	5.0	5.7
Switzerland	15.8	0.0	0.0	0.0	0.0	3.4
United Kingdom	5.3	22.2	16.7	10.5	5.0	11.4
United States	15.8	22.2	41.7	21.1	10.0	20.5
Others	21.1	16.7	25.0	47.4	75.0	38.6
% of Total	**21.6**	**20.5**	**13.6**	**21.6**	**22.7**	**100.0**

NOTE: The Top Ten countries earned 54, or 61.4% of the Nobel Peace prizes awarded.

Summary

In summary, the dominant country credited Nobel Prizes was the United States. In the scientific categories—Chemistry, Medicine, Physics and, later, Economics—the United Sates started slowly, but since 1941 its awards in these categories have increased sharply up to about 44% of total awards.

This change can be attributed, in part, to the flight of many scientists (mostly Jewish) from Germany, Italy, and the occupied countries during the Nazi era. When they fled to the West, especially to the United States, they brought advanced European knowledge and experience with them. The influence of this knowledge migration persisted for generations, making the United States the leading scientific country in the world. Hitler, when told that scientists (mostly Jews) were emigrating, reacted with indifference and discounted the scientific cost to his regime. He did not realize the eventual impact of this pattern.

After 100 years of Nobel Prizes in science, the United States leads with 34.8% of the awards in Chemistry, 46.9% in Medicine, 42.6% in Physics and 63% in Economics. Ten countries—the United States and nine European countries—have accounted for about 90% of the Nobel Prizes in the scientific categories. These 10 countries, however, account for only about 60% of the awards in the Literature and Peace categories. Nevertheless, the United States is the leading country in the Peace prize category with the United Kingdom second, and France third. In the Literature category, France leads with the United States second.

It should also be noted that these 10 countries comprise only 11% of the world's total population, but are among the highest in terms of per capita Gross National Product, life expectancy, and educational level, according to U.N. statistics. The ten countries have also won more than 80% of all Nobel Prizes awarded.

LEADING INSTITUTIONS WHERE NOBEL PRIZE WINNERS WERE EDUCATED

The 22 leading institutions where Nobel Laureates were educated and received their highest academic degrees are presented in Table 13 and Figure 4. A review of the data reveals huge differences among these institutions; the best known and most prestigious universities have several times more graduates winning Nobel prizes than the rest of academia. For example, Cambridge University in the United Kingdom has produced 58 Nobel Laureates while the University of Copenhagen has had only nine.

There are, of course, many other institutions with no Nobel Laureates at all. Top universities seem to produce Nobel Laureates because they can afford to select the best teachers and students; they also have the financial means to provide better equipped laboratories to carry out top-quality basic research. Therefore, such universities as Cambridge attract students and teachers from all over the world, partly because they can meet the best experts, including Nobel prize winners, in various disciplines. Thus, the premier education centers in the United States and Europe can better prepare graduates for the highest levels of research.

Not all laureates, of course, have performed their Nobel prize research at the same institution from which they were graduated. Cambridge University, for example, has its 58 Nobel Prizes, but more than 70 Laureates (about 10% of the total) acknowledge some sort of tie to Cambridge. Take Piotr Kapitsa, Nobel Prize winner in Physics in 1978. He received his Ph.D. degree at Cambridge, but credited the research that led to his Nobel Prize to the Academy of Science in Moscow.

A close look at the data indicates a specialization of universities in certain Nobel categories. Cambridge University leads in all scientific categories except economics; the University of Chicago leads in the field of economics. In fact, about half of all Nobel prize Laureates in economics have ties to the University of Chicago.

Table 13
LEADING EDUCATIONAL INSTITUTIONS OF NOBEL PRIZE WINNERS BY CATEGORY

Institute	Chem.	Med.	Phys.	Peace	Lit.	Econ.	Total
Cambridge Univ.	14	16	21	2	2	3	58
Harvard Univ.	10	14	9	3	1	6	43
Columbia Univ.	5	10	11	1	0	7	34
Univ. of Chicago	3	2	9	0	0	11	25
Univ. of California (all)	13	3	3	1	0	4	24
Oxford Univ.	6	5	1	4	2	3	21
Univ. of Paris	3	6	2	6	1	1	19
Univ. of Munich	9	3	5	0	0	0	17
M.I.T.	5	0	8	0	0	3	16
Univ. of Berlin	4	3	6	1	0	1	15
Univ. of Göttingen	5	3	5	1	1	0	15
Cal Tech	3	2	9	0	0	0	14
Johns Hopkins Univ.	0	9	0	1	0	2	12
Princeton Univ.	2	0	6	1	0	3	12
Yale Univ.	1	7	2	0	1	1	12
Univ. of Wisconsin	3	4	3	0	0	1	11
Univ. of London	3	6	1	0	0	0	10
Univ. of Uppsala	3	0	2	4	1	0	10
Cornell Univ.	0	3	3	1	2	1	10
Univ. of Illinois	2	4	4	0	0	0	10
Univ. of Copenhagen	0	5	2	0	2	0	9
École Normale Super.	1	0	5	0	2	1	9

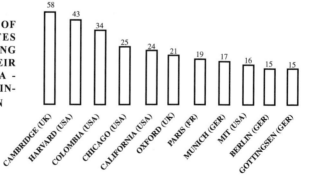

Fig 4. NUMBER OF LAUREATES ACCORDING TO THEIR EDUCATIONAL INSTITUTION

UNIVERSITIES/INSTITUTES WHOSE RESEARCHERS HAVE RECEIVED NOBEL PRIZES

Researchers working in 10 countries hold some 90% of all the Nobel Prizes awarded from 1901 to 2000 in the scientific categories (Chemistry, Medicine, Physics and Economics). Tables 13 and 14 show the institutions in which Nobel Laureates have achieved their highest educational degree as well as the universities credited with Nobel Prizes. Note that in many cases the two tables are not identical.

Close to 50% of the Nobel Prizes awarded in the science categories were earned by researchers affiliated with only 18 universities in the United States, the United Kingdom, Germany, and France. As noted before, there is specialization among these universities: the University of Chicago in Economics with nine Nobel Laureates; the University of California (especially its Berkeley campus), Max-Planck Institute, and Cambridge which excel in Chemistry; Harvard and Rockefeller Universities are prominent in Medicine; Stanford stands out in Physics. The top three universities in all scientific categories are: Harvard, California (at five of its campuses), and Cambridge.

It should be pointed out that these same top universities, because of their corps of Nobel Laureates, tend to attract the younger generation of scientific talent. As a result of this or for other reasons, these universities tend to have greater research budgets and are better equipped to provide for the needs of its scientific faculties. For example, the Burger Precision Camera only existed at M.I.T. Max Perutz and John Kendrew were therefore better equipped than other scholars anywhere else to study the structure of globular proteins —hemoglobin and myoglobin—for which they won the Nobel Prize in Chemistry in 1962.

Only a small portion of scientists working for such private companies as IBM or Bell Laboratories have been awarded Nobel Prizes: Two in Chemistry (1.5%), eight in Medicine (4.7%), 18 in Physics (11.1%) and one in Economics (2.2%). It should also be mentioned that in the other two Nobel categories—Literature and Peace—universities have likewise not been materially involved.

Table 14
SCIENTIFIC NOBEL PRIZES CREDITED TO UNIVERSITIES/INSTITUTIONS: 1901-2000

University	Chem.	Med.	Physics	Econ.	Total
Harvard (USA)	5	12	8	4	29
California (USA)	11	4	8	3	26
Cambridge (UK)	9	5	7	3	24
Max-Planck (Germany)	10	5	3	0	18
Rockefeller (USA)	5	11	0	0	16
Chicago (USA)	1	1	4	9	15
Stanford (USA)	3	1	10	1	15
Cal Tech (USA)	3	5	6	0	14
London, UK	2	7	3	1	13
M.I.T., USA	1	4	5	2	12
Columbia, USA	1	3	5	2	11
Princeton, USA	0	1	7	2	10
Oxford, UK	4	5	0	0	9
Cornell, USA	3	0	4	0	7
Berlin, Germany	5	0	2	0	7
Heidelberg, Germany	4	1	2	0	7
Washington, USA	0	5	1	1	7
Sorbonne, France	2	1	3	0	6
Inst. Pasteur, France	0	6	0	0	6
TOTAL	69	77	78	28	252
% of Total	51.1	44.8	48.2	60.9	48.9
Private companies	2	8	18	1	29

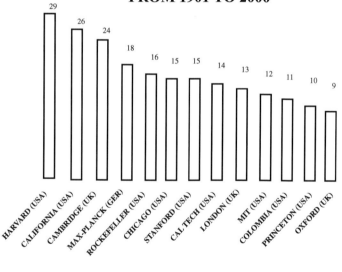

Fig 5. NUMBER OF NOBEL PRIZES CREDITED TO MAJOR INSTITUTIONS OF HIGHER LEARNING FROM 1901 TO 2000

AGE AT PUBLICATION AND THE INTERVAL TO WINNING THE NOBEL PRIZE

Successful scientific work has to be accompanied by immediate publication of the findings; the date of acceptance of an article for publication is the proof of priority of discovery in the biological sciences.

There have been cases of scientists delaying publication of their findings, and as a result losing out on a Nobel Prize. Furthermore, publication does not imply immediate recognition of the importance of the work done, since according to Alfred Nobel's Will, the findings have to be verified first before obtaining the prize. In fact, the importance of many scientific discoveries reported in the scientific literature is appreciated only over the long run.

Table 15
AVERAGE AGE (YEARS) OF PUBLISHING AND RANGE AND INTERVAL TO NOBEL PRIZE

	Publication Age Average	Range	Interval
Physics	37.3	20 - 59	15.4
Chemistry	40.7	26 - 63	15.0
Medicine	41.1	21 - 67	15.2
Peace	54.3	26 - 83	9.1
Literature	57.4	26 - 78	6.3
Economics	59.0	21 - 80	8.2

The average age of scientists publishing a discovery that led to winning the Nobel Prize was the youngest in Physics (37.3 years), but the interval between publication and the Nobel Prize was 15.4 years. For example, Albert Einstein was born in 1879 and won the Nobel Prize in Physics in 1922 (for 1921) for a paper he wrote in 1905. In other words, he wrote the paper when he was 26-years-old and was recognized for it 17-years later when he was 43. Interestingly, Einstein was nominated for the award every year from 1910 to 1922 (except for 1911 and 1915).

The paper that gained him the Nobel Prize was for his theory of the photoelectric effect and not for his better-known theory of relativity. Few scientists at the time could comprehend the latter, especially when no proof was yet available. In fact some of the very well known physicists of the time called Einstein's theory of relativity, "Jewish physics," as if it had nothing to do with science.

Recently new observations using the Hubble telescope have indicated that the antigravity theory that Albert Einstein postulated more than 70 years ago was, in fact, correct. This proof on its own could have qualified him for a second Nobel Prize, since antigravity may be the most powerful force in the universe.

Another example of the discrepancy between the age of publishing the results of a discovery and the award of a Nobel prize involves Subrahmanyan Chandrasekhar of the United States. He was scorned in the early 1930's for suggesting the existence of black holes and was regarded as a fool for it. One-half a century later his theory was proven right; he was awarded the Nobel Prize in Physics in 1983. Similarly, Ernst Ruska was 27-years-old when he invented the electron microscope in 1933. Some 53-years later, in 1986, he was awarded the Nobel Prize in Physics at the age of 80.

The second youngest average age for publication of a discovery was in Chemistry —at 40.7 years; the mean interval between publication and gaining the Nobel award was 15 years. Here, too, some extreme cases can be noted. Lars Onsager was awarded the Nobel Prize in 1968, 40 years after his discovery of the reciprocal relations fundamental to the study of non-equilibrium thermodynamics.

The third youngest winners were in the field of Medicine with an average age of 41.1. The interval between publication and award of a Nobel Prize was similar to that found in Physics and Chemistry. A further example: Francis Peyton Rous was awarded the Medicine Prize in 1966 some 56 years after his discovery of tumor-inducing viruses in chickens.

It seems, therefore, that in the biological sciences, the interval between publication and winning the award takes more time than in the other disciplines. Generally, publication of great discoveries in the categories of physics, chemistry, and medicine, have been done mostly by young scientists. There have been some older ones as well. Max Planck was 43 when he articulated the quantum law of physics; Dorothy Hodgkin was 46 when she discovered the chemical structure of B12.

The oldest Laureates at the time of publication were those in the field of Economics (an average of 59.0 years of age), but their wait for recognition was relatively short (only an average of 8.2 years). There have been exceptions, of course. Mathematician John Nash—profiled in the 2001 Academy Award-winning film, *A Beautiful Mind,* had to wait 45 years for his Nobel prize for work he had done at the age of 21.

The shortest interval between publication and award has been in the category of Literature (6.3 years), but these Laureates published their serious works at a relatively advanced age (57.4). The reason for the short delay in recognition in Economics and Literature may be that their Nobel prize was based on a *series* of publications—a lifetime's work—rather than on a specific publication detailing a particular discovery.

In the category of Peace, publication has usually meant much less. These prizes are in recognition of actual acts such as peace treaties or the work of an organization. But there have been exceptions in this area as well. Linus Pauling won in 1962 for his campaign against the dangers of radioactive fallout from weapons testing and the use of nuclear weapons in war; Eli Wiesel won in 1986 for his writings and teachings about the meaning of the Holocaust.

The range of age of publication was younger and shorter for Physics (20 to 59), followed by Chemistry (26-63). Economics is in third position with Peace and Literature following.

AGE OF NOBEL PRIZE-WINNERS: 1901-2000

The previous discussion dealt with the age of publication and the interval between publication and the award of a Nobel Prize. Below is a table dealing with the age of Prize winners at the time they accepted their award.

Table 16
AVERAGE AGE AND RANGE (YEARS) WHEN NOBEL PRIZE WAS AWARDED

Category	Average Age	Age Range
Physics	52.4	25-84
Chemistry	55.5	35-83
Medicine	56.3	32-87
Peace	62.0	32-87
Literature	63.8	42-85
Economics	66.5	51-82

The data shown in Table 16 indicate that the *youngest* Nobel Prize winners were in the category of Physics (which also had the highest age range), followed by Chemistry and Medicine. The Laureates in Peace and Literature were older by seven to ten years while the oldest group comprised the Economics prize-winners.

The youngest Nobel Prize winner was William Lawrence Bragg from the United Kingdom. He won in the year 1915 at the age of 25 in Physics for work on crystal structure he did with his father, with whom he shares the award. By contrast, the oldest Laureates received their prizes at the age of 87 were: Francis Peyton Rous in Medicine in 1966 and Joseph Rotblat in Peace in 1995.

The shortest-lived winner was William Vickery of the United States. He won the Nobel Prize in Economics in 1996 at the age of 83 and died three days after he had learned of his award. Christian Mommsen was 85 when he was awarded the prize for Literature in 1902 for his monumental work, *History of Rome*, which he had completed in 1886.

Another peculiar case is that of the Swedish poet, Erik Axel Karlfeldt. He was born in 1864 and won the Nobel Prize in 1918. But he refused it. He preferred to devote himself to the affairs of the Swedish Academy, as both a member and as its secretary from 1904 until his death in 1931. After he died, the Academy decided to give him his Nobel Prize posthumously.

In the graph below, note the gaps between the average age of publishing the results of a discovery versus the age of the recipient at the time the prize was awarded.

Fig 6. AGE (YEARS) AT PUBLICATION AND AGE WHEN NOBEL PRIZE AWARDED

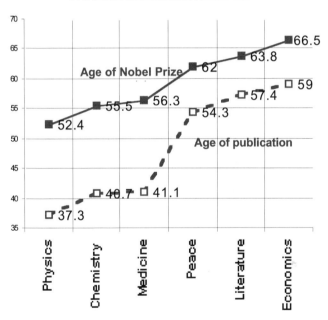

WOMEN AS WINNERS OF THE NOBEL PRIZE DURING THE FIRST 100 YEARS

Only 29 women have won the Nobel Prize—4.3% of the total awarded—compared to 672 or 93.3% for men. Even though Madam Marie Curie won the Nobel Prize in scientific categories twice, few other women (less than 3%) followed the example she set (see Fig. 7 and Table 1).

Of the 29 Nobel Prizes won by women, 34% have been in the Peace category, 31% in Literature, 17.2% in Medicine, 10.3% in Chemistry, 6.9% in Physics, and none in Economics. American women have earned 11, or 37.9% of these awards, while women of France, the United Kingdom, and Sweden have each won three awards (10.4%).

The age of obtaining the prize was within as broad a range for the women as for the men—32 to 80 years. But only 10 (34.5%) of the women had a third academic degree (Ph.D., M.D., etc.) while nine (31%) did not have *any* academic degree. As for religion, the 29 women include one Buddhist, two freethinkers, and six Jews (20.7%); the other 20 (69%) follow various denominations of Christianity, except there is no Muslim woman (see Table 17).

The contributions of some of the 20th Century's most prominent women have seemingly been ignored, e.g., Rachel Carson, the environmentalist, and Ava Helen, who contributed with her husband, Linus Pauling, to the ban on nuclear weapon testing. Despite her effort, he alone was awarded the Nobel Peace Prize in 1963. Another example is Jocelyn Bell. As a graduate student, she was the first to discover a source of radiation from space that had not previously been detected. Later, additional research building on her work brought about the discovery of a new type of star—a pulsar. As a result, Antony Hewish and Martin Ryle won the Nobel Prize in physics in 1974. Several scientists argued at the time that Jocelyn

Bell should have been included in the award as well.

The nuclear physicist Lise Meitner worked with Otto Hahn for many years on a project which earned him the Nobel Prize for Chemistry in 1945 (for 1944). She received no recognition from the Swedish Academy for her contribution. In another example, the famous Swedish author of children's books, Astrid Lindgren (1908-2002), created and expanded the freckle-faced, free-spirited character of Pippi Longstocking. Her books were translated into 76 languages and sold more than 120 million copies. Throughout her life she preached respect for the rights of children and animals as well as equality between the sexes. Her work earned her 24 successive nominations for the Nobel Prize in Literature, but she was rejected each time on the grounds that the Literature prize was not intended for authors who write exclusively for children!

The case of Marie Curie best illustrates the potential of women as scientists. She was born in Poland in 1867 and left home at an early age to pursue a scientific career in France. A woman of great courage, she faced the dual bias of being female as well as a foreigner. Nevertheless she was the first woman to earn a Ph.D. and then teach at the Sorbonne. Marie Curie later became the first woman to receive two Nobel Prizes—the first in Physics in 1903 and the second in Chemistry in 1911. As a result, she is generally regarded as one of the most important scientists ever—male or female! The work she and her partners did led to improved cancer treatment as well as the development of the atom bomb.

It is interesting to note that during the first 100 years of Nobel Prizes, there has actually been a *decline* in awards to women. This, despite the gains they have made in other fields of life and the number of new opportunities that have arisen. For whatever it may be worth, nine of the 29 Nobel winners (31%) were not married or had been divorced at the time of their award, while seven (24.1%) did not have children. It suggests that the commitment to intellectual success restricts a full family life.

A commitment to success in a field for which Nobel Prizes are awarded imposes a particular toll on women. The most fruitful period of life in which people excel intellectually, especially in science, seems to be between 20 and 30 years of age. These, of course, are also prime childbearing years.

Given the fact that the burden of raising children still falls mainly to women, real balance in intellectual achievements will occur only when both sexes share equally in this task. If adequate daycare centers and educational facilities are also available, then everyone will benefit when women can reach their full potential, provided of course that prejudice against women ceases and more women are made part of the Nobel judging committees.

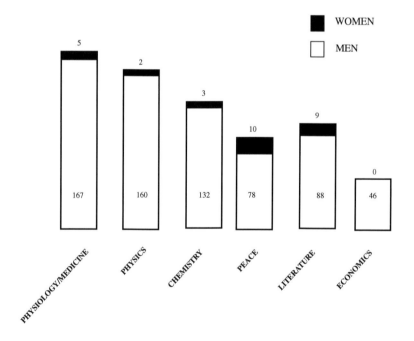

Fig 7. NUMBER OF NOBEL PRIZE WINNERS BY GENDER: 1901-2000

Table 17
WOMEN AWARDED THE NOBEL PRIZE: 1901-2000

Name	Category	Date	Born/Birth Place	Death	Nat./Ed. Place *	Rel.**	Ed./Degree
Curie, Marie	Chem.	1911	1867 Poland	1934	Poland France	Cath.	France Ph.D.
Joliot-Curie, Irene	Chem.	1935	1897 France	1956	France	Prot.	France D.Sc.
Hodgkin, Dorothy Crowfoot	Chem.	1964	1910 Egypt	1994	UK	Chris.	UK Ph.D.
Cori, Gerty Theresa Radnitz	Med.	1947	1896 Czech.	1957	Czech. American	Jewish	Czech. M.D.
Yalow, Rosalyn Sussman	Med.	1977	1921 USA	----	American	Jewish	USA Ph.D
McClintock, Barbara	Med.	1983	1902 USA	1992	American	Cong.	USA Ph.D.
Levi-Montalcini, Rita	Med.	1986	1909 Italy	----	Italy American	Jewish	Italy M.D.
Elion, Gertrude Belle	Med.	1988	1918 USA	1999	American	Jewish	USA M.S.
Curie, Marie	Phys.	1903	1867 Poland	1934	Polish	Cath.	France Ph.D.
Goeppert-Mayer, Maria	Phys.	1963	1906 Poland	1972	German	Chris.	German Ph.D
von Suttner, Bertha Fellicie Sophie Kinsky	Peace	1905	1843 Austria	1914	Austrian	ARelig.	----
Addams, Laura Jane	Peace	1931	1860 USA	1935	American	Presb.	USA A.B.
Balch, Emily Greene	Peace	1946	1867 USA	1961	American	Unit.	USA A.B.
Corrigan, Mairead	Peace	1976	1944 N. Ire.	----	N. Ire.	Cath.	N.Ire. None
Williams, Elizabeth	Peace	1976	1943 N. Ire.	----	N. Ire.	Cath.	N. Ire. None
Mother Teresa	Peace	1979	1910 Turkey	1997	Yugos. India	Cath.	India None
Myrdal, Alva Reimer	Peace	1982	1902 Swed.	1986	Swedish	Luth.	Swed. M.A.
Aung San, Suu Kyi	Peace	1991	1945 Burma	----	Burmese	Budd.	UK B.A.
Menchu Tum, Rigoberta	Peace	1992	1959 Guate.	----	Guate.	Chris.	Guate. None
Williams, Jody	Peace	1997	1950 USA	----	USA	----	USA M.A.
Lagerlof, Selma Ottilia Lovisa	Literature	1909	1858 Swed.	1940	Swed.	Free-Thinker	Swed. B.A.
Deledda, Grazia	Literature	1926	1871 Italy	1936	Italy	Cath.	None
Undset, Sigrid	Literature	1928	1882 Den.	1949	Den. Nor.	Cath.	None
Buck, Perl	Literature	1938	1892 USA	1973	USA	Presb.	USA M.A.
Mistral, Gabriela	Literature	1945	1889 Chile	1957	Chile	Cath.	Chile Teacher
Sachs, Leonie Nelly	Literature	1966	1891 German	1970	German Swed.	Jewish	None
Gordimer, Nadine	Literature	1991	1923 S. Africa	----	S. Africa	Jewish	None
Morrison, Toni	Literature	1993	1931 USA	----	USA	Chris.	USA M.A.
Szymborska, Wislawa	Literature	1996	1923 Poland	----	Poland	----	Poland B.A.

* Nationality/Country of Education
** Religion

COLLABORATION AND SIMULTANEOUS WORK LEADING TO NOBEL PRIZES

An examination of the level of collaboration between Laureates was undertaken. It was assumed that increased *numbers* of winners would indicate that greater collabortation was needed over the years to produce important findings leading to the award of a Nobel prize.

Table 18
NUMBER OF NOBEL PRIZE WINNERS IN 20–YEAR PERIODS BETWEEN 1901 AND 2000

	1901-1920	1921-1940	1941-1960	1961-1980	1981-2000
Chemistry	18	22	24	32	39
Medicine	18	24	36	51	43
Physics	24	22	28	43	45
Peace	22	19	16	22	28
Literature	20	18	17	22	20
Economics*	--	--	--	18	28

* Nobel Prizes in Economics were initiated in 1969

Table 18 clearly shows that collaboration in the scientific Nobel categories is increasing. For example, when Maurice Wilkins was asked why he and Rosalind Franklin missed the discovery of the double helix—even after Franklin had the crucial X-ray photographs in her own hands—he replied that they could not cooperate together. Francis Crick, on the other hand, understood that as a physicist he needed the collaboration of James Watson, a biologist. As he himself noted: "If Jim had been killed by a tennis ball" he was "reasonably sure he would not have solved the problem (of the double helix) on his own."

Table 18 also shows that nearly *twice* the number of Nobel Prizes were awarded in Chemistry, Medicine, and Physics between 1961 and 2000 compared to the 1901 to 1940 period. This suggests that new discoveries now require more sophisticated research, involving more collaboration and far higher costs than ever before. Take the European Organization for Nuclear Research (CERN) as a model. It was created and is funded by the European community. No private university or company could afford to build and maintain the facilities that CERN has assembled in Switzerland, and no single scientist could undertake the ongoing projects that CERN currently sponsors. For example, it has the largest machine for the acceleration of electrons and positrons in the world today (forming a ring of 27km in diameter). As a result, scientists from all over the world collaborate in large teams (sometimes over 400 per team). These teams may include specialists in a variety of disciplines such as physics, chemistry, medicine, and so forth.

A significant success of CERN has been the verification of the existence of the W and Z particles (UA1 experiment), which involved many physicist and engineers using huge equipment. While in the past a single scientist could succeed with a "crazy" idea on a tiny budget, this is no longer likely to happen. Now, committees are formed to approve experimental work; they are much less likely to risk large sums on a "crazy" idea. In other words, much of the individual freedom that scientists knew in the past has become restricted now.

It seems that in the future more teamwork will be needed in nearly all aspects of the biological sciences. The human genome project is a case in point. Because of the complexity of such investigations, it may be that only the leader of a scientific group would be awarded the Nobel Prize. Such a leader may not be the classical scientific genius, but one with the ability in human resources management to organize and control a team of individuals. This will probably require scientists with higher numbers in the Emotional Quotient (EQ) rather than the more traditional Intelligent Quotient (IQ).

By contrast, the other Nobel categories—Literature and Peace—have seen no drastic change in the number of Laureates winning over the years, suggesting that collaboration is of much less importance in these fields.

OTHER AWARDS EARNED BY NOBEL PRIZE WINNERS BETWEEN 1901 AND 2000

The other intellectual awards earned by Nobel Prize winners have been researched and divided into two categories—before and after their Nobel Prizes were awarded.

Table 19
NUMBER OF AWARDS BEFORE AND AFTER OBTAINING THE NOBEL PRIZE

Category	Before NP*	After NP*	# Laureates	Average Before	Average After
Chemistry	420	327	135	3.1	2.4
Medicine	665	407	172	3.9	2.4
Physics	374	345	162	2.3	2.1
Peace	136	74	88	1.6	0.8
Literature	256	83	97	2.6	0.9
Economics	67	19	46	1.5	0.3
Total	**1918**	**1255**	**700**	**2.7**	**1.8**

Note NP stands for Nobel Prize

As can be seen from Table 19, the number of awards earned by Laureates in all categories *before* they received their Nobel Prize was much greater than that afterwards. It may be postulated that after winning what is considered the highest possible recognition for intellectual achievement, there was less incentive for the Laureates to continue at the same pace of achievement; or that the inevitable effects of aging may have played a role.

The largest number of outside awards were earned in the category of Medicine, whereas the smallest number was for Peace. The reason, here, is probably that the awards for Medicine concern the welfare of all human beings in every country, whereas those for Peace concern specific regional problems, which do not affect other parts of the world. Likewise, research in Physics does not usually have a direct or immediate impact on the daily human affairs and this may be a reason for the relatively smaller number of "other awards".

Finally, the very small number of "other awards" in Economics can be attributed to the fact that Nobel Prize in this category were only initiated in 1969 and there have been just 32 years (compared to 100 years for the other categories) in which these "other awards" could have been earned.

ACADEMIC DEGREES OF NOBEL PRIZE WINNERS BETWEEN 1901 AND 2000

It was interesting to determine whether there are differences in the academic degrees obtained by Nobel Laureates in the different categories. Our findings are surprising; there seems to be significant differences among the categories.

In the scientific categories (Chemistry, Medicine, Physics and Economics), for example, more than 90% of the Laureates had a third academic degree—either earning a doctor of philosophy (Ph.D.), a general doctorate (Dr.), a medical doctorate (M.D.), or Doctorate in Philosophy (D.Phil.).

A Ph.D. was the most common academic degree of the scientific Laureates, except for Medicine—77% Ph.D. Laureates in Chemistry, 77.8% in Physics, 87% in Economics, and 40% in Medicine. On the other hand, less than a third of the Laureates had a third academic degree in the Peace category and when they did, it was mainly a Ph.D.; nearly a third of them had no academic degree, whatsoever. In the Literature category, only 8.1% had a third academic degree, while about half did not have any academic degrees at all (see Table 20). Among those who did have an academic degree, they say it was achieved in response to family pressure to ensure a "practical" profession.

It would seem, therefore, that Laureates in the Peace category and especially those in Literature were born with sheer special talent or were able to develop it on their own through the circumstances of their life. Such talent, it would appear, does not require any academic degree to flourish.

Table 20
ACADEMIC DEGREES OF NOBEL PRIZE WINNERS

Degree	Chem.	Med.	Phys.	Peace	Lit.	Econ.	Total
B.A.	1	0	2	13	25	1	42
D.Sc.	7	6	10	0	1	2	26
Dr.	5	3	9	9	3	2	31
Dr. Eng.	2	0	0	0	0	0	2
M.A.	4	1	5	8	9	1	28
M.D.	4	85	1	0	0	0	90
M.Sc.	1	2	2	0	0	0	5
Ph.D.	104	53	126	13	2	40	338
Ph.D.+D.Sc.	4	2	2	0	0	0	8
Ph.D.+M.D.	1	14	0	2	0	0	17
Engineer	0	1	1	1	2	0	5
M.B.	0	2	0	0	0	0	2
M.D.+D.Sc.	0	2	0	1	0	0	3
B.Sc.	0	0	3	1	2	0	6
Law degree	0	0	0	11	6	0	17
D.Phil	2	1	0	0	2	0	5
None	0	0	1	29	46	0	76
Total	**135**	**172**	**162**	**88**	**98**	**46**	**701**
%/No degree	0.0	0.0	0.6	33.0	46.9	0.0	--
%/1st degree[1]	0.7	0.6	3.7	29.6	35.7	2.2	--
%/2nd degree[2]	3.7	2.9	4.3	9.0	9.3	2.1	--
%/3rd degree[3]	95.6	96.5	91.4	28.4	8.1	95.7	--

1   1st degree= B.A., B.Sc., Engineer, Law degree.
2   2nd degree= M.A., M.Sc., M.B.
3   3rd degree= Ph.D., Dr., M.D., D.Phil.

RELIGION OF NOBEL PRIZE WINNERS

A review of the Nobel awards between 1901 and 2000 reveals that 654 Laureates belong to 28 different religions. Most (65.4%) have identified Christianity in its various forms as their religious preference. While separating Roman Catholic from Protestants among Christians proved difficult in some cases, available information suggests that more Protestants were involved in the scientific categories and more Catholics were involved in the Literature and Peace categories.

Atheists, agnostics, and freethinkers comprise 10.5% of total Nobel Prize winners; but in the category of Literature, these preferences rise sharply to about 35%. It can be speculated that the latter have a greater urge to be totally free of any formal religious attachments so that they can better express universal ideas.

A striking fact involving religion is the high number of Laureates of the Jewish faith—over 20% of total Nobel Prizes (138); including: 17% in Chemistry, 26% in Medicine and Physics, 40% in Economics and 11% in Peace and Literature each. The numbers are especially startling in light of the fact that only some 13 million people (0.2% of the world's population) are Jewish. By contrast, only 5 Nobel Laureates have been of the Muslim faith—0.8% of total number of Nobel prizes awarded—from a population base of about 1.2 billion (20% of the world's population) (see Tables 21A, 21B, 21C and Fig. 8).

How can such a few number of Jews produce so many Nobel prize winners? One explanation may be the effect of being a minority without a homeland producing an extraordinary desire to excel. Jewish people were not allowed to settle down as farmers for hundreds of years in Europe; they were only permitted to participate in commerce and education. As a result, doctors serving important people could save themselves from deportation. The same tradition continues to the present day.

Another additional explanation of the disproportionate number of Jewish Nobel Laureates is related to persecution of Jews over the years, culminating during World War II. The Holocaust, alone, claimed nearly half of the Jewish nation. Given the evidence of the brain migration, it can be argued that Darwin's principle of the survival of only the fittest may have been at work. In other words, pogroms and the Holocaust forced a genetic selection for the better fit, which was much more drastic than for any other faith.

It should also be noted that the Jewish population in Israel, representing nearly half of the world's Jewish population, has not produced any Nobel Laureates in any of the scientific categories. It is thought that the reason has to do with the importance of financial aid for basic scientific research. Israel is still engaged in wars and security problems and cannot afford to invest the sums required to develop all that is required to compete in basic scientific research. On the other hand, a country such as Israel is prone to stick to more practical aspects of research, e.g., Israel holds the second place in the world in high-tech industry.

100 YEARS OF NOBEL PRIZES

Table 21A
RELIGION OF NOBEL PRIZE WINNERS BETWEEN 1901 AND 2000—NUMBERS

Religion	Chem.	Med.	Physics	Peace*	Lit.	Econ.	Total	%Total
Anglican	1	4	10	4	3	1	23	3.5
Ath. & Agnostic	8	14	3	3	17	1	46	7.0
Freethinker	1	1	4	0	15	1	22	3.4
Baptist	0	3	0	1	0	1	5	0.8
Brahmin	0	0	0	0	1	0	1	0.2
Buddhist	1	0	3	2	1	0	7	1.1
Calvinist	2	1	0	0	0	0	3	0.5
Catholic	10	16	10	16	23	1	76	11.6
Christian	44	33	35	11	0	10	133	20.3
Congregation.	0	6	3	1	0	0	10	1.5
Duch-Menonite	0	0	1	0	0	0	1	0.2
Duch-Reform	0	0	0	1	0	0	1	0.2
E. Orthodox	0	0	2	1	5	1	9	1.4
Episcopalian	0	2	0	2	1	0	5	0.8
Evangelical	1	2	0	0	0	0	3	0.5
G. Orthodox	0	1	0	0	0	0	1	0.2
Hindu	0	1	2	0	0	0	3	0.5
Jewish	22	44	38	9	10	15	138	21.1
Lutheran	8	7	8	6	3	2	34	5.2
Methodist	3	4	2	5	1	0	15	2.3
Muslim	1	0	1	2	1	0	5	0.8
Neo-Pagan	0	0	0	0	1	0	1	0.2
Presb.	0	7	5	4	1	0	17	2.6
Protestant	23	18	19	12	8	4	84	12.8
Quaker	0	1	1	1	0	0	3	0.5
Shinto	0	0	0	1	0	0	1	0.2
Unitarian	2	3	0	1	0	1	7	1.1
Total	127	168	147	83	91	38	654	100.0
% of total	19.4	25.7	22.5	12.7	13.9	5.8	100.0	

*An additional 19 Peace Nobel Prizes were awarded to international organizations.

Table 21B
RELIGION OF NOBEL PRIZE WINNERS BETWEEN 1901 AND 2000—PERCENTAGES

Religion	Chem.	Med.	Physics	Peace*	Lit.	Econ.
Anglican	0.8	2.4	6.8	4.8	3.3	2.6
Ath. & Agnostic	6.3	8.3	2.0	3.6	18.7	2.6
Freethinker	0.8	0.6	2.7	0.0	16.5	2.6
Baptist	0.0	1.8	0.0	1.2	0.0	2.6
Brahmin	0.0	0.0	0.0	0.0	1.1	0.0
Buddhist	0.8	0.0	2.0	2.4	1.1	0.0
Calvinist	1.6	0.6	0.0	0.0	0.0	0.0
Catholic	7.9	9.5	6.8	19.3	25.3	2.6
Christian	34.6	19.6	23.8	13.3	0.0	26.3
Congregation.	0.0	3.6	2.0	1.2	0.0	0.0
Duch-Menonite	0.0	0.0	0.7	0.0	0.0	0.0
Duch-Reform	0.0	0.0	0.0	1.2	0.0	0.0
E. Orthodox	0.0	0.0	1.4	1.2	5.5	2.6
Episcopalian	0.0	1.2	0.0	2.4	1.1	0.0
Evangelical	0.8	1.2	0.0	0.0	0.0	0.0
G. Orthodox	0.0	0.6	0.0	0.0	0.0	0.0
Hindu	0.0	0.6	1.4	0.0	0.0	0.0
Jewish	17.3	26.2	25.9	10.8	11.1	39.5
Lutheran	6.3	4.2	5.4	7.2	3.3	5.3
Methodist	2.4	2.4	1.4	6.0	1.1	0.0
Muslim	0.8	0.0	0.7	2.4	1.1	0.0
Neo-Pagan	0.0	0.0	0.0	0.0	1.1	0.0
Presbyterian	0.0	4.2	3.4	4.8	1.1	0.0
Protestant	18.1	10.7	12.9	14.5	8.8	10.5
Quaker	0.0	0.6	0.7	1.2	0.0	0.0
Shinto	0.0	0.0	0.0	1.2	0.0	0.0
Unitarian	1.6	1.8	0.0	1.2	0.0	2.6
Total	**100.0**	**100.0**	**100.0**	**100.0**	**100.0**	**100.0**

*An additional 19 Peace Nobel Prizes were awarded to international organizations.

Fig 8. NOBEL PRIZE WINNERS BY RELIGION (1901-2000)

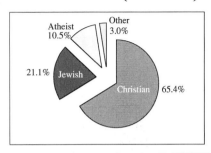

Table 21c
ILLUSTRATIVE COMPARISON OF THE RELATIVE SUCCESS OF TWO RELIGIOUS GROUPS IN PRODUCING NOBEL PRIZE WINNERS

ISLAMIC
(1,200,000,000 Muslims [about 20% of the world's population] with less than 1% of Nobel Prizes)

Chemistry	Physics	Literature	Peace:
1999 - Ahmed Zewail	1979 - Abdus Salam	1988 - Najib Mahfouz	1978 - Mohamed Anwar El-Sadat
			1994 - Yasser Arafat

JEWISH
(13,000,000 Jews [about 0.2% of the world's population] with more than 20% of Nobel Prizes)

Chemistry
- 1905 - Adolph Von Baeyer
- 1906 - Henri Moissan
- 1910 - Otto Wallach
- 1915 - Richard Willstatter
- 1918 - Fritz Haber
- 1943 - George Charles de Hevesy
- 1961 - Melvin Calvin
- 1962 - Max Ferdinand Perutz
- 1971 - Gerhard Herzberg
- 1972 - William Howard Stein
- 1977 - Ilya Prigogine
- 1979 - Herbert Charles Brown
- 1980 - Paul Berg
- 1980 - Walter Gilbert
- 1981 - Roald Hoffmann
- 1982 - Aaron Klug
- 1985 - Herbet A. Hauptman
- 1985 - Jerome Karle
- 1989 - Sidney Altman
- 1992 - Rudolph Marcus
- 1998 - Walter Kohn
- 2000 - Alan J. Heeger

Medicine
- 1908 - Ilya Metchnikoff
- 1908 - Paul Erlich
- 1914 - Robert Barany
- 1922 - Otto Meyerhof
- 1922 - willem einthoven
- 1930 - Karl Landsteiner
- 1931 - Otto Warburg
- 1936 - Otto Loewi
- 1944 - Joseph Erlanger
- 1944 - Herbert Spencer Gasser
- 1945 - Ernst Boris Chain
- 1946 - Hermann Joseph Muller
- 1950 - Tadeus Reichstein
- 1952 - Selman Abraham Waksman
- 1953 - Hans Krebs
- 1953 - Fritz Albert Lipmann
- 1958 - Joshua Lederberg
- 1959 - Arthur Kornberg
- 1964 - Konrad Bloch
- 1965 - Francois Jacob
- 1965 - Andre Lwoff
- 1967 - George Wald
- 1968 - Marshall W. Nirenberg
- 1969 - Salvador Luria
- 1970 - Julius Axelrod
- 1970 - Sir Bernard Katz
- 1972 - Gerald Maurice Edelman
- 1975 - David Baltimore
- 1975 - Howard Martin Temin
- 1976 - Baruch S. Blumberg
- 1977 - Rosalyn Sussman Yaow
- 1978 - Daniel Nathan
- 1980 - Baruj Benacerraf
- 1984 - Cesar Milstein
- 1985 - Michael Stuart Brown
- 1985 - Joseph L. Goldstein
- 1986 - Stanley Cohen [and Rita Levi-Montalcini]
- 1988 - Gertude Elion
- 1989 - Harol Varmus
- 1994 - Alfred Gilman
- 1994 - Martin Rodbell
- 1995 - Edward B. Lewis
- 1997 - Stanley Prusiner
- 2000 - Eric R. Kandel

Physics
- 1907 - Albert Abraham Michelson
- 1908 - Gabriel Lippmann
- 1921 - Albert Einstein
- 1922 - Niels Bohr
- 1925 - James Franck
- 1925 - Gustav Hertz
- 1943 - Otto Stern
- 1944 - Isidor Issac Rabi
- 1945 - Wolfgang Pauli
- 1952 - Felix Bloch
- 1954 - Max Born
- 1958 - Igor Tamm
- 1958 - Ilya Frank
- 1959 - Emilio Segre
- 1960 - Donald A. Glaser
- 1961 - Robert Hofstadter
- 1962 - Lev Davidovich Landau
- 1963 - Eugene Wigner
- 1965 - Richard Phillips Feynman
- 1965 - Julian Scwinger
- 1967 - Hans Beth
- 1969 - Murray Gell-Mann
- 1971 - Dennis Gabor
- 1973 - Brian David Josephson
- 1975 - Benjamin Mottleson
- 1976 - Burton Richter
- 1978 - Arno Allan Penzias
- 1979 - Stephen Weinberg
- 1979 - Sheldon Glashow
- 1979 - Steven Weinberg
- 1988 - Leon Lederman
- 1988 - Melvin Schwartz
- 1988 - Jack Steinberger
- 1990 - Jerome Friedman
- 1992 - Georges Charpak
- 1995 - Martin Perl
- 1995 - Frederick Reines
- 1997 - Claude Cohen-Tannoudji

Economics
- 1969 - Ragnar Frisch
- 1970 - Paul Anthony Samuelson
- 1971 - Simon Kuznets
- 1972 - Kenneth Joseph Arrow
- 1975 - Leonid Kantorovich
- 1976 - Milton Friedman
- 1978 - Herbert A. Simon
- 1980 - Lawrence Robert Klein
- 1985 - Franco Modigliani
- 1987 - Robert M. Solow
- 1990 - Harry Markowitz
- 1990 - Merton Miller
- 1992 - Gary Becker
- 1993 - Rober Fogel
- 1997 - Myron Scholes

Literature
- 1910 - Paul Heyse
- 1927 - Henri Bergson
- 1958 - Boris Pasternak
- 1966 - Shmuel Yosef Agnon
- 1966 - Nelly Sachs
- 1976 - Saul Bellow
- 1978 - Isaac Bashevis Singer
- 1981 - Elias Canetti
- 1987 - Joseph Brodsky
- 1991 - Nadine Gordimer

Peace
- 1911 - Alfred Fried
- 1911 - Tobias M. C. Asser
- 1968 - Rene Cassin
- 1973 - Henry Kissinger
- 1978 - Menachem Begin
- 1986 - Elie Wiesel
- 1994 - Shimon Peres
- 1994 - Yitzhak Rabin
- 1995 - Joseph Rotblat

BIRTH DATES OF LAUREATES BY SEASONS AND ASTROLOGICAL SIGNS

We were able to uncover the dates of birth of 684 Laureates, out of a total of 700. An analysis of these birth dates reveals that they were evenly distributed through three seasons—summer, spring and autumn. Winter, however, saw 22% fewer births (see Table 22). Before too much is made of this fact, it should be realized that a similar distribution is found in the population at large. The reason seems to be that couples throughout the world prefer to avoid raising babies in the very cold weather of Northern hemisphere winters.

As for the astrological signs, no significant differences were found among the Laureates of the six prize categories. As it turns out, the largest numbers were born under the sign of Gemini (May 22 to June 21) and Virgo (August 23 to September 22) while Capricorn (December 23 to January 20) was the least represented. Again, the probable reason is that more births, in general, occur under the first two signs than the latter (because of Northern Hemisphere winter).

Interestingly, Capricorn has the highest representation (27.8%) in the Peace category. However, statistical analysis suggests that this deviation, based on such a small body of data, may also occur by chance. Therefore, additional data are needed to provide a more meaningful reason for this phenomena (see Table 23).

Table 22
BIRTH DATES OF LAUREATES ACCORDING TO CATEGORY AND SEASON

Category	Autumn	Spring	Summer	Winter	Total-No.
Chemistry—No.	37	34	35	25	131
Chemistry—%	28.2	26.0	26.7	19.1	100
Economics—No.	7	13	18	6	44
Economics—%	15.9	29.6	40.9	13.6	100
Literature—No.	25	26	28	18	97
Literature—%	25.8	26.8	28.9	18.5	100
Medicine—No.	45	39	47	40	171
Medicine—%	26.3	22.8	27.5	23.4	100
Peace—No.	27	25	12	20	84
Peace—%	32.1	29.8	14.3	23.8	100
Physics—No.	38	41	45	33	157
Physics—%	24.2	26.1	28.7	21.0	100
Total—No.	**179**	**178**	**185**	**142**	**684**

Table 23
BIRTH DATES ACCORDING TO CATEGORIES AND ASTROLOGICAL SIGNS

Sign	Chem.	Econ.	Lit.	Med.	Peace	Phys.	Total
Aquarius - No.	9	1	6	12	6	14	48
Aquarius - %	18.8	2.1	12.5	25.0	12.5	29.2	
Aries - No.	12	3	8	16	5	14	58
Aries - %	20.7	5.2	13.8	27.6	8.6	24.1	
Cancer - No.	11	5	14	11	2	22	65
Cancer - %	16.9	7.7	21.5	16.9	3.1	33.8	
Capricorn - No.	5	3	5	7	10	6	36
Capricorn - %	13.9	8.3	13.9	19.4	27.8	16.7	
Fishes - No.	10	2	5	16	5	9	47
Fishes - %	21.3	4.3	10.6	34.0	10.6	19.1	
Gemini - No.	10	6	10	26	6	13	71
Gemini - %	14.1	8.5	14.1	36.6	8.5	18.3	
Leo - No.	11	4	8	6	5	12	46
Leo - %	23.9	8.7	17.4	13.0	10.9	26.1	
Libra - No.	12	2	13	13	12	14	66
Libra - %	18.2	3.0	19.7	19.7	18.2	21.2	
Sagittarius - No.	12	2	7	18	6	16	61
Sagittarius - %	19.7	3.3	11.5	29.5	9.8	26.2	
Scorpio - No.	8	3	7	16	7	11	52
Scorpio - %	15.4	5.8	13.5	30.8	13.5	21.2	
Taurus - No.	13	6	10	9	11	14	63
Taurus - %	20.6	9.5	15.9	14.3	17.5	22.2	
Virgo - No.	18	7	4	21	9	12	71
Virgo - %	25.4	9.9	5.6	29.6	12.7		16.9

100 YEARS OF NOBEL PRIZES

COMMENTARY

LUCK, GENIUS, AND ENVIRONMENT

A typical Nobel Prize winner is not easy to describe. Yet there are some common attributes that apply to most: highly talented; very good student, although mostly not at the genius level; strong sense of curiosity; intuitive; creative; consistent; devoted; and courageous in opposing conventional prejudices. Interestingly, many of the Laureates knew their destiny in life, even as children.

Most of the Laureates' achievements result from hard work and careful preparation. As Louis Pasteur once said: "Chance favors the prepared mind." Or, in the words of Peyton Rous (Nobel Laureate in Medicine, 1966) "a prepared mind [makes] its own chances."

Few experiments have proven risky for the Laureate himself. Such was the case for Werner Forssman (Nobel Laureate in Medicine, 1956). He inserted a catheter into the crook of his arm and up to his heart. It was important to his investigation, but dangerous and against medical rules. Similarly, Laureates may have to make extraordinary sacrifices. For example, Aung San Suu Kyi (Peace, 1991) stayed in Burma in danger while leaving her family behind in England.

The Role of Luck
Some achievements that led to winning the Nobel Prize were made possible by pure luck, or a combination of a moment of inspiration and luck. Here are a few examples:

- Marie Curie, as noted above, was born in Poland. Because women were not allowed to attend institutions of high learning in Poland, she went to study at the Sorbonne in France. When Marie graduated, she intended to return to Poland to become a teacher. This would clearly have ended her career as a scientist. Instead, she fell in love with Pierre Curie, a promising scientist. As a result of this stroke of good fortune, she decided to remain in France and study for a doctoral degree, becoming the first woman in Europe to earn a Ph.D. In fact, she earned a first place in her science examinations, despite the handicap of learning in a foreign language. The research for her Ph.D. involved an investigation into the phenomena of radiation, the discovery that led to her first Nobel Prize in 1903 which she shared with her husband. In fact, she became the first scientist of either gender to win two Nobel Prizes. She won her second in Chemistry in 1911 for her discovery of the elements, radium and polonium.

- Alexander Fleming won the Nobel Prize for his discovery of penicillin. Fleming was born in 1881 to a Scottish sheep-farming family. He excelled in school, but was not considered a genius.

His scientific breakthrough began in 1928 when he was investigating his theory that nasal mucus had antibacterial properties. He smeared a microscope slide with Staphylococcus bacteria, left it in his laboratory, and went for a two-week vacation. Upon his return, he noticed that bacteria growing near a mold had died; the mold that had accidentally contaminated the slide was unknown to him. It appears that a spore of a rare variant called *Penicillium notatum* had somehow and luckily drifted in from a laboratory on the floor below. In a moment of inspiration he correctly concluded that the mold had released a substance which had killed the bacteria. This substance, which he named penicillin, later turned out to be the most effective lifesaving drug ever produced.

Fleming, it turns out, was not the first to describe the antibacterial properties of penicillin. John Tyndall (in 1875) and D. A. Gratia (in 1925) preceded him. Fleming, however, was the first to *recognize* the immense importance of the discovery, and he published his findings in the *British Journal of Experimental Pathology* in 1929. Interestingly, he never conducted the most important experiment connected to his discovery, namely injecting penicillin into mice that had been previously infected with bacteria; more significantly, he abandoned his study of penicillin in 1932.

Luckily, a specimen of Fleming's mold was acquired by a team of scientists at Oxford University. The team included Howard Florey (an Australian-born physiologist) and Ernst Boris Chain (a chemist who had fled Nazi Germany). They and their colleagues were able to purify sufficient penicillin to undertake the experiments that Fleming had been unable to do. They inoculated mice with lethal doses of bacteria and then injected them with penicillin, and found that it totally cured them. Later, they were able to show that patients with a variety of infections were cured by injections of penicillin. Florey, Chain, and their colleagues continued their effort to mass-produce penicillin for use during World-War II. For their combined efforts, which saved millions of lives, Fleming, Florey, and Chain were awarded the Nobel Prize in 1945.

- Carl David Anderson was awarded the Nobel Prize in Physics in 1936 for his discovery of the positron, an important element in understanding atomic structure. Anderson confessed later that his discovery was obtained by accident rather than a methodical application of reason and perservering effort.

Sometimes, research aimed at one goal has its direction changed to a different more important target. Such was the case of C. T. R. Wilson (Physics, 1927). He developed his "cloud chamber" for the study of weather and light; instead, it turned out to be an important instrument for the examination of the basic components of matter.

- Another recent example of chance at work occurred to Professor Hideki Shirakawa of the University of Tsukuba in Japan. He shared the Nobel Chemistry Prize in 2000 for the discovery and development of conductive polymers.

We have always been taught that plastics, unlike metals, do not conduct electricity. As a result, they have been used to insulate copper wires in electric cables. However, Shirakawa's Nobel Prize was awarded for the revolutionary discovery that plastics can, after modification, be made electrically conductive. When something defies common wisdom and works, it is put to use; conductive plastics are already being employed in solar cells, mobile telephones, "smart" window panes, and offer the prospect of many more applications in the future.

Yet, the discovery started with a mistake made by one of Shirakawa's graduate students, who had been asked to warm a plastic compound. The student mistakenly used a much higher temperature than intended; this mistake allowed the plastic to become more conductive to electricity. Prof. Shirakawa, in a moment of inspiration, realized the importance of this accident and acted to perfect the finding.

- Another case of a Nobel Laureate favored by luck involves Crick and Watson, winners of the Nobel Prize for the double-helix structure of DNA. At the time, Rosalind Franklin was producing the world's best X-ray diffraction pictures of DNA. Her colleague, Maurice Wilkins, showed Watson one of Franklin's best pictures of DNA. Watson later recalled that "The instance I saw the picture my mouth fell open," since it "gave several of the vital helical parameters." In other words, he could visualize the structure in 3-dimensions. Rosalind Franklin died in 1958 of cancer at the age of 37. Since the Nobel Prize was awarded in 1962, only Maurice Wilkins was able to share the award with Crick and Watson.

  If Rosalind Franklin had lived, the prize would surely have been given to her instead of Wilkins, since she not only had produced the key pictures of DNA, but had correctly criticized Watson and Crick's early work. Her criticism helped them to later find the right solution. Drawings in her own notebook indicated that she herself was trying to get the right solution as well. But, she never did. She missed the three dimension molecular models that Watson and Crick correctly assumed.

- Another case is a combination of vision, courage, and luck, initiated by a Dutch chemist named Paul Krutzen. His work led him to suggest that man-made chemicals were a threat to the Earth's ozone shield. Many scientists at that time were very skeptical about this theory. However, skepticism faded when a "hole" in the ozone layer was found over Antarctica.

  Krutzen put the blame on nitrogen oxides, but an American, F. Sherwood Rowland, and his Mexican postdoctoral student, Mario Molina, identified by good fortune the correct chemicals: chlorofluorocarbons (CFCs). These chemicals break up in the atmosphere, releasing ozone-splitting chlorine atoms. As a result, the protocol of the 1987 Montreal conference on the environment banned the further use of CFCs; a Nobel Prize followed for the three scientists in 1995. It shows that the world has, indeed, become a small village in two aspects: First, three scientists of three different nationalities were able to solve an important problem; and secondly, they demonstrated that what happens in one corner of the world can effect the whole planet.

- The spark of inspiration can occur at any moment unexpectedly and in many cases while occupied with other matters. However, the moment of inspiration does not come out of a vacuum. Previous hard work invested in a specific field and an active subconscious can offer powerful assistance. Such was the case with Linus Pauling who had struggled for several years with the structure of the alpha-helix molecule. Then, while sick in bed he was able to fold a piece of paper to solve its structure. His discovery led to the Nobel prize in Chemistry in 1965. Similarly, Erwin Schrödinger (Physics, 1933) was on a Christmas vacation in the Alps with his mistress when he had an inspiration that produced his prize-winning work. Another case was of Mullis Kary Banks (Chemistry, 1993). His moment of inspiration, leading to the invention of the Polymerase Chain Reaction (PCR), came while he was driving (The PCR method changed molecular biology forever). Finally, there is the example of Richard Feynman (Physics, 1965). The inspiration leading to his discovery was a wobbling plate he observed while eating in a cafeteria at Cornell University.

The Role of Genius
Is the Nobel Laureate a genius? Or does his or her success depend on the proper education and environment? Indeed, only some Laureates were of the genius type. Albert Einstein (Physics, 1921) comes to mind. As noted above, the case of John Nash (Economics, 1994) combined a case of genius with schizophrenia. His story became the basis for the film, *A Beautiful Mind*. Ironically, the film itself won its own distinction when it was awarded an Oscar as Best Picture of 2001 by the Academy of Motion Picture Arts and Sciences.

Even when the Laureate *is* a recognized genius, it may not show up at the early stages of a career. Albert Einstein, who is regarded as one of the most important scientists in the 20th century and the greatest physicist who ever lived, was only an average pupil at school. When his father went to speak with the schoolmaster about what profession his son should choose, the teacher replied that it did not matter because Albert would never make much of a success of anything. Albert dropped out of school at 15; he could not stand the discipline and in any case his father urged him to enter a practical profession. Later, he would even fail his entry examination to the university and had to study and prepare for a year before he eventually passed it. At the university, he was bored and missed many lectures. He graduated with less than medium grades and could not get a position commensurate with his degree.

So in 1902 he took a job as a minor clerk in the Swiss Patent Office. There he wrote some of the papers which revolutionized physics. He was awarded the Nobel Prize in 1922 for 1921 for the law of photoelectric effect (first published in 1905). Interestingly, his much better known theory of relativity, demonstrating that space is "curved," was never recognized for a Nobel Prize, despite its completion in 1915 and its confirmation in 1919. Even more significantly, Einstein is considered the father of the atom bomb and nuclear power because of his theoretical equation, $E=mc^2$, and his support for their development.

Another example of a genius who had an indifferent school career is Jack Kilby. He shared the Nobel Prize in Physics in 2000, but was never accepted at M.I.T. as a teenager and never earned a Physics degree. Rather, he worked as an engineer and was able to solve various practical electronic problems with ingenious solutions. For instance, he invented the silicon chip after working for Texas Instruments for two weeks. Later he would develop applications for his invention in pocket calculators, digital watches, improved computers, space probes, pacemakers, dishwashers, and the Internet.

There is also a possibility of collective genius being produced when a group of scientists meet and produce new ideas in a brainstorming session, ideas that no one was able to develop on his or her own.

Many of the conferences taking place in many fields around the world may in fact contribute to this effect. Such was the case of the Solvay Conferences, initiated in 1911, that brought many distinguished physicists together and proved to have an important impact.

The Role of Environment

Our study of the first 100 years of Nobel prizes has suggested that those born and educated in an undeveloped country have a very slim chance of winning a Nobel Prize, particularly in the scientific categories. Furthermore, regardless of one's genius and despite the place of birth, only those educated at one of the top universities in the world are likely to receive a Nobel Prize. Being a graduate of a top university opens the way to acceptance at the best research institutions, which are in the forefront of scientific knowledge and advances.

The environment at home of a child probably also has a role in helping to determine Nobel success. Those born to a wealthy family with a proper tradition of education seem to have had a better chance than those born in poverty and deprivation. But not always. Quite a number of the Laureates lost their fathers, or even parents, at a very early age, or grew up in a divorced family. For example:

- Albert Camus (Literature, 1957) lost his father when he was four and was brought up by his illiterate mother in a house where no books were available.
- Jean Paul Sartre (Literature, 1964) lost his father when he was 9 months old.
- Yasunari Kawabata (Literature, 1968) lost his parents when he was only few days old and was raised by his grandparents.
- Yasser Arafat (Peace, 1994) lost his mother when he was 4 and was thrown out of his house by his father later in his life.

Therefore, the stress imposed on children may stimulate their mental ability. With regard to the prize for Literature, it seems the talent is a genetic gift given to an author or poet at birth. The Nobel Prize in this category is not based on one successful book, but on a lifetime of contributions. By contrast, in the biological scientific categories (Chemistry, Medicine and Physics), one successful important finding can be enough to earn a Nobel Prize.

MAJOR INNOVATIONS OF NOBEL PRIZE LAUREATES BETWEEN 1901 AND 2000

As the long recognized highest and most prestigious intellectual prize is awarded each year, it is important to remember the contributions made by the recipients. They have truly made a difference.

- **Max Karl Ernst Ludwig Planck** established and developed the theory of elementary quanta in 1900/1 and was awarded the Nobel Prize in Physics in 1918.

- **Willem Einthoven** invented the electrocardiogram in 1901 and was awarded the Nobel Prize in Medicine in 1924.

- **Karl Landsteiner** classified blood groups, also in 1901, but waited until 1930 to be awarded the Nobel Prize in Medicine.

- **Albert Einstein** revolutionized theoretical physics during a prolific period of work between 1905 and 1915 and was awarded the Nobel Prize in Physics in 1922 (for 1921).

- **Richard Willstätter** was first to explain how chlorophyll works in plants during a period of study between 1905 and 1914 and was awarded the Nobel Prize in Chemistry in 1915.

- **Heike Kamerlingh-Onnes** first demonstrated superconductivity in 1907/8 and was awarded the Nobel Prize in Physics in 1913.

- **Woodrow Thomas Wilson** and **Lèon-Victor Auguste Bourgeois** were awarded the Nobel Peace Prizes of 1919 and 1920 for their work in the formation of the League of Nations.

- **Frederick Banting** and **John Macleod** discovered insulin in 1922 and were promptly awarded the Nobel Prize for Medicine in 1923.

- **Edward Appleton** discovered radio waves in 1924, but he had to wait until 1947 for his Nobel Prize in Physics. His discovery led to worldwide radio broadcasts, radar, and eventually opened the whole field of radio-physics to study.

- **Alexander Fleming, Ernst Boris Chain,** and **Walter Florey** were awarded the Nobel Prize in Medicine in 1945. Fleming was recognized for his 1929 discovery of penicillin while the others were recognized for their work in implementing his discovery. It is believed that penicillin has saved more than 50 million lives.

- **Linus Pauling** for developing quantum chemical bonding theory between 1928 and 1932, for which he was awarded the 1954 Nobel Prize in Chemistry. In 1962, he won a second Nobel Prize for Peace for his campaign against radioactive fallout.

- **Walter Norman Haworth** discovered vitamin C in 1932 and was awarded the Chemistry prize in 1937.

- **Ernest O. Lawrence** invented the cyclotron in 1932. The cylotron permitted very high acceleration of nuclear material, leading to important medical and biological applications. He was awarded the Physics prize in 1939.

- **Ernst Ruska** invented the electron microscope in 1933, but had to wait until 1986 to receive the Physics prize!

- **Dennis Gabor** invented holography in 1948 and was awarded the Physics prize in 1971. Holographic photography has proven useful in medical diagnosis, map making, computing, and photographic storage.

- **John Enders, Thomas Weller** and **Frederick Robbins** discovered how the polio virus grows in 1947 and 1948 for which they won the Nobel Prize in Medicine in 1954.

- **John Bardeen, William Shockley,** and **Walter Brattain** worked on semiconductors and discovered the transistor effect in 1948 and 1949. Their research led to the invention of the silicon chip, transistor radios, digital clocks, and communication satellites. They were awarded the Nobel Prize in Physics in 1956.

- **Francis Crick, James Watson** and **Maurice Wilkins** revealed the double helix structure of DNA in 1953, the basis of the genetic inheritance of all living things. They won the Nobel Prize in Medicine in 1962.

- **Charles Townes, Nicolai Basov,** and **Alexandr Prokhorov** did fundamental work in quantum electronics between 1952 and 1954. They were awarded the Nobel Prize in Physics in 1964. Townes's infrared telescope, for example, is 100 times more powerful than any other similar device.
- **George Catlett Marshall** was awarded the Nobel Peace Prize in 1953 for what came to be called the "Marshall Plan"—American loans and technical assistance to European nations devastated by the effects of World War II.
- **John Bardeen, Leon Cooper,** and **John Robert Schrieffer** developed the theory of superconductivity in 1957. This theory explained why materials lost electrical resistance at temperatures close to zero, an important finding for further development of a number of products. They received the Physics Prize in 1972.
- **Ernest Norman Borlaug** led the "Green Revolution" between 1963-67 with his development of a high-yield, disease-resistant dwarf wheat strain to provide relief from famine in developing countries. He was awarded the Nobel Peace Prize in 1970 for his work.
- **Zhores Alferov, Jack S. Kilby,** and **Herbert Kroemer** were awarded the Physics prize in 2000 for their work between 1958 and 1970 that led to the foundation of modern information technology, particularly for their invention of rapid transistors, laser diodes, and integrated circuits.
- **Peter Doherty** and **Rolf Zinkernagel** won the Nobel Prize in Medicine in 1996 for their discoveries in the 1970s concerning the specificity of cell mediated immune defense.
- **Paul Crutzen, Sherwood Rowland,** and **Mario Molina** proved the threat of chlorofluorocarbons (commonly used in aerosol cans) to the ozone layer which provides protection to the planet from ultraviolet radiation. That work in 1974 led to the Nobel Prize in Chemistry in 1995.

- **Paul Berg, Frederick Sanger,** and **Walter Gilbert** determined the base sequences in nucleic acids in 1977. This seminal work led to the development of interferon, growth hormones, cloning, and genetic engineering. They were awarded the Nobel Prize in Chemistry in 1980.

- **Mikahail Sergryevich Gorbachev** was awarded the Nobel Peace Prize in 1990 for decisive and dramatic changes in the relationship between the Soviet Union and its satellite nations and the West.

- **Steven Chu, Claude Coen-Tannoudji,** and **William D. Philips** developed methods over a 10-year period to cool and trap atoms with laser lights. This work led to the 1997 Nobel Prize in Physics.

- **Doctors Without Borders** were awarded the Nobel Peace Prize in 1999 for three decades of bringing medical help to victims of famine, war, and genocide.

- **Alan J. Heeger, Alan G. MacDiarmid,** and **Hideki Shirakawa** discovered and developed electrically conductive polymers in 1998. This material is used today in mobile phones, computers, and other electronic equipment. They were awarded the Nobel Prize in Chemistry in 2000 for their effort.

NOBEL PRIZES WITHIN FAMILIES (1901-2000)

Curies.
The Curies prove to be the most prolific family in the history of the Nobel Prizes:
1. Marie, and her husband, Pierre Curie, won in Physics in 1903. Marie won another Nobel Prize in Chemistry in 1911.
2. Irène, their eldest daughter, and her husband, Frédéric Joliot-Curie, were awarded the Chemistry Prize in 1935.
3. Henry Labouisse, the husband of Irène's daughter (Eve), accepted the 1965 Peace Prize on behalf of UNICEF.

Braggs
William Henry and his son, William Lawrence Bragg, working as a team, won in Physics in 1915.

Thomsons
Joseph John Thomson (Physics, 1906) and his son, George Paget Thomson (Physics, 1937).

von Eulers
Hans von Euler-Chelpin won a Chemistry prize in 1929 and his son, Ulf Svante Von Euler, won in Medicine in 1970.

Coris
Carl Ferdinand Cori and his wife, Gerty Cori, for Medicine in 1947.

Tinbergens
Jan Tinbergens (Economics, 1969) and his brother, Niko (Medicine, 1973).

Bohrs
Niels Bohr (Physics, 1922), and his son, Aage Bohr (Physics, 1975).

Siegbahns
Karl Manne Siegbahn (Physics, 1924) and his son, Kai Manne Siegbahn (Physics, 1981).

Myrdals
Gunnar Myrdal (Economics, 1974) and his wife, Alva (Peace, 1982).

Chandrasekhars
Raman V. Chandrasekhara (Physics, 1930) and his nephew, Subrahmanyan C. (Physics, 1983).

WINNERS OF MORE THAN ONE NOBEL PRIZE—OR REJECTING IT

Winning one Nobel Prize in the intellectual world is much more than winning the lottery, since it provides not only substantial financial benefits but also instant recognition and worldwide fame. To win *two* Nobels is something so rare and so special that it deserves a separate discussion.

- Marie Curie of France was the first Laureate to win *two* Nobel Prizes. She shared her first Nobel Prize in 1903 when she was 36. It was awarded in Physics for her investigation of the phenomena of radiation. She won her second Nobel in Chemistry in 1911 for the discovery of radium and polonium.
- Linus Carl Pauling of the United States was the first individual to receive two unshared Nobel Prizes in two *different* categories. He won his first Nobel in Chemistry in 1954 when he was 53 years old for his work on chemical bonds and molecular structures. He won his second Nobel in Peace just eight years later for his campaign against the dangers of radioactive fallout in weapons testing and from nuclear war.
- John Bardeen of the United States won two Nobel Prizes in Physics in the years 1956 and 1972. His first came at the age of 48 for his work on semiconductors; his second at the age of 64 for his work in the field of superconductivity.
- Frederick Sanger of the United Kingdom won two Nobel Prizes in Chemistry in the years 1958 and 1980. He won the first when he was 40 for the structure of insulin and the second at 62 for determining the base sequences of nucleic acids.

The case of Robert Burns Woodward of the United States is of interest because he won the Nobel Prize in 1965 in Chemistry for his outstanding achievements in the art of organic synthesis of such substances as quinine, cholesterol, cortisone, strychnine, and chlorophyll. His death at the early age of 62 probably prevented him from earning a second prize in Chemistry for his work in the organic synthesis of important substances.

As for those who have declined the prize, the case of Erik Axel Karlfeldt of Sweden has already been mentioned. He refused to accept the Nobel Prize in 1918 in Literature because of his position as Secretary of the Swedish Academy. Upon his death in 1931, however, his Prize was finally awarded. Karlfeldt remains the *only* individual ever awarded a Nobel prize posthumously.

Jean-Paul Sartre, the famous French philosopher, was awarded the Nobel Prize in Literature. He declined it on the grounds that he wanted to remain an "anybody." He felt that it could not happen as a Nobel Laureate. His dedication to freedom also led him to reject such possessions as a wife or children. The Nobel committee ignored his refusal, however, and delivered the award to him.

Le Duc Tho of the Democratic Republic of Vietnam was supposed to share the Nobel Peace Prize of 1973 with American Henry Kissinger. Le Duc Tho declined the prize under pressure that arose when the negotiated cease fire was not maintained by North Vietnam. Kissinger, claiming that President Richard M. Nixon deserved the award more than he, did not go to Oslo for the ceremony. On the other hand, the Russian writer Boris Pasternak, was awarded the Nobel Prize in Literature in 1958. At first, he indicated his acceptance, but later had to refuse it. Soviet authorities did not like his portrayal of Communist society in his novel, *Dr. Zhivago,* which had been published in the West without official approval. The Nobel Committee, aware of the situation in Moscow, rejected Pasternak's refusal and awarded him the prize anyway.

Finally, there is the matter of Oreste Piccioni, one of many who perhaps deserved a Nobel Prize, but never received one. Piccioni studied under Enrico Fermi and proved that a mesotron was *not* the carrier of the strong force holding the nuclei of atoms together. After immigrating to the United States, Piccioni continued his research, conferring at one point with Owen Chamberlin and Emilio Segré. He said that his suggestions led to their discovery of antiprotons for which both won a Physics Nobel in 1959. Piccioni later filed a civil law suit seeking money as well as a public acknowledgment of the importance of his contribution. But the case was dismissed as being beyond the statute of limitations. Worse, from Piccioni's standpoint, he and three others discovered the existence of the antineutron. This, too, was ignored by the Nobel Committee. While he did receive an award for his seminal contributions to particle physics from the Academia Nazionale Delle Scienze of Italy in 1999, it was clearly not the Nobel he coveted.

BRAIN MIGRATION

As mentioned above, about 10 western countries have won about 90% of the Nobel Prizes in science. Scientists working at 18 universities in just four countries have received about 50% of all the scientific Nobel Prizes. This leads to the question of whether a brain migration occurred during the first 100 years of the Nobel Prizes. Data for each of the six categories (Chemistry, Medicine, Physics, Economics, Literature and Peace) are presented in Tables 24 through 29.

Chemistry

There was a brain migration of scientists in the Chemistry category on a scale of about 20%, especially to the United States. Thirty-one (23%) of the Chemistry Laureates credited a different nationality, state, or institution other than their country of birth. About a third of these Laureates were Jewish; they fled anti-Semitism. Eight Laureates, most of them Jewish, left Germany and Austria before and during World War II. But there were other significant examples from other countries: George de Hevesy, born in Hungary and educated in Germany, fled from anti-Semitism to Denmark and Sweden.

On the other hand, some of the scientists who emigrated were born in countries that could not offer the top level education and research that leads to a Nobel Prize. The details of Marie Curie's experiences have been noted above. Another example is Ahmed Hassan Zewail. He was born in Egypt, but continued his studies and research in the United States, where he was awarded the Nobel Prize in Chemistry in 1999.

This migration helped to replace Germany as the leading country in chemistry science with the United Kingdom and the United States. For example, during the years 1901 to 1940, Germany led the world with about 40% to 50% of the Laureates in chemistry, while the United

States had only 5% to 9% during this period. Afterwards, Germany dropped to 7% to 16%, while the United States increased its percentage to 35% and 59% of the Chemistry Laureates.

Table 24
BRAIN MIGRATION IN CHEMISTRY

Name	Year Birth	Nationality	Education	Credited University	Credited State	Religion
Rutherford, Sir Ernest	1908 NZ	British	New Zealand	Victoria, Manchester	UK	Protestant
Oswald, Friedrich W.	1909 Latvia	Latvian	Latvia	Leipzig	Germany	Christian
Curie, Marie	1911 Poland	Pol/Fr	France	Sorbonne	France	Catholic
Zsigmondy, Richard A.	1925 Austria	Aus/Ger	Germany	Goettingen	Germany	Protestant
Karrer, Paul	1937 Russia	Russ/Swiss	Switzerland	Zurich	Switzerland	Protestant
Kuhn, Richard	1938 Austria	Aus/Ger	Germany	Max-Planck/Heid.	Germany	Protestant
Ruzicka, Leopold S.	1939 Yugo.	Yugo.	Germany	Fed. Instit.Tech.	Switzerland	Christian
Hevesy, George C. de Von	1943 Hungary	Hungarian	Germany	Stockholm	Hungary	Jewish
Giauque, William F.	1949 Canada	American	USA	U.C. Berkeley	USA	Christian
Heyrovsky, Jaroslav	1959 Czech.	Czech.	UK/Czech.	Polar. Instit. Of Czech.	Czech.	Christian
Perutz, Max Ferdinand	1962 Austria	Aus/British	UK	Cambridge	UK	Jewish
Hodgkin, Dorothy C.	1964 Egypt	UK	UK	Oxford	UK	Christian
Onsager, Lars	1968 Norway	Nor/Amer.	Nor/America	Yale	USA	Protestant
Hassel, Odd	1969 Norway	Norweg.	Nor/Germany	Kjemisk Instit. Oslo	Norway	Lutheran
Herzberg Gerhard	1971 Germany	Ger/Canadian	Germany	Nat.Res.Coun., Ottawa	Canada	Jewish
Cornforth, Sir John W	1975 Australia	British	Aus/UK	Sussex Brighton	Aus/UK	Protestant
Prelog, Vladimir	1975 Yugo.	Yugo/Swiss	Czech.	Eid. Tech.Hoch., Zurich	Switzerland	Agnostic
Prigogine, Ilya	1977 Russia	Russ/Belg.	Belgium	Libre de Bruxelles	Belgium	Jewish
Hoffman, Roald	1981 Poland	Pol/Amer.	USA	Cornell	USA	Jewish
Klug, Aaron	1982 Lithuania	S. Afr./Brit.	S. Africa/UK	Cambridge	UK	Jewish
Taube, Henry	1983 Canada	Can/Amer.	Can/USA	Stanford	USA	Lutheran
Lee, Yuan Tseh	1986 Taiwan	Chin/Amer.	Taiwan/USA	U.C. Berkeley	USA	Buddhist
Polanyi John Charles	1986 Germany	Can/British	UK	Univ. of Toronto	Canada	Christian
Pederse, Charles John	1987 Korea	Kor/Amer.	USA	Du Pont,Wilmington	USA	Catholic
Altman, Sidney	1989 Canada	Can/Amer.	USA	Yale	USA/Canada	Jewish
Marcus, Rudolph A.	1992 Canada	Can/Amer.	Canada	Cal Tech	USA	Jewish
Olah, George Andrew	1994 Hungary	Hun/Amer.	Hungary	Univ. So. Cal.	USA	Christian
Molina, Mario	1995 Mexico	Mexico	Mexico	MIT	USA	Catholic
Kohn, Walter	1998 Austria	Fr/American	USA	U.C. Santa Barbara	USA	Jewish
Zewail, Ahmed Hassan	1999 Egypt	Egypt/Amer.	Egypt/USA	Cal Tech	Egypt/USA	Muslim
MacDiarmid, Alan G.	2000 NZ	American	USA	Univ. of Penn.	USA	Jewish

Medicine

In the category of Medicine the pattern of brain migration was similar to that in Chemistry. However, the *scale* of migration here was the largest: 55 (or 32%) Nobel Laureates have a nationality, state, or institution credited that differs from their homeland. Again a third of them were Jewish, and again the bulk of migration was from the less to the more developed countries, especially to the United States.

While the Nobel statistics used in this book are reliable, some of them do not reveal as much detail as would be desired. For example, some of the Nobel prizes in Medicine were credited to the native countries of the Laureates, although their research was carried out in other countries.

Table 25
BRAIN MIGRATION IN MEDICINE

Name	Year	Birth	Nationality	Education	Credited University	Credited State	Religion
Ross, Sir Ronald	1902	India	UK	UK	Univ. College Liverpool	UK	Anglican
Mechnikov, Ilya Ilyich	1908	Russia	Russian	Russia	Institut Pasteur, Paris	Russia	Jewish
Carrel Alexis	1912	France	French	France	Rockefeller Instit.	France	Catholic
Barany, Robert	1914	Austria	Aus/Swed.	Austria	Vienna University	Austria	Jewish
Macleod, John J.R.	1923	UK	UK	UK	Univ. of Toronto	Canada	Presb.
Einthoven, Willem	1924	E. Indies	Netherlander	Netherlands	Leyden University	Netherlands	Jewish
Landsteiner, Karl	1930	Austria	Austrian	Austria	Rokefeller Instit. NY	Austria	Catholic
Loewi Otto	1936	Germany	Ger/Amer.	France	Univ. of Graz	Austria	Jewish
Szent-Gyorgyi, Albert	1937	Hungary	Hungarian	Hungary, UK	Szeget U. Hungary	Hungary	?
Florey, Sir Howard W.	1945	Australia	British	UK	Oxford University	UK	Protestant
Chain Ernst Boris, Sir	1945	Germany	Ger/British	Germany	Oxford University	UK	Jewish
Houssay, Bernardo A.	1947	Argentina	Argentinian	Argentina	Inst. Bio. Exper. Med.,	Argentina	Christian
Cori, Carl Ferdinand	1947	Czech	American	Czech	Washington, MO	USA	Christian
Cori, Gerty T. R.	1947	Czech	American	Czech	Washington, MO	USA	Jewish
Reichstein, Tadeus	1950	Poland	Swiss	Switzerland	Basel University	Switzerland	Jewish
Theiler, Max	1951	S. Africa	S. Africa	UK	Rockefeller Fnd. NY	S. Africa	Protestant
Waksman, Selman A.	1952	Russia	American	USA	Rutgers Univ., NJ	USA	Jewish
Krebs Hans Adolf, Sir	1953	Germany	Ger/British	Germany	Univ. of Sheffield	UK	Jewish
Lipmann Fritz Albert	1953	Germany	Ger/Amer.	Germany	Harvard & Mass. GH	USA	Jewish
Cournand Andre F.	1956	France	Fr/Amer.	France	Columbia Univ.	USA	Agnostic
Bovet Daniel	1957	Switz.	Swed/Ital.	Switz/Rome	Chief Inst.Pub. Health	Italy/USA	Calvinist
Ochoa, Severo	1959	Spain	American	Spain	New York University	USA	Christian
Burnet, Sir Frank M.	1960	Australia	Australia	Australia, UK	Walter&Eliza Hall	Australia	Presb.
Medawar, Sir Peter Brian	1960	Brazil	British	UK	University of London	UK	Christian
Von Bekesy, Georg	1961	Hungary	American	Hungary	Harvard University	USA	Christian
Wilkins, Maurice H. F.	1962	N. Zealand	British	UK	University of London	UK	Agnostic
Eccles, John Carew, Sir	1963	Australia	Australian	UK	Australian Nat.Univ.	Australia	Catholic
Bloch Konrad E.	1964	German	Ger/Amer.	USA	Harvard University	USA	Jewish
Huggins, Charles B.	1966	Canada	American	Canada, USA	Chic. Ben May Lab.	USA	Baptist
Granit, Ragnar Arthur	1967	Finland	Swedish	Finland	The Karolinska Instit.	Sweden	Lutheran
Khorana, Har Gobind	1968	India	American	India, UK	Univ. of Wisc.Madison	USA	Hindu
Delbruck Max	1969	Germany	Ger/Amer.	Germany	CalTech.	USA	Protestant
Luria, Salvador Edward	1969	Italy	American	Italy	M.I.T.	USA	Jewish
Katz Bernard	1970	Germany	Ger/Brit.	German,UK	University of London	UK	Jewish
Frisch, Karl von	1973	Austria	German	Germany	University of Munich	Germany	Catholic
Lorenz, Konrad Z.	1973	Austria	Austrian	Austria	Osterreichische Akademie	Austria	Catholic
Tinbergen, Nikolaas	1973	Netherlands	British	Netherlands	Oxford University	UK	Agnostic
Claude, Albert	1974	Rumania	Belgium	Belgium	Univ. Catholique de Louvain	Belgium	Catholic
Palade, George Emil	1974	Rumania	USA	Rumania	Yale University, CT	USA	G. Ortho.
de Duve, Christian R.M.	1974	UK	Bel/Amer.	Belgium	Rockefeller Univ.	USA	Catholic
Dulbecco, Renato	1975	Italy	American	Italy	Imp.Cancer Res. Fund Lab.	USA	Catholic
Guillemin Roger	1977	France	Fr/Amer.	France,Canada	The Salk Institute	USA	Agnostic
Schally, Andrew Victor	1977	Poland	American	Canada	Veterans Admin. Hosp. LA	USA	Christian
Cormack, Allan Macleod	1979	S. Africa	American	S. Africa	Tufts Univ., MA	USA	Christian
Benacerraf, Baruj	1980	Venezuela	American	USA	Harvard University	USA	Jewish
Hubel, David Hunter	1981	Canada	American	Canada	Harvard University	USA	Unitarian
Wiesel Torsten N.	1981	Sweden	Swed/Amer.	Sweden	Harvard University	USA	Protestant
Milstein, Cesar	1984	Argentina	Brit/Argen.	Argentina, UK	Cambridge, UK	UK, Argen.	Agnos/Jew
Jerme Niels Kaj	1984	UK	Brit/Danish	Denmark	Basel Instit. for Immun.	Denmark	Christian
Levi-Montalcini, Rita	1986	Italy	Ital/Amer.	Italy	Instit. Cell Biol., C.N.R.,	Italy, USA	Jewish
Tonegawa, Susumu	1987	Japan	Japanese	Japan, USA	M.I.T.	Japan	?
Fischer, Edmond Henry	1992	China	Amer/Swiss	Switzerland	Wash. Seattle, WA	USA, Swiss	?
Doherty, Peter C.	1996	Australia	Australian	UK, Australia	Tenn. Memphis, TN	Australia	Methodist
Kandel, Eric	2000	Austria	American	USA	Columbia University	USA	?

Physics

A similar trend to the above two categories occurred in Physics: 33, or 20% of the Laureates have a nationality, state, or institution credited that is different from their homelands. Again about a third of the winners were Jews who fled from anti-Semitism in their homelands. For example, Albert Einstein left Germany and Enrico Fermi (with a Jewish wife) fled from Italy. The bulk of immigrating scientists, as was found in the fields of Chemistry and Medicine, left less developed countries especially for the United States.

With the establishment of CERN (European Organization for Nuclear Research) in Switzerland, this trend of migrating physicists to the United States has been reduced. Indeed, in some cases the flow was reversed. Carlo Rubbia moved to Switzerland to work at CERN from the United States and was able to use their superior facilities to confirm the existence of W and Z particles. That work earned him the Nobel Prize in 1984.

Table 26
BRAIN MIGRATION IN PHYSICS

Name	Year	Birth	Nationality	Education	Credited University	Credited State	Religion
Curie, Marie	1903	Poland	Pol/Fr.	France	Ecole	France	Catholic
von Lenard, Phillipp E.A.	1905	Hungary	German	Germany	Kiel	Germany	Protest.
Michelson, Albert A.	1907	Germany	Ger/Amer.	USA	Chicago University	USA	Jewish
Lippmann, Gabriel Jonas	1908	Luxem.	French	Fr./Germany	Sorbonne	France	Jewish
Marconi, Guglielmo	1909	Italy	Italian	Italy	Marc. Wireless Tel.Co, UK	Italy	Catholic
Bragg William Lawrence	1915	Australia	British	Australia, UK	Victoria, UK	UK	Anglican
Einstein Albert	1921	Germany	Swiss/Amer.	Sweden	Max-Plank Inst.	Switzerland	Jewish
Franck James	1925	Germany	Ger/Amer.	Germany	Goettingen University	Germany	Jewish
Sir Raman, C. V.	1930	India	Indian	India	Calcutta	India	Hindu
Schrodinger, Erwin	1933	Austria	Austrian	Austria	Berlin Univ., Germany	Austria	Catholic
Fermi, Enrico	1938	Italy	Ital/Amer.	Italy	Rome Univ.	Italy	Agnostic
Stern Otto	1943	Germany	Ger/Amer.	Germany	Carneggie Instit. of Tech.	USA	Jewish
Rabi, Isidor Isaac	1944	Austria	Aus/Amer.	USA	Columbia Univ., NY	USA	Jewish
Pauli, Wolfgang Ernst	1945	Austria	Aus/Swiss	Germany	Princeton Univ., NJ	Austria	Catholic
Yukawa, Hideki	1949	Japan	Japanese	Japan	Kyoto Imp. U..& Colum. U.	Japan	Buddhist
Walton, Ernest T. S.	1951	Ireland	Irish	Ireland, UK	Trinity Col., Dublin	Ireland	Methodist
Born Max	1954	Germany	Ger/British	Germany	Edinburgh University	UK	Jewish
Brattain, Walter Houser	1956	China	American	USA	Bell Telephone Lab.	USA	Quaker
Lee, Tsung-dau	1957	China	Chin/Amer.	China, USA	Columbia Univ., NY	China	?
Yang, Chen Ning	1957	China	Chin/Amer.	China, USA	Instit. for Adv. Study, Princeton	China	?
Segre, Emilio Gino	1959	Italy	Ital/Amer.	Italy	U.C., Berkeley	USA	Jewish
Wigner, Eugene Paul	1963	Hungary	Hung/Amer.	Germany	Princeton Univ., NJ	USA	Jewish
Goeppert-Mayer, Maria	1963	Poland	Ger/Amer.	Germany	U.C. La Jolla	USA	Christian
Prokhorov, Alexander M.	1964	Australia	Australian	Russia	Lebedev Inst. Phys.	Russia	E. Ortho.
Gabor, Dennis	1971	Hungary	Hung/British	Germany	Imp. Col.Sci.& Tech.	UK	Jewish
Esaki, Leo	1973	Japan	Japanese	Japan	IBM /T. J. W. Res. Cen.	Japan	Buddhist
Giaever, Ivar	1973	Norway	Norweg/Amer	Norway, USA	General Electric CO.	USA	Lutheran
Salam, Abdus	1979	Pakistan	Pak/British	UK	Imperial Col., London	Pakistan	Muslim
Chandrasekhar, Subrahmanyan	1983	India	Ind/Amer.	India, UK	Univ. of Chicago	USA	Hindu
Rubbia, Carlo	1984	Italy	Italian	Italy	CERN, Geneva	Italy	Catholic
Taylor, Richard E.	1990	Canada	Can/Amer	Canada, USA	Stanford Univ., CA	Canada	Christian
Charpak, Georges	1992	Poland	Pol/Fr.	France	Ecole de PhysiqueParis & Cern	France	Jewish
Tsui, Daniel C.	1998	China	American	USA?	Princeton Univ., NJ	USA	Christian

Economics

As has been noted previously, Nobel Prizes in Economics were established in 1968 by the Bank of Sweden in memory of Alfred Nobel. As a result, the 46 Nobel Prizes in this category are much fewer than in other categories.

In this category, 12 Laureates (26%) credited different nationality, state, or institutions than their homeland. About 25% of the Laureates who had migrated and 36% of the Laureates in this category were Jewish.

Again, the bulk of migrated Laureates came from the less to the more developed countries and especially to the United States, helping that country to dominate this category.

Table 27
BRAIN MIGRATION IN ECONOMICS

Name	Year	Birth	Nationality	Education	Credited University	Credited State	Religion
Rvon Hayek, F.A.	1974	Austria	Aus/Brit/Amer	Austria	Univ. of London?	UK	Catholic
Vickrey, William	1996	Canada	Can/Amer.	USA?	Columbia Univ., NY	USA	?
Scholes, Myron S.	1997	Canada	Can/Amer	Canada, USA	Long Term Cap.Mgt., CT	USA	Jewish
Mundell, Robert A.	1999	Canada	Canada	Canada, USA	Columbia Univ., NY	Canada	?
Debreu, Gerard	1983	France	Fr/American	France	U.C., Berkeley	USA	Christian
Harsanyi, John C.	1994	Hungary	American	Hungary, USA	U.C., Berkeley	USA	Christian
Sen, Amartya	1998	India	India	India,UK	Trinity College, UK	India	?
Modigliani, Franco	1985	Italy	Ital/Amer.	Italy,USA	M.I.T.	USA	Jewish
Koopmans, Tjulling C.	1975	Neth.	Neth./Amer.	Netherlands	Yale Univ.	USA	Christian
Kuznets, Simon Smith	1971	Russia	Russ/Amer.	USA	Harvard Univ.	USA	Jewish
Leontief, Wassily W.	1973	Russia	Russ/Amer.	Germany	Harvard Univ.	USA	E. Ortho.
Lewis, Sir William A.	1979	St.Lucia	St.Lucia/Brit.	St.Lucia, UK	Princeton Univ.	UK	?

Literature

In the Nobel category of Literature, there have been 17 cases of brain migration (17.5%). Six of them (35%) were Jews who fled from anti-Semitism in their homeland. In other cases, the writers were fleeing from tyrannical regimes inimical to the free exchange of ideas. For example, Thomas Mann left Germany, Alexander Solzhenitsyn was exiled from the USSR, Isaac Bashevis Singer left Poland, and Gao Xingjian was forced to depart his native China.

Table 28
BRAIN MIGRATION IN LITERATURE

Name	Year	Birth	Nationality	Education	Credited State	Religion
Kipling, Joseph Rudyard	1907	India	British		UK	Methodist
Undset, Sigrid	1928	Denmark	Dan/Nor.		Norway	Catholic
Mann, Paul Thomas	1929	German	Ger/Czech/Amer.		German	Protestant
Hesse, Herman	1946	German	Ger/Swed.		Switzerland	Lutheran
Camus, Albert	1957	Algeria	French	France	France	Atheist
Seferis, Giorgos	1963	Turkey	Greek	France	Greece	E. Ortho.
Agnon, Shmuel Yosef	1966	Austria	Aus/Israeli		Israel	Jewish
Sachs, Leonie Nelly	1966	German	Ger/ Swed.		Sweden	Jewish
Solzhenitsyn, Alexander	1970	Russia	Russ/Amer.	Russia	Russia	E. Ortho
White, Patrick V. M.	1973	UK	Australian	UK	Australia	None
Bellow, Saul	1976	Canada	Can/Amer.	USA	USA	Jewish
Singer, Bashevis	1978	Poland	Pol/Amer.	Poland	USA	Jewish
Milosz, Czelaw	1980	Lith	Pol/Amer.	Poland	USA/Pol	Catholic
Canetti, Elias	1981	Bulgaria	Au/Br		UK	Jewish
Simon, Claude	1985	Madagascar	French		France	Christian
Brodsky, Joseph	1987	Russia	Rus/Amer.		USA	Jewish
Gao, Xingjian	2000	China	Chin/French		France	

Peace

In the Peace category, there have been only nine cases (or just 10%) of individuals born in a country other than the one in which they gained the award. Of these nine, five were Jewish and all had fled anti-Semitism in their homeland—Menachem Begin, Shimon Peres, Joseph Rotblat, Elie Wiesel, and Henry Kissinger. Of the other four, Albert Schweitzer and Mother Tereza followed a call to leave their homelands to serve humanitarian causes in Africa and India; Yasser Arafat eventually came to lead the Palestinian people in the Middle East; and Sean MacBride took his experience in Northern Ireland to promote human rights and the liberation of Namibia (see Table 29 below).

Table 29
BRAIN MIGRATION IN PEACE

Name	Year	Birth	Nationality	Education	Credited State	Religion
Schweitzer, Albert	1952	Germany	Ger/Fr.	France	France	Lutheran
Kissinger, Henry	1973	Germany	Ger/Amer.	USA	USA	Jewish
MacBride, Sean	1974	France	Irish	Ireland	Ireland	Catholic
Begin, Menachim W.	1978	Poland	Israeli	Poland	Israel	Jewish
Teresa, Mother	1979	Turkey	Yugo/ Indian	India	India	Catholic
Wiesel, Elie	1986	Romania	Rom/Fr/Amer.		USA	Jewish
Arafat, Yasser	1994	Egypt	Palestinian	Egypt	Palestine	Muslim
Peres, Shimon	1994	Poland	Israeli		Israel	Jewish
Rotblat, Joseph	1995	Poland	Pol/British	Poland	UK	Jewish

MARRIAGE, DIVORCE, AND CHILDLESSNESS AMONG NOBEL LAUREATES

Differences appear among the various Nobel prize categories in the numbers and percentages of Laureates who have married, divorced, and remained childless. It suggests that different types of people succeed in different fields.

The extremes, perhaps not unsurprisingly, are found in the categories of Literature and Peace. The former has the highest rate of divorce and remarriage, while both Literature and Peace share top place in the childlessness list. Of course, the Peace category has included Laureates whose religious faith forbade them from marrying and thus having children, e.g., Mother Teresa and the Dalai Lama. Celebacy also explains why this category includes the highest percentage of single individuals (see Table 30 below for details).

Table 30
PERCENTAGE OF MARRIAGES, DIVORCES, AND CHILDLESSNESS AMONG LAUREATES

Status	Chem.	Med.	Physics	Peace	Lit.	Econ.
1 Marriage	82.2	77.3	79.2	84.5	49.0	68.9
2 Marriages	8.5	14.5	18.2	0.0	31.3	22.2
3 Marriages	2.3	1.7	0.7	0.0	6.3	0.0
4 Marriages	0.8	0.0	0.0	0.0	2.1	0.0
5 Marriages	0.0	0.0	0.0	0.0	1.0	0.0
Single	6.2	6.4	2.0	15.5	10.4	8.9
1 Divorce	6.2	7.6	5.2	6.0	22.9	13.3
2 Divorces	1.6	0.6	0.7	0.0	4.2	0.0
3 Divorces	0.0	0.0	0.0	0.0	4.2	0.0
Childless	10.1	13.4	10.4	32.1	27.2	11.1

NOBEL LAUREATES IMPRISONED OR KILLED

The following Nobel Laureates were imprisoned during their careers for some aspect of their intellectual life:

- **Carl von Ossietzky** was the leader of the German Peace Society and a journalist who exposed German military activities from 1926. This caused his imprisonment several times. Because of his attacks on the Nazi regime in 1933, he was sent to a concentration camp and died under arrest in 1938. He was awarded the Nobel Peace Prize in 1935 as "a symbol [of the] struggle for peace rather than its champion."

- **Lev Davidovich Landau** was arrested in 1938 by Joseph Stalin, accusing him of being a "German spy." In 1962, he was awarded the Nobel Prize in Physics.

- **Pyotr Leonidovich Kapista** was another citizen of the USSR placed under house arrest in 1945 by Stalin. Imprisonment came after the United States developed the first atom bomb and lasted eight years. Kapista was awarded the Nobel Prize in Physics in 1978.

- **Otto Hahn, Max von Laue,** and **Werner Heisenberg** all played a key role in trying to develop a German atom bomb during World War II. They were placed under arrest by the British and taken to England to learn about their findings as well as to prevent their seizure by the Russians. While in prison, Otto Hahn was awarded the Nobel prize in Chemistry (1944).

- **Nelson Mandela**, leader of the African National Congress in South Africa, was arrested in 1962 and sentenced to life in prison. In 1990, he was released and a year later was elected president of his country. He was awarded the Nobel Peace Prize in 1993.

- **Wole Soyinka** was a prisoner for several years during Nigeria's civil war. While in prison, he created some of his best works of poetry. He was awarded the Nobel Prize in Literature in 1986.

- **Alexander Solzhenitsyn** was a prisoner in the Soviet Union during Stalin's regime. This experience led him to write his famous book, *The Gulag Archipelago*. He won the Nobel Prize in Literature in 1970.

- **Aung San Suu Kyi** was put under house arrest in 1988 by the governing junta of Burma. They feared her fight for freedom in the country (now Myanmar) would lead to their loss of power. In 1995 she was released temporarily, but decided not to leave the country to visit her family in England (even with her husband about to die). She was afraid that once she left, she would not be allowed to return. She was awarded the Nobel Peace Prize in 1991 and released from house arrest in 2002.

- **Dae-Jung Kim** was sentenced to death in South Korea in 1981. Under international pressure, the sentence was changed to life imprisonment. He was later released and in 1997 was elected president of South Korea. He was awarded the Nobel Peace Prize in 2000 for his work for democracy, human rights, and reconciliation with North Korea.

- **Daniel Carleton Gajdusek** is the one case where a Nobel Laureate was sentenced to prison for *criminal* rather than political activities. He was awarded the Nobel Prize in Medicine in 1976 for studies in the North South Pacific on "slow viruses." A year later, he was sentenced to 18 months in prison for sexually abusing a teenage boy he had brought back from the islands.

Among the Nobel Laureates who have been killed after receiving their awards are the following:

- **Dag Hammarskjold** was Secretary General of the United Nations when he won the Nobel Peace Prize in 1961. In the same year, he was killed in an airplane crash while negotiating peace in the Congo. The Soviet Union had accused him of supporting the United States in this conflict, but no firm evidence of USSR involvement in his death ever surfaced.

- **Martin Luther King, Jr.** was leader of the Southern Christian Leadership Conference, a civil rights organization in the United

States. He was awarded the Nobel Peace Prize in 1964 at the age of 35. He was assassinated in 1968.

- **Muhamed Anwar el-Sadat** was president of Egypt when he shared the Nobel Prize for Peace (1978) for negotiating and signing an historic agreement between Egypt and Israel. He was 60 years of age. Three years later, a Muslim fanatic killed him while he was reviewing a military parade. Despite this, the peace between Egypt and Israel continues to be maintained by his successor.

- **Yitzhak Rabin** was the Prime Minister of Israel when he shared the 1994 Nobel Prize with Yasser Arafat for involving himself in the historic process that led to the formation of the Palestinian Authority. Rabin was 72 years of age. He was murdered a year later by a fanatic Jew. The assassination effectively brought the peace process to a halt.

HAVE THE GOALS OF ALFRED NOBEL BEEN FULFILLED IN THE PAST 100 YEARS?

It is difficult to evaluate the benefit to the world made by the sheer existence of the Nobel Prizes. That said, one needs to keep in mind that life expectancy has nearly doubled during these years, due to disease control. There has also been an increase in the standard of living of most countries and death from starvation has been reduced in spite of an immense increase in the world's population. In the past 50 years no world war has occurred, probably because of the paradox of fear from the nuclear weapons. In each of these advancements, Nobel Laureates have made substantial contribution. Nevertheless, it has to be noted that some of the global problems of today—pollution, HIV, tuberculosis, global warming, obesity—are all a result of the increase in standard of living and population size.

Generally, we think, Alfred Nobel would be satisfied with the results of his initiative, although some revisions would inevitably be considered given the enormous changes over the past 100 years. Take food and agriculture. As Norman Borlaug pointed out, he received his Nobel Prize in 1970 for peace, not for food production and hunger alleviation. Borlaug often speculated that if Alfred Nobel had written his Will 50 years earlier, when Europe was suffering from the widespread potato famine of 1845 to 1851, he would have chosen food and agriculture as his first priority for a prize. Even today, part of the world still suffers from a lack of food (500 million people live on less than $1 per day).

Five categories were defined by Alfred Nobel in 1895: Physics, Chemistry, Literature, Peace, and Physiology or Medicine. In the last category, Alfred Nobel was very much influenced by the important work of Louis Pasteur, who was not even a doctor, but a medical chemist. As such, he considered the subject of Physiology before Medicine.

Since then, however, prizes in this category have been awarded only to research into human health rather to clinical work. In 1968, an additional category of Economic Sciences was added in Alfred Nobel's name.

There are, of course, many other new fields that no one would have thought of in Alfred Nobel's time. They include:
- Psychology
- Environment sciences
- Aviation
- Anthropology
- Computer sciences

and more. Because these fields were not made part of the original Nobel prize categories, many prominent contributors to our world have missed out on an award. Take Sigmund Freud who revolutionized our thinking about the role of the subconscious, and Jean Piaget, who explored the secrets of learning, both never received the Nobel Prize.

Then, there are the famous inventors who have been left out of the Nobel parade as well. The Wright brothers first airplane flight in 1903 was never recognized. Thomas Alva Edison, who invented the electric light bulb, the phonograph, the microphone, and more was ineligible for consideration within the constraints of the original categories. Nikola Tesla, who discovered the rotating magnetic field, and Philo Farnsworth, an inventor of television, were skipped. Mathematician Alan Turing, a pioneer in the theoretical basis of computers, and Edwin Hubble, who discovered that the universe is expanding and proposed that it was created by the Big Bang, were also excluded from consideration. The same goes for the first environmentalist, Rachel Carson. The story of Tim Berns-Lee follows the same pattern. He single-handedly established the Internet. Could a development that impacts the lives of more than 500 million people around the world on a daily basis be ignored?

The author feels that in order to catch up with progress, more discreet fields of intellectual exploration should be added to the list of Nobel Prizes awarded—as was the case with Economics. He also urges consideration for recognizing extraordinary inventions in any area.

Another source of continuing concern is the small number of women receiving Nobel Prizes. On average, in all categories and excluding organizations, only 4% (or 29) of Nobel Prize winners have been women, compared with 93% (671) for men. In the scientific categories—Physics, Chemistry and Medicine—not even 3% of the winners have been women. As noted before, no woman has ever been honored in the Economics category. Even in the fields of Peace and Literature, where women are supposedly better positioned to win, less than 10% of the prizes have gone to their gender.

Interestingly, the number of women achieving Nobel recognition has been declining since Marie Curie won her two Nobels. This, at a time when women have been able to level the playing field in nearly every area of endeavor. This situation calls for the attention of educators and, perhaps, of the judging committees. At the very least, more women should participate in the judging committees.

Judging is another area worthy of review. Generally, the judging committees have done a fair job, within the limitations imposed upon them. Although it is relatively easy to be nominated for a Nobel Prize, the committees have properly denied some bizarre nominations, e.g. both Stalin and even Hitler were nominated for the Peace prize.

There have also been cases where Nobel Prizes should never have been awarded at all. Three examples are in the category of Medicine: Johannes Fibiger (1926), Julius von Jauregg Wagner (1927), and Antonio Egas Muniz (1949). Fibiger won for discovering a parasite that was erroneously believed to cause cancer; von Jauregg for supposedly curing mental illness through induced fever (by infecting patients with malaria); and Egas Muniz for the invention of prefrontal lobotomies which were subsequently found to be ineffective.

Another case involves Konrad Zacharias Lorenz, who won a Nobel for Medicine in 1973. He had claimed in 1940 that in order to save the purity of the white race all inferior races should be eliminated. His concept was subsequently adopted by Adolf Hitler. In addition,

German Fritz Haber was awarded the chemistry Nobel Prize in 1918 for his discovery of a method to extract ammonia from nitrogen in the air. This was indeed important for agriculture in the fertilization of soils and a contributing factor to the diminution of starvation. However, this invention allowed Germany to continue the First World War for a much longer period than otherwise might have been possible. Moreover, Fritz Haber, as a German patriot, introduced poison gas into the War without regard to its prohibition by international law.

In both cases, the Nobel committee ignored the information about these two and awarded them their Nobel Prizes. By contrast, one of the members of the Norwegian parliament resigned from the Nobel Peace committee in protest of the award to Yasser Arafat in 1994. He claimed that a terrorist who was responsible for the killing of innocent people should not be honored.

There have also been additional serious misjudgments in the awards. Examples include: C. H. Best, who did the key work in isolating insulin, but was deprived of the Nobel Prize by his senior professor; Jocelyn Bell, who first spotted pulsars, but did not share the Nobel Prize awarded to her professor; and Jonas Salk, who was the first to make a polio vaccine that saved countless children from being crippled. He was overlooked because of intrigues. Dimitri Mendeleev, the famous Russian chemist, who developed the well known periodic chart of elements, was also deprived of the Nobel Prize for similar reasons.

Another recent example of what appears to be an error of the Nobel Committee involves the mapping of the human genome. It was completed in 2000, far ahead of schedule. President Clinton of the United States and Prime Minister Blair of the United Kingdom held a press conference to mark what *Science* called the most important scientific achievement of 2000. But the Nobel Prize Committee simply ignored it.

In literature, many well known authors have been left on the sidelines. Leo Tolstoy, Bertolt Brecht, James Joyce, and Virginia Woolf, to name a few, were all ignored by the Nobel committee during their lifetimes.

In the Peace category, it seems hard to accept that Gandhi, who was the most important advocate of nonviolent change in the 20th century was overlooked. On the other hand, there is a tendency to award the Nobel Peace Prize on the basis of a *signature* to a peace treaty, rather on the complete implementation of its terms. Here are some examples:

- Henry Kissinger won the prize in 1973 for signing a peace treaty with North Vietnam. Kissinger's opposite on the North Vietnam side, Le Duc Tho, declined his prize in the same year.
- Oscar Sanches Arias of Costa Rica won in 1987 for brokering a stop to the war between the Contras and the Sandanistas in Nicaragua.
- Prime Minister Yitzhak Rabin and Foreign Minister Shimon Peres of Israel shared the 1994 Peace Prize with Yasser Arafat, Chairman of the Palestinian Authority.
- David Trible and John Hume (1998) were rewarded for their efforts to end the conflict in Northern Ireland.

In none of these cases was peace actually established.

One of the cases, however, where the Nobel Peace Prize proved to be very effective was in East Timor. With the award of the prize to Carlos Belo and José Rahmos-Horta in 1996, the problems of the region came to the attention of the world and independence for East Timor eventually followed in May 2002.

SUMMARY AND CONCLUSIONS

1. In the 100 years since the Nobel Prizes were first established, 719 have been awarded:
   - 135 in Chemistry
   - 172 in Medicine
   - 162 in Physics
   - 107 in Peace
   - 97 in Literature and
   - 46 in Economics (the latter was first initiated in 1969.)

2. Researchers in 10 well-developed countries—involving only 11% of the world's population—have earned about 90% of Nobel Prizes in the scientific categories of Chemistry, Medicine, Physics and Economics and about 60% of those in the categories of Literature and Peace. It seems, therefore, that only a small proportion of the world's brainpower is involved in solving the many problems facing the planet. These 10 countries are distinguished by their long intellectual tradition.

3. There are about 18 leading universities in the 4 top countries whose researchers have gained about 50% of the Nobel Prizes. In some cases, universities have developed specialization in certain fields; e.g., the University of Chicago is leading in Nobel Prizes awarded in Economics. Only a small proportion of scientists working for private companies have been awarded Nobel Prizes.

4. Based on the data available, scientists born in an undeveloped country and educated there have a very slim chance of getting a Nobel Prize, regardless of the individual's genius.

5. Those countries facing hunger or fighting diseases cannot afford to invest in basic research, nor can they support high-grade

institutions capable of carrying out top-level research. For these reasons it seems that the number of Nobel Prizes per nation may indicate its scientific and cultural level. Therefore, the wealthier countries should contribute to improve conditions in the less fortunate countries. Such an activity would ultimately benefit the rich countries themselves. Problems of the third world (HIV, ebola, malaria, starvation, pollution, and more) may affect the rich countries as well. Worse, how these problems impact the third world are not properly investigated. The most talented students of these countries immigrate to the more attractive ones in the West, where they focus their talent on the problems of the wealthy countries instead of their own. Thus, the gap between rich and poor countries increases. The key problem seems to be how to provide free and high-quality education to keep the talented students at home.

6. Is the Nobel Laureate a genius? In most cases it does not appear so. Rather, Nobel Laureates seem to be a combination of talent, very strong motivation, hard work, and a little bit of luck. In some cases discoveries were achieved accidentally, e.g., penicillin—the most effective lifesaving medicine ever produced.

7. Women, who comprise 50% of the world's population, have won less than 5% of the Nobel Prizes. Indeed, women have advanced over the past 100 years in many fields, gaining ever increasing numbers of high positions. But when it comes to Nobel Prizes, there has been a *decline*. It may be that the main problem is biological—the prime years to excel, especially in science, are when women are most fertile. The main burden of raising children, of course, still falls on women, while men are able to continue their studies and personal development. This fact highlights the need for child-rearing to be shared equally by both sexes. If women are to fulfill their intellectual potential, inexpensive day care and education facilities need to be provided. In addition, in order to avoid the possibility of intended or unintended sex discrimination, more women should be asked to participate in the Nobel judging committees.

8. There are very high correlations (r =0.9) between the number of Nobel Prizes obtained by each country in the scientific categories. This means that excellence in one category is dependent on success in the others, especially for Chemistry, Medicine, and Physics. In the top countries producing Nobel Prize winners, there is a long tradition and proper infrastructure for scientific research.

9. Even the correlation between the number of Laureates of each country in the scientific categories and the equivalent number in the Peace category is high (r =0.8), while the correlation with the Literature category is much lower (r =0.6). In the latter category, only 8.1% have a third academic degree (Dr., Ph.D., M.D., and the like) compared to more than 90% in the scientific categories, and only one-third in the Peace category. This is presumably because to excel as an author or a poet depends on natural talent—something a person is born with—and does not require the type of training that leads to an academic degree. A Ph.D. was the most common degree among the scientific Laureates, except understandably for Medicine.

10. With regard to the question of the role of democracy vs. tyranny, some 17 democratic countries have seen their citizens awarded about 95% of the Nobel Prizes in the scientific categories and 65% to 70% in the Literature and Peace categories. This strongly indicates that without democracy, progress is diminished and the human race is endangered.

11. About 20% to 30% of scientists who earned Nobel Prizes were born in countries other than the one in which they researched their prize-winning work; in the Literature and Peace categories the numbers were 10% to 20%. This supports the concept that there has been a clear brain migration to the more developing countries. About a third of migrating Laureates of all six Nobel categories were of the Jewish faith, fleeing some form of anti-Semitism in their homeland.

12. The distribution of the Nobel Prizes among nations has shifted over the years, especially during and after World War II. Germany and France were the leading countries in scientific Nobel Prizes between 1901 and 1940. For example, Germany was leading with 50% of Nobel Prizes in Chemistry during 1901-1920, and 36% in 1921-1940, while during the same periods of time the United States had only 5.6% and 9.1%, respectively. But during and after World War II this pattern changed dramatically, primarily because of migration so that during the 1981 to 2000 period, Germany's share of the Chemistry prizes had dropped to only 7.3%, while that of the United States had risen to 58.5%. A similar trend was observed in other scientific categories.

13. Average age of publication that led to the Nobel Prize was as follows:

    - Physics—37.3 years
    - Chemistry—40.7 years
    - Medicine—41.1 years
    - Literature—57.4 years
    - Economics—59.0 years
    - Peace—54.3 years (mostly for signed peace agreements rather than for publication.)

    According to Alfred Nobel's Will the prizes were supposed to be distributed "to those who, during the *preceding year* (emphasis added) shall have conferred the greatest benefit on mankind." In reality, this has seldom happened since work done has to be proved first.

    The data indicate that the interval between publication date and winning the prize was about 15 years for the biological sciences (Physics, Chemistry and Medicine) and 6.3 to 9.5 years for the other three categories (Economics, Literature, and Peace). For example, Albert Einstein was 26 when he wrote his paper on photoelectric effect, but waited 17 years for the Nobel Prize. Another theory of his—the effect of antigravity—deserved another Nobel Prize, but it was proved correct only recently (2001), more than 70 years after he proposed it and long after he had died.

14. The average age of Laureates as well as the range of ages of those who have received Nobel prizes is of interest. The youngest have been in Physics and the oldest in Economics. Here are the numbers followed by the range of their ages:

    - Physics—52.4 years-of-age (ranging from 25 to 84 years)
    - Chemistry—55.5 years-of-age (35 to 83 years)
    - Medicine – 56.3 years-of-age (32 to 87 years)
    - Peace – 62.0 years-of-age (32 to 87 years)
    - Literature – 63.8 years-of-age (42 to 85 years)
    - Economics - 66.5 years-of-age (51 to 82 years).

15. The top 20 countries in terms of Gross National Product per Capita, or the United Nations Index, are also the countries whose citizens have the longest life spans and which have produced a great number of Nobel Prize winners. No statistically valid connection was found between the size of a population and the number of Laureates credited to that country.

16. Several of the Nobel Prize winners were raised by divorced parents, or lost one or even both parents at a very young age, e.g., Albert Camus, Jean-Paul Sartre, and Yashunari Kawabata; the first two were raised by their mothers and the latter by his grandparents. It could be, therefore, that such stress imposed at an early stage of life may even have had a positive effect, in certain cases, in stimulating early maturation.

17. According to the data, an increasing proportion of Nobel Prizes in the science categories have been awarded to *teams* of researchers. The reason for this appears to be that the discovery of new scientific knowledge demands increasingly large investments in sophisticated instruments and equipment, which also require teams of researchers to operate. Such has been the case for research on the human genome or the investigations being done at the European Organization for Nuclear Research (CERN). As a result, in the future Nobel Prize may be awarded to the leader of a team, who may excel as an organizer rather than as a scientific genius. The ability to work in such a team is associated more with the Emotional Quotient (EQ) than with the traditional Intelligent Quotient (IQ). This trend tends to limit the freedom of

a single scientist to choose and operate his own project.

18. A review of dates of birth shows that winter produced about 22% fewer births. However, this phenomenon is not exclusive to Nobel Laureates as it also occurs in the population at large. Couples in the Northern hemisphere clearly prefer not to risk raising newborns during the coldest season. Differences were found among Nobel categories in astrological signs. However, such differences are not significant in such a small sized sample and may occur just by chance.

19. The highest number of awards earned by Laureates *in addition to* their Nobel Prize, was found in the category of Physiology and Medicine; the lowest was in the Peace category. The additional awards were mostly earned *before* receiving the Nobel Prize.

20. In Literature, fiction writers have won 52 Nobel Prizes, poets 28, and playwrites 11. Philosophers have won only four and historians just two Nobel Prizes for their writings. The question of whether there are any reasons for these differences remains open.

21. In the category of Medicine, the principal prize-winning works during the first fifty years of the Nobel awards were in physiology (10%) and bacteriology (10%); in the next fifty years, biochemistry predominated. About one-third of the prize-winning works in Medicine (59) have been connected with DNA.

    In Chemistry, about 12% (16) of the prize-winning work has been involved with genetics. Ten prize-winning investigations have involved vitamin research (four in Chemistry, six in Medicine) and only two have been awarded in the field of psychiatry.

22. In the category of Peace, 19 prizes have been awarded to organizations such as the International League for Permanent Peace and the International Peace Bureau at Bern.

23. Literature Laureates have the highest rates of divorce and remarriage, while Peace Laureates have the highest proportion of single people, no doubt because the faiths of some prevents marriage (e.g., Mother Teresa, the Dalai Lama). These two categories also have the highest proportion of childless individuals.

24. It is interesting to note that the life expectancy of Laureates far exceeds that of the population at large. A comparison of the longevity of Nobel Laureates was conducted for the years 1969 to 2000. The longevity of Laureates is as follows:

    Economics – 83.1 years; 55.4% are still alive
    Physics – 80 years; 80.6% are still alive
    Chemistry – 80 years; 77.6% are still alive
    Literature – 79 years; 54.6% are still alive
    Medicine – 78 years; 73% are still alive
    Peace – 77.4 years; 65.7% are still alive (Four Laureates have been assassinated).

    The reason for the long lives of Nobel Laureates may be attributed to their love of their interesting work, something that keeps their minds active and transfers presumably to their physical health as well.

25. There have been three Nobel Prizes awarded to husband-wife teams and one to a father-son team; in four cases, a father and son, and in one case a mother and daughter, received the Nobel award in the same category, but at different times. There has been one case of two brothers and another involving a husband and wife receiving Nobel Prizes in different categories and at different times.

26. The number of scientists, writers, researchers, and other intellectuals have increased by many thousands times over the years. For example, there were only about 2000 physicists in 1901 while there are several hundred thousand today. As a result, competition has become much more intense and therefore the prestige of the Nobel Prize has become much greater than ever before.

27. About 66% of the Laureates belong to the Christian faith in its various forms. It seems that more Protestants were involved in the scientific categories, whereas more Catholic Laureates appear in the Literature and Peace categories. Over 20% of the Laureates belong to the Jewish religion (17% in Chemistry, 26% each in Medicine and Physics; 40% in Economics), about 138

Laureates in total. This is striking in the fact that there are only some 13 million Jews in the world. By comparison, the Muslim faith includes a population of 1.2 billion, but only 5 (0.8%) have won Nobel Prizes. Interestingly, atheists, agnostics and free-thinkers comprise 10.5% of total Nobel Prize winners; in Literature, the percentage rises to 35%.

28. Tracking the educational level of the parents of the science laureates reveals that about half of them (especially fathers) were college graduates, whereas this proportion was much less in the other Nobel categories. However, in most cases the influence of parents and close relatives seems to be crucial regardless of their education. As Ahmed Zewail (Chemistry, 1999), whose Egyptian parents were not college graduates, recalls: "The family's dream was to see me receive a high degree abroad and to become a university professor. On the door of my room a sign was placed reading 'Dr. Ahmed,' even though at that point I was far from becoming a doctor."

29. The world faces various severe problems such as hunger, pollution, disease, war, climatic change, and more. In 1895, Alfred Nobel selected five categories for prizes. It is difficult to evaluate the benefit to the world provided by the Nobel Foundation. However, the world has made enormous progress during the 100 years of Nobel prizes and the Nobel Laureates have contributed greatly to this progress. Without question, the Nobel Prizes are regarded as the most prestigious intellectual awards in the world. Nevertheless, some very important achievements have been overlooked by the Nobel committees and some awards have been given for unworthy claims. Moreover, new fields of science and culture have emerged during these 100 years, which could not have been foreseen at the time of Alfred Nobel (e.g., computers). Therefore, new categories of Nobel Prizes should be established.

APPENDIX

List of Nobel Prize Winners in Chemistry	108
List of Nobel Prize Winners in Physiology or Medicine	114
List of Nobel Prize Winners in Physics	120
List of Nobel Prize Winners in Economics	126
List of Nobel Prize Winners in Literature	128
List of Nobel Prize Winners in Peace	133
Selected Bibliography	138

NOBEL PRIZE WINNERS IN CHEMISTRY: 1901-2000

Year	Name/ Contribution	Born	Place	Prize Age	Death	Nat.	Country Credited	Univ. Credited	Degree
1901	Van't Hoff, Jacobus Henricus Discovery of the laws of chemical dynamics & osmotic pressure	1852	Neth.	49	1911	Dutch	Germany	Berlin	Ph.D.
1902	Fischer, Emil Herman Work on sugar & purine synthesis	1852	Germ.	50	1919	German	Germany	Berlin	Ph.D.
1903	Arrhenius, Svante August Electrolytic theory of dissociation	1859	Swed.	44	1927	Swed.	Sweden	Stockholm	Ph.D
1904	Ramsay, Sir William Discover of inert gaseous elements in air and place in periodic system	1852	UK	52	1916	British	UK	London	Ph.D
1905	Von Baeyer, Adolf J. F. Wilhelm Work on organic dyes and hydro-aromatic compounds	1835	Germ.	70	1917	German	Germany	Munich	Ph.D
1906	Moissan, Ferdinand F. H. Isolation of the elements fluorine and adoption of electric furnace	1852	France	54	1907	French	France	Sorbonne	D.Sc.
1907	Buchner, Eduard Discovery of cell free fermantation (enzymes)	1860	Germ.	47	1917	German	Germany	Ag.College Berlin	Ph.D
1908	Rutherford, Sir Ernest Disintegration of elements and chemistry of radioactive substances	1871	NZ	37	1937	British	UK	Victoria (Manchester)	M.A.
1909	Oswald, Friedrich Wilhelm Catalysis and conditions of chemical equilibrium and velocities	1853	Latvia	56	1932	Latvia	Germany	Leipzig	Ph.D
1910	Wallace, Otto Alicyclic compounds	1847	Germ.	63	1931	German	Germany	Goettingen	Ph.D
1911	Curie, Marie (Sklodowska, Maria) (F) Discovery of the elements radium and polonium	1867	Poland	44	1934	Poland French	France	Sorbonne	Ph.D Female
1912	Grignard, Francois A. Victor Discovery of reagent to greatly advance organic chemistry	1871	France	41	1935	French	France	Nancy	D.Sc.
1912	Sabatier, Paul Method of hydrogenating organic compounds	1854	France	58	1941	French	France	Toulouse	D.Sc.
1913	Werner, Alfred Linkage of atoms in molecules opened new fields	1866	France	47	1919	French Swiss	Switzerland	Zurich	Ph.D
1914	Richards, Theodore William Determined accurate atomic weight of large number of elements	1888	USA	46	1928	American	USA	Harvard	Ph.D
1915	Willstätter, Richard Martin Research on plant pigments, especially chlorophyll	1872	Germ	43	1942	German	Germany	Munich	Ph.D
1918	Haber, Fritz Synthesis of ammonia production from its elements	1868	Germ.	50	1934	German	Germany	Fritz-Haber Institute	Ph.D
1920	Nernst, Walther Hermann Recognition of work in thermo-chemistry	1864	Germ.	77	1941	German	Germany	Berlin	Ph.D
1921	Soddy, Frederick Contributions to the chemistry of radioactive substances	1877	UK	44	1956	British	UK	Oxford	M.A.
1922	Aston, Francis William Discovery of isotopes in various non-radioactive elements	1877	UK	45	1945	British	UK	Cambridge	B.A.
1923	Fragl, Fritz Invention of micro-analysis of organic substances	1859	Austria	64	1930	Austrian	Austria	Graz	M.D.

NOBEL PRIZE WINNERS IN CHEMISTRY: 1901-2000
[CONTINUED]

Year	Name/Contribution	Born	Place	Prize Age	Death	Nat.	Country Credited	Univ. Credited	Degree
1925	Zsigmondy, Richard Adolf *Heterogenous nature of colloid solutions*	1865	Austria	60	1929	Aus/Germ	Germany	Goettigen	Ph.D.
1926	Svedberg, The (Theodor) *Work on disperse systems*	1884	Sweden	42	1971	Swed.	Sweden	Uppsala	Ph.D.
1927	Wieland, Heinrich Otto *Investigation of bile acids and related substances*	1877	Germany	50	1957	Germ.	Germany	Munich	Ph.D.
1928	Windaus, Adolf Otto Reinhold *Sterols and their connection with vitamins*	1876	Germany	52	1959	Germ	Germany	Goettigen	Ph.D.
1929	Von Euler-Chelpin, Hans K.A.S.	1873	Germany	56	1964	Germ. Swed.	Sweden	Stockholm	Ph.D.
	Harden, Sir Arthur *Fermentation of sugar and fermentative enzymes*	1865	UK	64	1940	British	UK	London	Ph.D.
1930	Fischer, Hans *Coloring matter of blood, synthesis of haemin & chlorophyll*	1881	Germany	49	1945	Germ.	Germany	Techniche Hochschule	Ph.D. M.D.
1931	Bergius, Friedrich K. R.	1884	Germany	47	1949	Germ.	Germany	Heidelberg/Farbenindustrie	Ph.D.
	Bosch, Carl *Development of chemical high-pressure methods*	1874	Germany	57	1940	Germ.	Germany	Heidelberg/Farbenindustrie	Ph.D.
1932	Langmuir, Irving *Discoveries and investigations in surface chemistry*	1881	USA	51	1957	American	USA	Gen. Elec. Co.	Ph.D.
1934	Urey, Harold Clayton *Discovery of heavy hydrogen*	1893	USA	41	1981	American	USA	Columbia	Ph.D.
1935	Joliot-Curie, Frédéric	1900	France	35	1958	French	France	Inst. du Radium	D.Sc.
	Joliot-Curie, Irène (F) *Synthesis of new radioactive elements*	1897	France	38	1956	French	France	Inst. du Radium	D.Sc.
1936	Debye, Peter J. W. *Dipole moments and diffraction of X-rays and electrons in gases*	1884	Neth.	52	1966	Dutch/American	Neth.	Berlin & Max-Planck Inst	Ph.D.
1937	Haworth, Sir Walter Norman *Investigations of cabohydrates and vitamin C*	1883	UK	54	1950	British	UK	Birmingham	Ph.D. D.Sc.
1937	Karrer, Paul *Carotenoids, flavin and vitamins A and B2*	1889	Russia	48	1971	Russian/Swiss	Switz.	Zurich	Dr.
1938	Kuhn, Richard *Work on carotenoids and vitamins*	1900	Austria	38	1967	Austrian/German	Germany	Heidelberg/Max-Planck Inst	Ph.D.
1939	Butenandt, Adolf F. J. *Work on sex hormones*	1903	Germany	36	1995	German	Germany	Berlin/Max-Planck Inst	Ph.D.
1939	Ruzicka, Leopold Stephen *Polymethylenes and higher terpenes (artificial testosterone)*	1887	Yugo.	52	1976	Yugo.	Switz.	Fed. Inst. of Technology	Dr. Ing.
1943	Hevesy, George C. de von *Isotopes as tracer elements in research of chemical processes*	1885	Hungary	58	1966	Hungary	Germany	Stockholm	Ph.D.
1944	Hahn, Otto *Discovery of the fission of heavy nuclei*	1879	Germany	65	1968	Germany	Germany	Max-Planck Inst	Ph.D.
1945	Virtanen, Artturi Ilmari *Inventions in agriculture including fodder preservation*	1895	Finland	50	1973	Finish	Finland	Helsinki	Ph.D.

Note: (F) stands for Female

NOBEL PRIZE WINNERS IN CHEMISTRY: 1901-2000
[CONTINUED]

Year	Name/ Contribution	Born	Place	Prize Age	Death	Nat.	Country Credited	Univ. Credited	Degree
1946	Northrop, John Howard	1891	USA	55	1987	American	USA	Rockefeller Inst. of Med.	Ph.D.
	Stanley, Wendell Meredith *Preparation of enzymes and virus proteins in pure form*	1904	USA	42	1971	American	USA	Rockefeller Inst. of Med.	Ph.D
1946	Summer, James Batcheller *Discovery that enzymes can be crytallized*	1887	USA	59	1955	American	USA	Cornell	Ph.D.
1947	Robinson, Sir Robert *Research on vegetable products particularly alkaloids*	1886	UK	61	1975	British	UK	Oxford	D.Sc.
1948	Tiselius, Arne Wilhelm Kaurin *Use of electrophoresis and discov-. eries about blood serum proteins*	1902	Sweden	46	1971	Swedish	Sweden	Uppsala	Ph.D.
1949	Giauque, William Francis *Behaviour of substances at extremely low temperature*	1895	Canada	54	1982	American	USA	Univ. Cal. Berkeley	Ph.D.
1950	Alder, Kurt	1902	Germany	48	1958	German	Germany	Cologne	Ph.D.
	Diels, Otto Paul Hermann *Discovery and development of the diene synthesis*	1876	Germany	74	1954	German	Germany	Kiel	Ph.D.
1951	McMillan, Edwin Mattison *Discovery of element 93, neptunium, the first after uranium*	1907	USA	44	1991	American	USA	Univ. Cal. Berkeley	Ph.D.
1951	Seaborg, Glenn Theodore *Discoveries about the transuranium elements (9 atomic elements)*	1912	USA	39	1999	American	USA	Univ. Cal Berkeley	Ph.D.
1952	Martin, Archer John Porter *Invention of partition chromatography*	1910	UK	42	--	British	UK	Nat. Inst. Med. Res.	Ph.D.
	Synge, Richard L. M. *Development of partition chromatography*	1914	UK	38	1994	British	UK	Rowett Res. Inst.	Ph.D.
1953	Staudinger, Hermann *Discoveries in macromolecular chemistry*	1881	Germany	72	1965	German	Germany	Freiburgh/ Inst. Macro Mul. Chem	Ph.D.
1954	Pauling, Linus Carl *Work on chemical bonds and molecular structure*	1901	USA	53	1994	American	USA	Cal Inst. of Tech.	Ph.D.
1955	Du Vigneaut, Vincent *Work on sulphur; first synthesis of polypeptide hormone*	1901	USA	54	1978	American	USA	Cornell	Ph.D.
1956	Hinshelwood, Sir Norman Cyril *Research into the mechanism of chemical reactions*	1897	UK	70	1967	British	UK	Oxford	M.A.
	Semenov, Nikolay Nikolaevich *Research into the mechanism of chemical reactions*	1896	Russia	90	1986	Russian	Russia	Inst. of Chemical Physics	Ph.D. Acad.
1957	Todd, Sir Alexander Robertus *Work on nucleotides and nucleotide coenzymes*	1907	UK	50	1997	British	UK	Cambridge	Ph.D.
1958	Sanger, Frederick (Nobel #1) *Structure of proteins, especially insulin*	1918	UK	40	----	British	UK	Cambridge	Ph.D.
1959	Heyrovsky, Jaroslav *Discovery of the polaro- graphic methods of analysis*	1890	Czech.	69	1967	Czech	Czech.	Polarographic Inst. of Czech.	Ph.D. D.Sc.
1960	Libby, Willard Frank *Use of carbon-14 for age deter- mination primarily in geology*	1908	USA	52	1980	American	USA	Univ. Cal Los Angeles	Ph.D.

NOBEL PRIZE WINNERS IN CHEMISTRY: 1901-2000
[CONTINUED]

Year	Name/Contribution	Born	Place	Prize Age	Death	Nat.	Country Credited	Univ. Credited	Degree
1961	Calvin, Melvin Carbon dioxide assimilation in plants (photosynthesis)	1911	USA	50	1997	American	USA	Univ. Cal Berkeley	Ph.D.
1962	Kendrew, Sir John Cowdery	1917	UK	45	1997	British	UK	Cambridge	Ph.D.
	Perutz, Max Ferdinand Studies of structures of globular proteins	1914	Austria	48	----	Austrian/British	UK	Cambridge	Ph.D.
1963	Natta, Giulio Discovery of chemistry and technology of high polymers	1903	Italy	60	1979	Italian	Italy	Inst. of Technology	Ph.D.
1963	Ziegler, Karl Discoveries about high polymers (catalysis polymerization)	1898	Germany	65	1973	German	Germany	Max-Planck Inst.	Ph.D.
1964	Hodgkin, Dorothy Crowfoot (F) Structure of important biochemical substances (B-12, penicillin)	1910	Egypt	54	1994	British	UK	Oxford	Ph.D.
1965	Woodward, Robert Burns The art of organic synthesis (quinine, penicillin, etc.)	1917	USA	48	1979	American	USA	Harvard	Ph.D.
1966	Mulliken, Robert Sanderson Chemical bonds and electronic structure of molecules	1896	USA	70	1986	American	USA	Chicago	Ph.D.
1967	Eigen, Manfred Techniques to measure rapid chemical reactions	1927	Germany	40	----	German	Germany	Max-Planck Inst.	Dr. Nat.
1967	Norrish, Ronald G. W.	1897	UK	70	1978	British	UK	Cambridge	Ph.D.
	Porter, George Studies of extremely fast chemical reactions	1920	UK	47	----	British	UK	Royal Inst. London	Ph.D.
1968	Onsager, Lars Discovery of reciprocal relations in thermodynamics processes	1903	Norway	65	1976	Norwegian/American	USA	Yale	Ph.D.
1969	Barton, Sir Derek H. R.	1918	UK	51	1998	British	UK	Imp. College of Sci & Tech.	Ph.D.
	Hassel, Odd Concept of conformation and its implication in chemistry	1897	Norway	72	1981	Norwegian German	Norway	Kjemisk Inst. Oslo	Ph.D.
1970	Leloir, Luis Federico Sugar nucleotides/role in biosynthesis of carbohydrates	1906	France	64	1987	Argentine	Argentina	Inst. Biochem Research	M.D.
1971	Herzberg, Gerhard Electronic structure/geometry of molecules, especially free radicals	1904	Germany	67	1999	German/Canada	Canada	Nat. Res. Council	Dr. Ing.
1972	Anfinsen, Christian Boemer Ribonuclease, connection of amino acids and conformation	1916	USA	56	1995	American	USA	Nat. Inst. of Health	Ph.D.
1972	Moore, Stanford	1913	USA	59	1982	American	USA	Rockefeller	Ph.D.
	Stein, William Howard Chemical structure and catalytic activity of ribonuclease molecule	1911	USA	61	1980	American	USA	Rockefeller	Ph.D.
1973	Fischer, Ernst Otto	1918	Germany	55		German	Germany	Tech. Univ. Munich	Ph.D.
	Wilkinson, Geoffrey Organometallic chemistry (sandwich compounds)	1921	UK	52	1996	British	UK	Imp. College of Sci & Tech.	Ph.D.
1974	Flory, Paul John Fundamental achievements in macro-molecules	1910	USA	64	1985	American	USA	Stanford	Ph.D.
1975	Cornforth, Sir John Warcap Streochemistry of enzyme-catalyzed reaction	1917	Austra.	58	----	Austra/British	UK/Austria	Sussex	D. Phil.

Note: (F) stands for Female

NOBEL PRIZE WINNERS IN CHEMISTRY: 1901-2000
[CONTINUED]

Year	Name/ Contribution	Born	Place	Prize Age	Death	Nat.	Country Credited	Univ. Credited	Degree
1975	Prelog, Vladimir *Stereochemistry of organic molecules and reactions*	1906	Yugo.	69	1998	Yugo./ Swiss	Swiss	Eld Tech. Hochshule	Dr.
1976	Lipscomb, William Nun *Structure of boranes/ chemical bonding*	1919	USA	57	----	American	USA	Harvard	Ph.D.
1977	Prigogine, Ilya *Theory of non-linear thermodynamics*	1917	Russia	60	----	Russian/ Belgian	Belgium	Libre de Bruxelles	Dr.
1978	Mitchell, Peter Denis *Biological energy transfer by chemiosmotic theory*	1920	UK	58	1992	British	UK	Glynn Res. Laboratory	Ph.D.
1979	Brown, Herbert Charles	1912	UK	67	----	British/ American	USA	Purdue	Ph.D.
	Wittig, Georg Fridriech Karl *Boron and phosphorus as important reagents*	1897	Germany	82	1987	German	Germany	Heidelberg	Ph.D.
1980	Berg, Paul	1926	USA	54	----	American	USA	Stanford	Ph.D.
	Gilbert, Walter *Biochemistry of nucleic acids, in particular recombinant-DNA*	1932	USA	48	----	American	USA	Biological Laboratory	Ph.D.
1980	Sanger, Frederick (Nobel #2) *Determining the base sequences of nucleic acids*	1918	UK	62	----	British	UK	Cambridge	Ph.D.
1981	Fukui, Fenichi	1918	Japan	63	1998	Japanese	Japan	Kyoto	Ph.D.
	Hoffman, Roald *Theories concerning the course of chemical reactions*	1937	Poland	44	----	Polish/ American	USA	Cornell	Ph.D.
1982	Klug, Aaron *Development of crystallographic electron microscopy*	1926	Lithuania	56	----	So. African/ British	UK	Cambridge	Ph.D.
1983	Taube, Henry *Electron transfer reaction, especially in metal complexes*	1915	Canada	68	----	Canadian/ American	USA	Stanford	Ph.D.
1984	Merrifield, Robert Bruce *For rapid synthesis of peptide chains*	1921	USA	63	----	American	USA	Rockefeller	Ph.D.
1985	Hauptman, Herbert Aaron *Direct methods of determination of crystal structures*	1917	USA	68	---	American	USA	Med. Foundation/Buffalo	Ph.D.
1985	Karle, Jerome *Mathematical methods for determining crystal structures*	1918	USA	67	----	American	USA	Naval Res.	Ph.D.
1986	Herschbach, Dudley Robert	1932	USA	54	----	American	USA	Harvard	Ph.D.
	Lee, Yuan Tseh	1936	Taiwan	50	----	Taiwanese/ American	Taiwan/ USA	Univ. Cal Berkeley	Ph.D.
	Polanyi, John Charles *Dynamics of elementary processes of chemical reaction*	1929	Germany	57	----	German/ British/ Canada	UK	Toronto	Ph.D.
1987	Cram, Donald James	1919	USA	68	----	American	USA	Univ. Cal Los Angeles	Ph.D.
	Lehn, Jean-Marie Pierre	1939	France	48	----	French	France	Univ. Louis Pasteur/Coll. du France	Ph.D.
	Pedersen, Charles John *Use of molecules with structure-specific interactions (enzymes)*	1904	Korea	83	1989	Korean/ American	USA	DuPont	M.S.
1988	Deisenhofer, Johann	1943	Germany	45	----	German	Germany	Texas	Ph.D.
	Huber, Robert	1937	Germany	51	----	German	Germany	Max-Planck Inst.	Ph.D.
	Michel, Hartmut *3-dimensional structure of photosynthetic reaction center*	1948	Germany	40	----	German	Germany	Max-Planck Inst.	Ph.D.

NOBEL PRIZE WINNERS IN CHEMISTRY: 1901-2000
[CONTINUED]

Year	Name/Contribution	Born	Place	Prize Age	Death	Nat.	Country Credited	Univ. Credited	Degree
1989	Altman, Sidney	1939	Canada	50	----	Canadian/American	USA/Canada	Yale	Ph.D.
	Cech, Thomas Robert	1947	USA	42	----	American	USA	Colorado	Ph.D.
	Discovery of catalytic properties of RNA								
1990	Corey, Elias James	1928	USA	62	----	American	USA	Harvard	Ph.D.
	Theory & methodology of organic synthesis								
1991	Ernst, Richard Robert	1933	Switz.	58	----	Swiss	Switz.	Eld. Tech. Hochshule	D. Sc.
	High resolution nuclear magnetic resonance (NMR) spectroscopy								
1992	Marcus, Rudolph Arthur	1923	Canada	69	----	Canadian/American	USA	Cal. Inst. Technology	Ph.D.
	Theory of electron transfer reactions in chemical systems								
1993	Mullis, Kary Banks	1944	USA	49	----	American	USA	La Jolla	Ph.D.
	Smith, Michael	1932	UK	61	----	British/Canadian	Canada	British Columbia	Ph.D.
	Polymerase chain reaction (PCR) method (duplication of DNA)								
1994	Olah, George Andrew	1927	Hungary	67	----	Hungarian/American	USA	Univ. of So. Cal.	Ph.D.
	Carbocation chemistry (higher octane fuel)								
1995	Crutzen, Paul	1933	Neth.	62	----	Dutch/German	Neth.	Max-Planck Inst.	Ph.D.
	Molina, Mario	1943	Mexico	52	----	Mexican/American	USA	MIT	Ph.D.
	Rowland, Frank Sherwood	1927	USA	67	----	American	USA	Univ. Cal Irvine	Ph.D.
	Discovered how chemical gases reduce atmospheric ozone								
1996	Curl Jr., Robert F.	1933	USA	63	----	American	USA	Rice	Ph.D.
	Kroto, Sir Harold W.	1939	UK	57	----	British	UK	Sussex	Ph.D.
	Smalley, Richard	1943	USA	53	----	American	USA	Rice	Ph.D.
	Discovery of fullerenes								
1997	Boyer, Paul D.	1918	USA	79	----	American	USA	Univ. Cal Los Angeles	Ph.D. D. Sc.
	Walker, John E.	1941	UK	56	----	British	UK	Cambridge	D. Phil.
	Synthesis of adenonosine triphosphate (ATP)								
1997	Skou, Jens C.	1918	Den.	79	----	Danish	Denmark	Aartus	M.D. Dr. Med
	Discovery of ion-transporting enzyme ("molecular pump")								
1998	Kohn, Walter	1923	Aust.	75	----	American/French	USA	Univ. Cal. Sta Barbara	Ph.D. D. Sc.
	Development of the density-functional theory								
1998	Pople, John A.	1923	UK	73	----	British	UK	Northwestern	Ph.D.
	Computational methods in quantum chemistry (computer program)								
1999	Zewail, Ahmed Hassan	1946	Egypt	53	----	Egyptian/American	Egypt/USA	Cal. Inst. of Technology	Ph.D.
	Chemical reactions using femtosecond spectroscopy								
2000	Heeger, Alan J.	1936	USA	64	----	American	USA	Univ. Cal. Sta. Barbara	Ph.D.
	MacDiarmid, Alan G.	1927	NZ	73	----	American	USA	Pennsylvania	Ph.D.
	Shirakawa, Hideki	1936	Japan	64	----	Japanese	Japan	Univ. of Tsukuba	Ph.D.
	Discovery of electrically conductive polymers								

NOBEL PRIZE WINNERS IN MEDICINE: 1901-2000

Year	Name/ Contribution	Born	Place	Prize Age	Death	Nat.	Country Credited	Univ. Credited	Degree
1901	von Behring, Emil Adolph Serum therapy, especially its application to diphtheria	1854	Germany	47	1917	German	Germany	Marburg	M.D.
1902	Ross, Ronald, Sir Proved Anopheles mosquito was the host of malaria	1857	India	45	1932	British	UK	Liverpool	M.D.
1903	Finsen, Niels Ryberg Treatment of disease with concentrated light rays	1860	Denmark	43	1904	Danish	Denmark	Finsen Med Light Instit.	M.D.
1904	Pavlov, Ivan Petrovich Physiology of digestion (conditioned reflexes)	1849	Russia	55	1936	Russian	Russia	Military Med Academy	M.D.
1905	Koch, Heinrich Hermann R. Work on tuberculosis—founder of modern bacteriology	1843	German	62	1910	German	Germany	Instit. For Infectious Diseases	M.D.
1906	Golgi, Camillo Ramòn y Cajal, Santiago Structure of the nervous system (Golgi staining technique)	1843 1852	Italy Spain	63 54	1926 1934	Italian Spanish	Italy Spain	Pavia Madrid	M.D. M.D.
1907	Laveran, Charles Luis Alphonse Role played by protozoa in diseases (malaria)	1845	France	62	1922	France	France	Institut Pasteur	M.D.
1908	Ehrlich, Paul Work on immunity, especially on diphtheria antitoxin (syphilis)	1854	Germany	54	1915	German	Germany	Goettingen & Royal Instit. Exper. Therapy	M.D.
1908	Mechnikov, Ilya Ilyich Work on immunity, especially "cellular" theory of immunity	1845	Russia	63	1916	Russian, French	Russia	Institut Pasteur	Dr.
1909	Kocher, Emil Theodor Physiology, patholoy & surgery of thyroid gland	1841	Switz	68	1917	Swiss	Switz	Berne	M.D.
1910	Kossel, Karl Martin L. A. Chemistry of the cell including nucleic substances	1853	German	57	1927	German	Germany	Heidelberg	M.D.
1911	Gullstrand, Allvar For work on dioptrics of the eye	1862	Sweden	49	1930	Swedish	Sweden	Uppsala	M.D.
1912	Carrel, Alexis For vascular studies and grafting blood vessels	1873	France	39	1944	French	France	Rockefeller Insit. for Med. Res.	M.D.
1913	Richet, Charles Robert Anaphylaxis= hypersensitivity induced by allergic reactions	1850	France	63	1935	French	France	Sorbonne	M.D.
1914	Bárány, Robert Physiology & pathology of medicine of the ear	1876	Austria	38	1936	Austrian Swedish	Austria	Vienna	M.D.
1919	Bordet, Jules J. B. Vincent Discoveries about immunity	1870	Belgium	49	1961	Belgian	Belgium	Brussels	M.D.
1920	Krogh, Schack A. S. Discovery of the regulation of motor mechanism of capillaries	1874	Denmark	46	1949	Danish	Denmark	Copenhagen	Ph.D.
1922	Hill, Archibald Vivian Discoveries of heat in muscles	1886	UK	36	1977	British	UK	London	Sc.D.
1922	Meyerhof, Otto Fritz Relationship of oxygen and lactic acid in muscle	1884	Germany	38	1951	German	Germany	Kiel	M.D.
1923	Banting, Sir Frederick Grant Macleod, John James Richard Discovery of insulin	1891 1876	Canada UK	32 47	1941 1935	Canadian British	Canada Canada	Toronto Toronto	M.D. Ph.D.
1924	Einthoven, Willem Mechanism of electrocardiogram	1860	East Indies	64	1927	Dutch	Neth	Leyden	Ph.D.
1926	Fibiger, Johannes Andreas Grib Spiroptera carcinoma (cancer research)	1867	Denmark	59	1928	Danish	Denmark	Copenhagen	M.D., Ph.D.

NOBEL PRIZE WINNERS IN MEDICINE: 1901-2000
[CONTINUED]

Year	Name/ Contribution	Born	Place	Prize Age	Death	Nat.	Country Credited	Univ.	Degree
1927	Wagner von Jauregg, Julius *Malaria innoculations in treatment of dementia paralytica*	1857	Austria	70	1940	Austrian	Austria	Vienna	Ph.D.
1928	Nicolle, Charles Jules Henri *For work on typhus*	1866	France	62	1936	French	France	Inst. Pasteur Tunis	M.D.
1929	Eijkman, Christiaan *Discovery of the antineuritic vitamin (beri-beri disease)*	1858	Neth	71	1930	Dutch	Neth.	Utrecht	M.D.
1929	Hopkins, Sir Frederick Gowland *Discovery of growth-stimulating vitamins (pioneer in nutrition)*	1861	UK	68	1947	British	UK	Cambridge	M.B.
1930	Landsteiner, Karl *Discovery of human blood groups*	1868	Austria	62	1943	Austrian	Austria	Rockefeller Insit.	M.D.
1931	Warburg, Otto Heinrich *Nature & action of respiratory enzyme (cytochrome oxidase)*	1883	Germany	48	1970	German	Germany	Max-Plank-Institut	M.D.
1932	Adrian, Baron Edgar D. Sherrington, Sir Charles S *Discoveries regarding the function of neurons in nerves*	1889 1857	UK UK	43 75	1977 1952	British British	UK UK	Cambridge Oxford	M.D. M.B.
1933	Morgan, Thomas Hunt *Function of chromosomes in transmission of heredity*	1866	USA	67	1945	American	USA	Cal. Instit. of Tech.	M.D. Ph.D.
1934	Minot, George Richards Murphy, William Parry Whipple, George Hoyt *Discoveries concerning liver therapy against anemias*	1885 1892 1878	USA USA USA	49 42 56	1950 1987 1976	American American American	USA USA USA	Harvard Harv./PBBH Rochester, NY	M.D. M.D. M.D.
1935	Spemann, Hans *Organizer effect in embryonic development*	1869	Germany	66	1941	German	Germany	Freiburg/ Breisgau	Dr.
1936	Dale, Sir Henry Hallet Loewi, Otto *Discoveries of chemical transmission of nerve impulses*	1875 1873	UK Germany	61 63	1968 1961	British German, American	UK Austria	Nat. Instit. Med Res Graz	M.D. M.D.
1937	Szent-Györgyi, Albert von N. *Biological combustion processes, re: vitamine C & fumaric acid*	1893	Hungary	44	1986	Hungarian American	Hungary	Szeget	M.D.
1938	Heymans, Corneille Jean F. *Role of sinus & aortic mechanism in the regulation of respiration*	1892	Belgium	46	1968	Belgian	Belgium	Ghent	M.D.
1939	Domagk, Gerhard *Antibacterial effects of prontosil (sulphonamide compound)*	1895	Germany	44	1964	German	German	Munster	M.D.
1943 1943	Dam, Carl Peter Henrik Doisy, Edward Adelbert *Discoveries related to vitamin K*	1895 1893	Denmark USA	48 50	1976 1986	Danish American	Denmark USA	Polytech. Inst. Saint Louis	D.Sc. Ph.D.
1944	Erlanger, Joseph Gasser, Herbert Spencer *Discoveries about functions of single nerve fibers*	1874 1888	USA USA	70 56	1965 1963	American American	USA USA	Washington Rock. Inst.	M.D. M.D.
1945	Chain, Sir Ernst Boris Fleming, Sir Alexander Florey, Sir Howard Walter *Work related to penicillin*	1906 1881 1898	Germany UK Australia	39 64 47	1979 1955 1968	Ger/Br. British Australian British	UK UK UK	Oxford London Oxford	Ph.D. M.D. Ph.D.
1946	Muller, Hermann Joseph *Mutations caused by X-rays*	1890	USA	56	1967	American	USA	Indiana	Ph.D.
1947	Cori, Carl Ferdinand Cori, Gerty Theresa Radnitz(F) *Catalytic conversion of glycogen*	1896 1896	Czech Czech	51 51	1984 1957	Czech/Am Czech/Am	USA USA	Wash., MO Wash., MO	M.D. M.D.

Note: (F) stands for Female

NOBEL PRIZE WINNERS IN MEDICINE:1901-2000
[CONTINUED]

Year	Name/ Contribution	Born	Place	Prize Age	Death	Nat.	Country Credited	Univ. Credited	Degree
1947	Houssay, Bernardo Alberto *Hormone of anterior pituitary lobe in metabolism of sugar*	1887	Argent.	60	1971	Argent.	Argentina	Buenos Aires	M.D.
1948	Müller, Paul Hermann *Discovery of high efficiency of DDT*	1899	Switz.	49	1965	Swiss	Switz.	Geigy Dye-Factory Co.	Dr.
1949	Egas Muniz, Antonio Caetano *Therapeutic value of leucotomy in certain psychoses*	1874	Portugal	75	1955	Portugal	Portugal	Lisbon	M.D.
1949	Hess, Walter Rudolph *Discovery of interbrain as coordinator of activities*	1881	Switz.	68	1973	Swiss	Switz.	Zurich	M.D.
1950	Hench, Philip Showalter	1896	USA	54	1965	American	USA	Mayo Clinic	M.D.
	Kendall, Edward Calvin	1886	USA	64	1972	American	USA	Mayo Clinic	Ph.D.
	Reichstein, Tadeus *Structure and effect of hormones of the adrenal cortex*	1897	Poland	53	1996	Polish/Swiss	Switz.	Basel	Ph.D.
1951	Theiler, Max *Discoveries concerning yellow fever and how to combat it*	1899	So. Af.	52	1972	So. Af.	So. Af./American	Rockefeller Foundation	M.D.
1952	Waksman, Selman Abraham *Discovery of streptomycin, the first antibiotic for TB*	1888	Russia	64	1973	Russian/American	USA	Rutgers	Ph.D.
1953	Krebs, Sir Hans Adolf *Discovery of citric acid cycle*	1900	Germany	53	1981	German/British	UK	Sheffield	M.D. M.S.
1953	Lipmann, Fritz Albert *Discovery of coenzyme-A*	1899	Germany	54	1986	German/American	USA	Harvard/Mass.Gen.	Ph.D.
1954	Enders, John Franklin	1897	USA	57	1985	American	USA	Harvard	Ph.D.
	Robbins, Frederick Chapman	1916	USA	38	----	American	USA	West. Reser.	M.D.
	Weller, Thomas Huckle *Related to the ability of poliomyelitis viruses to grow in cultures*	1915	USA	39	----	American	USA	Harvard	M.D.
1955	Theorell, Axel Hugo Theodor *Nature and mode of action of oxidation enzymes*	1903	Sweden	52	1982	Swedish	Sweden	Nobel Med. Instit.	M.D.
1956	Cournand, Andre F.	1895	France	61	1988	Fr/Am	USA	Columbia	M.D.
	Forssmann, Werner T. O.	1904	Germany	52	1979	German	Germany	Mainz/BK	M.D.
	Richards, Dickinson Woodruff *Heart catheterization & changes in circulatory systems*	1895	USA	61	1973	American	USA	Columbia	M.D.
1957	Bovet, Daniel *Synthetic compounds inhibiting the action of body substances*	1907	Switz.	50	1992	Swiss/It.	Italy	Instit. Public Health	D.Sc.
1958	Beadle, George Wells *Contributions in the field of biochemical and microbial genetics*	1903	USA	55	1989	American	USA	Cal. Instit. of Tech	Ph.D.
1958	Lederberg, Josua *Recombination and organization of bacterial genetic material*	1925	USA	33		American	USA	Wisconcin	Ph.D.
1958	Tatum, Edward Lowrie *Discoveries that genes act by regulating chemical processes*	1909	USA	49	1975	American	USA	Rockefeller Insit.	Ph.D.
1959	Kornberg, Arthur	1918	USA	41	----	American	USA	Stanford	M.D.
	Ochoa, Severo *Mechanisms in the biological synthesis of RNA and DNA*	1909	Spain	50	1993	Sp./Am	USA	New York	M.D.
1960	Burnet, Sir Frank MacFarlane	1899	Australia	61	1985	Australian	Australia	Hall Instit.	M.D./Ph.D
	Medawar, Sir Peter Brian *Discovery of aquired immunological tolerance*	1915	Brazil	45	1987	British	UK	London	D.Sc.

NOBEL PRIZE WINNERS IN MEDICINE: 1901-2000
[CONTINUED]

Year	Name/Contribution	Born	Place	Prize Age	Death	Nat.	Country Credited	Univ. Credited	Degree
1961	Von Békésy, Georg Mechanisms of stimulation within the cochlea (hearing)	1899	Hungary	62	1972	Hung. American	USA	Harvard	Ph.D.
1962	Crick, Francis Harry Compton	1916	UK	46	----	British	UK	Cambridge	Ph.D.
	Watson, James Dewey	1928	USA	34	----	American	USA	Harvard	Ph.D.
	Wilkins, Maurice Hugh F. Structure of nucleic acids and their transfer in living material	1916	NZ	46	----	British	UK	London	Ph.D.
1963	Eccles, Sir John Carew	1903	Australia	60	1997	Aust./Br	Australia	Aus. Nat. Univ.	Ph.D.
	Hodgkin, Sir Alan Lloyd	1914	UK	49	1998	British	UK	Cambridge	----
	Huxley, Sir Andrew Fielding Ionic mechanisms the nerve cell membrane (nerve impulses)	1917	UK	46	----	British	UK	London	M.A.
1964	Bloch, Konrad E.	1917	Germany	47	----	Germ./Am	USA	Harvard	Ph.D.
	Lynen, Feodor Felix Konrad Mechanism of cholesterol and fatty acids metabolism	1911	Germany	53	1979	German	German	Max-Plank/M	Ph.D.
1965	Jacob, Francois	1920	France	45	----	French	France	Inst.Pasteur/P	M.D., D.Sc.
	Lwoff, André Michael	1902	France	63	1994	French	France	Inst.Pasteur/P	M.D., D.Sc.
	Monod, Jacques Lucien Fundamental living processes such as adaptation, reproduction, etc.	1910	France	55	1976	French	France	Inst. Pasteur/P	D.Sc.
1966	Huggins, Charles Brentom (1) Hormonal treatment of prostate cancer (androgens vs. estrogens)	1901	Canada	65	1998	Can/Am	USA	Ben May Lab.	M.D.
1966	Rous, Francic Peyton Tumor-inducing viruses in chickens	1879	USA	87	1970	American	USA	Rockefeller Inst.	M.D.
1967	Granit, Ragnar Arthur	1900	Finland	67	1991	Fin./Swed	Sweden	Karolinska Inst.	M.D.
	Hartline, Halden Keffer	1903	USA	64	1983	American	USA	Rockefeller Inst.	M.D.
	Wald, George Physiological and chemical visual processes in the eye	1906	USA	61	1997	American	USA	Harvard	Ph.D.
1968	Holley, Robert William	1922	USA	46	1993	American	USA	Cornell	Ph.D.
	Khorana, Har Gobind	1922	India	46	----	Ind./Am	USA	Wisconsin	Ph.D.
	Nirenberg, Marshall Warren Interpretation of the genetic code; its function in protein synthesis	1927	USA	41	----	American	USA	NIH	Ph.D.
1969	Delbrück, Max	1906	Germany	63	1981	Germ/Am	USA	Cal Instit. Tech.	Ph.D.
	Hershey, Alfred Day	1908	USA	61	1997	USA	USA	Carnegi Instit.	Ph.D.
	Luria, Salvador Edward Replication mechanism and genetic structure of viruses	1912	Italy	57	1991	It/Am	USA	MIT	Ph.D.
1970	Axelrod, Julius	1912	USA	58	----	American	USA	NIH	Ph.D.
	Katz, Sir Bernard	1911	Germany	59	----	Ger/Br	UK	London	M.D., Ph.D.
	Von Euler, Ulf Svante Humoral transmitters of the nerve and mechanism of operation	1905	Sweden	65	1983	Swedish	Sweden	Karolinska Inst.	M.D.
1971	Sutherland, Earl Wilbur, Jr. Mechanisms of the action of hormones	1915	USA	56	1974	American	USA	Vanderbilt	M.D.
1972	Edelman, Gerard Maurice	1929	USA	43	----	American	USA	Rockefeller Inst.	M.D.
	Porter, Rodney Robert Chemical structure of antibodies	1917	UK	55	1985	UK	UK	Oxford	----
1973	Frisch, Karl von	1886	Austria	87	1982	Austrian	German	Munich	Ph.D.
	Lorenz, Konrad Zacharias	1903	Austria	70	1989	Austrian	Austria	Ost. Akademie	M.D., Ph.D.
	Tinbergen, Nikolaas Behavior patterns of bees; imprinting geese; and gulls and wasps	1907	Neth.	66	1988	Dutch	UK	Oxford	Ph.D.

NOBEL PRIZE WINNERS IN MEDICINE: 1901-2000
[CONTINUED]

Year	Name/Contribution	Born	Place	Prize Age	Death	Nat.	Country Credited	Univ. Credited	Degree
1974	Claude, Albert	1912	Romania	62	1983	Rom/Am	Belgium	Louvain	M.D.
	de Duve, Christian Rene M. J	1917	UK	57	----	Belg/Am	Belgium	Rockefeller Inst.	M.D.
	Palade, George Emil	1912	Romania	62	----	Rom/Am	USA	Yale	M.D.
	Structural and functional organization of the cell								
1975	Baltimore, David	1938	USA	37	----	American	USA	M.I.T.	Ph.D.
	Dulbecco, Renato	1914	Italy	61	----	It/Am	USA	Imp. Cancer	M.D.
	Temin, Howard Martin	1934	USA	41	1994	American	USA	Wisconsin	Ph.D.
	Interaction between tumor viruses and genetic material of the cell								
1976	Blumberg, Baruch Samuel	1925	USA	51	----	American	USA	Can. Res. Inst.	M.D., Ph.D.
	Gajdusek, Daniel Carleton	1923	USA	53	----	American	USA	NIH	M.D.
	Origin and spread of infectious diseases (Hepatitis-B, Kuru)								
1977	Guillemin, Roger	1924	France	53	----	Fr/Am	USA	Salk Instit.	M.D., Ph.D.
	Schally, Andrew Victor	1926	Poland	51	----	Pol/Can	USA	VA Hosp, LA	Ph.D.
	Discoveries on peptide hormone production of the brain								
	Yalow, Rosalyn Sussman (F)	1921	USA	56	----	American	USA	VA Hosp, NY	Ph.D.
	Radioimmunoessays of peptide hormones (insulin)								
1978	Arber, Werner	1929	Switz.	49	----	Swiss	Switz	Biozentrum, Basel	Ph.D.
	Nathans, Daniel	1928	USA	50	----	American	USA	Johns Hopkins	M.D.
	Smith, Hamilton Othanel	1931	USA	47	----	American	USA	Johns Hopkins	M.D.
	Discovery of restricted enzymes; application to molecular genetics								
1979	Cormack, Allan Macleod	1924	So. Af.	55	1998	So. Af/Am	USA	Tufts	M.Sc.
	Hounsfield, Sir Godfrey N.	1919	UK	60	----	British	UK	EMI	Engineer
	Invention of X-ray system for computerized axial tomography								
1980	Benacerraf, Baruj	1920	Venez.	60	----	Venez/Am	USA	Harvard	M.D.
	Dausset, Jean Baptiste Johachim	1916	France	64	----	France	France	Univ. de Paris	M.D.
	Snell, George Davis	1903	USA	77	1996	American	USA	Jackson Lab	D.Sc.
	Genetic structures on cell surface regulating immunological reactions								
1981	Hubel, David Hunter	1926	Canada	55	----	Can/Am	USA	Harvard	M.D.
	Sperry, Roger Wolcott	1913	USA	68	1994	American	USA	Cal Tech	Ph.D.
	Wiesel, Torsten N.	1924	Sweden	57	----	Swed/Am	USA	Harvard	M.D.
	Information processing in the visual system								
1982	Bergstrom, Sune	1916	Sweden	66	----	Swedish	Sweden	Karolinska Inst.	M.D.
	Samuelsson, Bengt Ingemar	1934	Sweden	48	----	Swedish	Sweden	Karolinska Inst.	M.D.
	Vane, John Robert	1927	UK	55	----	British	UK	Wellcome Lab	D.Phil.
	Prostaglandins and related biologically active substances								
1983	McClintock, Barbara (F)	1902	USA	81	1992	American	USA	Cld Spr. Harbor	Ph.D.
	Discovery of mobile genetic elements aiding gene function								
1984	Jerne, Niels Kaj	1911	UK	73	1994	Br/Dan/Sw	Denmark	Instit. Imunology	M.D.
	Köhler, Georges J.F.	1946	Germany	38	1995	German	Germany	Instit. Imunology	M.D.
	Milstein, César	1927	Argentina	57	----	Arg/Br.	UK/Argent.	Cambridge	M.D., Ph.D
	For theories and techniques of immunology								
1985	Brown, Michael Stuart	1941	USA	44	----	American	USA	Texas, Dallas	M.D.
	Goldstein, Joseph Leonard	1940	USA	45	----	American	USA	Texas, Dallas	M.D.
	Regulation of cholesterol metabolism and treatment								
1986	Cohen, Stanley	1922	USA	64	----	American	USA	Vanderbilt	Ph.D.
	Levi-Montalcini, Rita (F)	1909	Italy	77	----	It/Am	Italy/USA	Instit. Cell Bio	M.D.
	Discoveries of mechanisms that regulate growth								

Note: (F) stands for Female

NOBEL PRIZE WINNERS IN MEDICINE: 1901-2000
[CONTINUED]

Year	Name/Contribution	Born	Place	Prize Age	Death	Nat.	Country Credited	Univ. Credited	Degree
1987	Tonegawa, Susumu *Genetic principle of generation of antibody diversity*	1939	Japan	48	----	Japan.	Japan	MIT	Ph.D.
1988	Black, Sir James W. *Important principles for drug treatments (beta-blockers)*	1924	UK	64	----	Brit	UK	King's College	M.D.
1988	Elion, Gertrude Belle (F) Hitchings, George Herbert *Important principles for drug treatments (malaria, leukemia)*	1918 1905	USA USA	70 83	1999 1998	American American	USA USA	Wellcome Lab. Wellcome Lab.	.M.S. Ph.D.
1989	Bishop, John Michael Varmus, Harold Eliot *Oncogenes in animal tumor viruses come from cellular genes*	1936 1939	USA USA	53 50	---- ----	American American	USA USA	Cal/SF Cal/SF	M.D. M.D.
1990	Murray, Joseph E. Thomas, Edward Donnall *Transplantation of organs to save lives (kidney, bone)*	1919 1920	USA USA	71 70		American American	USA USA	B&W Hosp Hutchinson CRC	M.D. M.D.
1991	Neher, Erwin Sakmann, Bert *Function of single ion channels in cells (diabetes, epilepsy)*	1944 1942	Germany Germany	47 49	---- ----	German German	Germany Germany	Max-Plank/Goet Max-Plank/Heid	Ph.D. M.D.
1992	Fischer, Edmond Henry Krebs, Edwin Gerhard *Reversible protein phosphorylation as a regulatory mechanism*	1920 1918	China USA	72 74	---- ----	Fr/Am American	USA/Switz USA	Washington Washington	Ph.D. M.D.
1993 1993	Roberts, Richard John Sharp, Philip Allen *Discoveries concerning of split genes*	1943 1944	UK USA	50 49	---- ----	Br/Am American	UK USA	NE Biolabs M.I.T.	Ph.D. Ph.D.
1994	Gilman, Alfred Goodman Rodbell, Martin *Discovery of G-proteins and their role in signal transduction in cells*	1941 1925	USA USA	53 69	---- 1998	American American	USA USA	Texas/ Dallas NIEH	M.D., Ph.D. M.D., Ph.D.
1995	Lewis, Edward B. Nüsselien-Volhard, Christiane Wieschaus, Eric F. *Genetic control of early embryonic development (malformation)*	1918 1942 1947	USA Germany USA	77 53 48	---- ---- ----	American German American	USA Germany USA	Cal. Inst Tech. Max-Plank/Tub Princeton	Ph.D. Ph.D. Ph.D.
1996	Doherty, Peter C. Zinkernagel, Rolf M. *Specifity of the cell mediated immune defense*	1940 1944	Australia Switz.	56 52	---- ----	Aus/Am Swiss	Australia Switz.	Tennessee/Mem Zurich	Ph.D.,D.Sc M.D.
1997	Prusiner, Stanley B. *Discovery of prions - a new biological principle of infection*	1942	USA	55	----	American	USA	Cal/SF	M.D., Ph.D.
1998	Furchgott, Robert Francis Ignarro, Louis J. Murad, Ferid *Nitric oxide as a signalling molecule in the cardiovascular system*	1916 1941 1936	USA USA USA	82 57 62	---- ---- ----	American American American	USA USA USA	Health Sc. Cen UCLA Texas/Houston	Ph.D.,D.Sc Ph.D. M.D., Ph.D.
1999	Blobel, Gunter *Proteins governing their transport and localization in the cell*	1936	Germany	63	----	American	USA	Rockefeller Univ	M.D., Ph.D.
2000	Carlsson, Arvid Greengard, Paul Kandel, Eric *Signal transduction in the nervous system*	1923 1925 1929	Sweden USA Austria	77 75 71	---- ---- ----	Swedish American American	Sweden USA USA	Goteborg Rockefeller Univ Columbia	M.D. Ph.D. M.D.

Note: (F) stands for Female

NOBEL PRIZE WINNERS IN PHYSICS: 1901-2000

Year	Name/ Contribution	Born	Place	Prize Age	Death	Nat.	Country Credited	Univ. Credited	Degree
1901	Roentgen, Wilhelm Conrad *Discovery of Roentgen rays*	1845	Germany	56	1923	German	Germany	Munich	Ph.D
1902	Lorentz, Hendrich Antoon	1853	Neth.	49	1928	Dutch	Neth.	Leiden	Ph.D
	Zeeman, Pieter *Influence of magnetism on radiation*	1865	Neth.	37	1943	Dutch	Neth.	Amsterdam	Ph.D
1903	Becquerel, Antoine Henri	1852	France	51	1908	French	France	Polytechnique	Ph.D
	Curie, Pierre	1859	France	44	1906	French	France	Ecole	D.Sc.
	Curie, Marie(F) *Discovery of spontaneous radioactivity*	1867	Poland	36	1934	Pol/Fr	France	Ecole	Ph.D
1904	Strutt, John W. (Lord Rayleigh) *Density of gases and discovery of Argon*	1842	UK	62	1919	British	UK	Royal Institute	B.A.
1905	Lenard, Phillipp Eduard A. von *Research on cathode rays*	1862	Hungary	43	1947	German	Germany	Kiel	Ph.D
1906	Thomson, Sir Joseph John *Conduction of electricity by gases*	1856	UK	50	1940	British	UK	Cambridge	B.A.
1907	Michelson, Albert Abraham *Spectroscopic and metrological investigation*	1852	German	55	1931	Ger/Am	USA	Chicago	M.D.
1908	Lippmann, Gabriel Jonas *Photographic reproduction of colors*	1845	Lux.	63	1921	French	France	Sorbonne	Ph.D/D.Sc.
1909	Braun, Carl Ferdinand	1850	Germany	59	1918	Germany	German	Strasbourg	Ph.D
	Marconi, Guglielmo *Wireless telegraphy*	1874	Italy	35	1937	Italian	Italy	Marconi Co. (UK)	--
1910	Van der Waals, Johness Diderik *Development of an equation of state for gases and liquids*	1837	Neth.	73	1923	Dutch	Neth.	Amsterdam	Dr.
1911	Wien, Wilhelm *Laws governing the radiation of heat*	1864	Germany	47	1928	German	Germany	Wurzburg	Ph.D
1912	Dalén, Niels Gustaf *Automatic regulators for illuminating lighthouses and buoys*	1869	Sweden	43	1937	Swedish	Sweden	Gas Co.	Engineer
1913	Kamerlingh-Onnes, Heike *Properties of matter at low temperatures, (liquid helium)*	1853	Neth.	60	1926	Dutch	Neth.	Leiden	Ph.D
1914	Laue, Max von *X-ray diffraction by crystals*	1879	Germany	35	1960	German	Germany	Frankfurt	Ph.D
1915	Bragg, Sir William Henry	1862	UK	53	1942	British	UK	London	M.A.
	Bragg William Lawrence *Study of chrystal structures by means of x-rays*	1890	Australia	25	1971	British	UK	Victoria (UK)	M.A.
1917	Barkla, Charles Glover *Discovery of charactaristic Roentgen radiation of the elements*	1877	UK	40	1944	British	UK	Edinburgh	D.Sc.
1918	Planck, Max Karl Ernst Ludwig *Elementary quanta theory*	1858	Germany	60	1947	German	Germany	Berlin	Ph.D
1919	Stark, Johannes *Doppler effect in canal rays and splitting of spectral lines*	1874	Germany	45	1957	German	Germany	Greifswald	Ph.D
1920	Guillaume, Charles Édouard *Anomalies of nickel steel alloys*	1861	Switz	59	1938	Sw/Fr	Switz	Bur. Measure	Ph.D
1921	Einstein, Albert *For services to theoretical physics, such as law of photoelectric effect*	1879	Germany	42	1955	Sw/Am	Switzerland	Max-Plank-Institut, Berlin	Ph.D
1922	Bohr, Niels Henrik David *Structure of atoms and radiation emanating from them*	1885	Denmark	37	1962	Danish	Denmark	Copenhagen	Ph.D

Note: (F) stands for Female

NOBEL PRIZE WINNERS IN PHYSICS: 1901-2000
[CONTINUED]

Year	Name/Contribution	Born	Place	Prize Age	Death	Nat.	Country Credited	Univ. Credited	Degree
1923	Millikam, Robert Andrews *Elementary charge of electricity and photoelectric effect*	1868	USA	55	1953	American	USA	Cal Tech	Ph.D
1924	Siegbahn, Karl Mann Georg *X-ray spectroscopy*	1886	Sweden	38	1978	Sweden	Sweden	Uppsala Univ.	D.Sc.
1925	Franck, James Hertz, Gustav Ludwig *Laws governing the impact of electrons on atoms*	1882 1887	Germany Germany	43 38	1964 1975	Ger/Am German	Germany Germany	Goettingen Halle	Ph.D Ph.D
1926	Perrin, Jean Baptiste *Structure of matter and discovery of sedimentation equilibrium*	1870	France	56	1942	French	France	Sorbonne	D.Sc.
1927	Compton, Arthur Holly *Discovery named after him of increased x-rays caused by electrons*	1892	USA	35	1962	American	USA	Chicago	Ph.D
1927	Wilson, Charles Thomson Rees *Electrically charged particles visible by vapor condensation*	1869	UK	58	1959	British	UK	Cambridge	B.Sc.
1928	Richardson, Sir Owen Williams *Discovery of law named after him (thermionic phenomenon)*	1879	UK	49	1959	British	UK	London	D.Sc.
1929	Broglie, Louis-Victor P. R. de *Discovery of wave nature of electrons*	1892	France	37	1987	French	France	Sorbonne	D.Sc.
1930	Chandrasekhara V., Sir Raman *Raman effect & scattering of light*	1888	India	42	1970	Indian	India	Calcuta	M.A.
1932	Heisenberg, Werner Karl *Creation of quantum mechanics*	1901	Germany	31	1976	German	Germany	Leipzig	Ph.D
1933	Dirac, Paul Adrien Maurice Schrödinger, Erwin *Productive forms of atomic theory*	1902 1887	UK Austria	31 46	1984 1961	Br/Am Austrian	UK Austria	Cambridge Berlin	Ph.D Ph.D
1935	Chadwick, Sir James *Discovery of neutron*	1891	UK	44	1974	British	UK	Liverpool	M.Sc.
1936	Anderson, Carl David *Discovery of the positron*	1905	USA	31	1991	American	USA	Cal Tech.	Ph.D
1936	Hess, Victor Franz *Dicovery of cosmic radiation*	1883	Austria	53	1964	Austrian	Austria	Innsbruck	Ph.D
1937	Davisson, Clinton Joseph Thomson, Sir George Paget *Discovery of diffraction of electrons by crystals*	1881 1892	USA UK	56 45	1958 1975	American British	USA UK	Bell Tel Lab. London	Ph.D B.Sc.
1938	Fermi, Enrico *New radioactive elements and nuclear reactions*	1901	Italy	37	1954	It/Am	Italy	Rome	Ph.D
1939	Lawrence, Ernest Orlando *Cyclotron for artificial radioactive elements*	1901	USA	38	1958	American	USA	UC Berkeley	Ph.D
1943	Stern, Otto *Molecular ray method and magnetic moment of proton*	1888	Germany	55	1969	Ger/Am	USA	Carnegie	Ph.D
1944	Rabi, Isidor Isaac *Magnetic properties of atomic nuclei (radar, atom bomb)*	1898	Austria	46	1988	Aust/Am	USA	Columbia	Ph.D
1945	Pauli, Wolfgang Ernst *Pauli Principle: No two electrons in same atom can exist in same state*	1900	Austria	45	1958	Aust/Sw	Austria	Princeton	Ph.D
1946	Bridgman, Percy Williams *Apparatus to produce extremely high pressure*	1882	USA	64	1961	USA	USA	Harvard	Ph.D

NOBEL PRIZE WINNERS IN PHYSICS: 1901-2000
[CONTINUED]

Year	Name/ Contribution	Born	Place	Prize Age	Death	Nat.	Country Credited	Univ. Credited	Degree
1947	Appleton, Sir Edward Victor Physics of the upper layer of atmosphere and Appleton layer	1892	UK	55	1965	British	UK	Sci./Ind Res.	B.A.
1948	Blackett, Patrick M. S. Development of Wilson cloud chamber and cosmic radiation	1897	UK	51	1974	British	UK	Victoria (UK)	M.A.
1949	Yukawa, Hideki Prediction of existence of mesons based on theoretical nuclear work	1907	Japan	42	1981	Japanese	Japan	Kyoto/Columbia	D.Sc.
1950	Powell, Cecil Frank Photographic method of studying nuclear processes (mesons)	1903	UK	47	1969	British	UK	Bristol	Ph.D
1951	Cockcroft, Sir John Douglas	1897	UK	54	1967	British	UK	AER (UK)	Ph.D
1951	Walton, Ernest Thomas Sinton Transmutation of atomic nuclei by accelerated atomic particles	1903	Ireland	48	1995	Irish	Ireland	Trinity (Dublin)	Ph.D
1952	Bloch, Felix	1905	Switz	47	1983	Sw/Am	USA	Stanford	Ph.D
	Purcell, Edward Mills New methods for nuclear magnetic precision measurements	1912	USA	40	1997	American	USA	Harvard	Ph.D
1953	Zernike, Frits (Frederik) Phase contrast method and phase contrast microscope	1888	Neth.	65	1966	Dutch	Netherlands	Groningen	Ph.D
1954	Born, Max quantum mechanics; statistical interpretation of wave function	1882	Germany	72	1970	Ger/Br	UK	Edinburgh	Ph.D
	Bothe, Walther Wilhelm Georg coincidence method	1891	Germany	63	1957	German	Germany	Heidelberg	Ph.D
1955	Kusch, Polycarp Demonstration of the magnetic moment of the electron	1911	Germany	44	1993	American	USA	Columbia	Ph.D
	Lamb, Willis Eugene, Jr. Discovery of the structure of the hydrogen spectrum	1913	USA	42	----	American	USA	Stanford	Ph.D
1956	Bardeen, John (See 1972)	1908	USA	48	1991	American	USA	Illinois	Ph.D
	Brattain, Walter Houser	1902	China	54	1987	American	USA	Bell Tel Lab.	Ph.D
	Shockley, William Bradford Semiconductors and discovery of the transistor effect	1910	UK	46	1989	American	USA	Beckman Instru.	Ph.D
1957	Lee, Tsung-dau	1926	China	31		Chi/Am	China	Columbia	Ph.D
	Yang, Chen Ning Parity laws and discovery of elementary particles	1922	China	35		Chi/Am	China	Priceton	Ph.D
1958	Cherenkov, Pavel Alekseyevich	1904	Russia	54	1990	Russian	Russia	Physics Instit.	Dr.
	Frank, Ilya Mikaylovich	1908	Russia	50	1990	Russian	Russia	Moscow/Phys Inst.	Dr.
	Tamm, Igor Evgenevich The Cherenkov effect	1895	Russia	63	1971	Russian	Russia	Moscow/Phys Inst.	Dr.
1959	Chamberlain, Owen	1920	USA	39	----	American	USA	UC Berkeley	Ph.D
	Segré, Emilio Gino Discovery of antiproton	1905	Italy	54	1989	It/Am	USA	UC Berkeley	Ph.D
1960	Glaser, Donald Arthur Invention of the bubble chamber	1926	USA	34	----	American	USA	UC Berkeley	Ph.D
1961	Hofstadter, Robert Electron scattering in atomic nuclei; structure of nucleons	1915	USA	46	1990	American	USA	Stanford	Ph.D
	Mössbauer, Rudolf Ludwig Resonance absorption of gamma radiation and Mossbauer effect	1929	Germany	32	----	German	German	Tech. (Munich)/ Cal Tech.	Ph.D

NOBEL PRIZE WINNERS IN PHYSICS: 1901-2000
[CONTINUED]

Year	Name/Contribution	Born	Place	Prize Age	Death	Nat.	Country Credited	Univ. Credited	Degree
1962	Landau, Lev Davidovich *Condensed matter especially liquid helium*	1908	Russia	54	1968	Russian	Russia	Acad Sci	Ph.D
1963	Jensen, Johannes Hans Daniel Goeppert-Mayer, Maria (F) *Nuclear shell structure*	1907 1906	Germany Poland	56 57	1973 1972	German Ger/Am	Germany USA	Heidelberg UC/San Diego	Ph.D Ph.D
1963	Wigner, Eugene Paul *Atomic nucleus; elementary particles; symmetry principles*	1902	Hungary	61	1995	Hun/Am	USA	Princeton	Dr.
1964	Basov, Nikolai Gennadievich Prokhorov, Alexander Mikhailovich Townes, Charles Hard *Quantum electronics; construction by maser-laser*	1922 1916 1915	Russia Australia USA	42 48 49	---- ---- ----	Russian Aust/Rus American	Russia Russia USA	Lebedev Instit. Lebedev Instit. M.I.T.	Ph.D Dr. Ph.D
1965	Feynman, Richard Phillips Schwinger, Julian Seymour Tomonaga, Shinichiro *Quantum electrodynamics for physics of elementary particles*	1918 1918 1906	USA USA Japan	47 47 59	1988 1994 1979	American American Japanese	USA USA Japan	Cal Tech Harvard Tokyo	Ph.D Ph.D D.Sc.
1966	Kastler, Alfred *Optical methods to study Hertzian resonances in atoms (laser)*	1902	France	64	1984	French	France	Paris	D.Sc.
1967	Bethe, Hans Albrecht *Nuclear reactions, especially concerning energy in stars*	1906	Germany	61	----	Ger/Am	USA	Cornell	Ph.D
1968	Alvarez, Luis Walter *Contributions to elementary particle physics and resonance states*	1911	USA	57	1988	American	USA	UC/Berkeley	Ph.D
1969	Gell-Mann, Murray *Classification of elementary particles and their interactions*	1929	USA	40	----	American	USA	Calif Tech.	Ph.D
1970	Alfven, Hannes Olof Gosta *Magnetohydrodynamics and application to plasma physics*	1908	Sweden	62	1995	Swedish	Sweden	Roy. Instit.Tech	Ph.D
	Neel, Louis Eugene Felix *Antiferromagnetism and ferromagnetism*	1904	France	66	----	French	France	Grenoble	D.Sc.
1971	Gabor, Dennis *Holographic method*	1900	Hungary	71	1979	Hun/Br	UK	Coll Sci.& Tech	Dr.
1972	Bardeen, John Cooper, Leon Neil Schrieffer, John Robert *Theory of superconductivity*	1908 1930 1931	USA USA USA	64 42 41	1991 ---- ----	American American American	USA USA USA	Illinois Brown Pennsylvania	Ph.D Ph.D Ph.D
1973	Esaki, Leo Giaever, Ivar *Tunneling phenomena in semiconductors and superconductors*	1925 1929	Japan Norway	48 44	---- ----	Japanese Nor/Am	Japan USA	IBM GE	Ph.D Ph.D
	Josephson, Brian David *Super current through tunnel barrier—Josephson effect*	1940	UK	33	----	British	UK	Cambridge	Ph.D
1974	Hewish, Antony *Radio astrophysics and discovery of pulsars*	1924	UK	50	----	British	UK	Cambridge	Ph.D
	Ryle, Sir Martin *Radio astrophysics and the aperture synthesis technique*	1918	UK	56	1984	British	UK	Cambridge	B.Sc.
1975	Bohr, Aage Niels Mottelson, Benjamin Roy Rainwater, Leo James *Collective and particle motion in atomic nuclei*	1922 1926 1917	Den USA USA	53 49 58	---- ---- 1986	Danish Am/Dan American	Denmark Denmark USA	Niels Bohr Instit. Nordita Columbia	Ph.D Ph.D Ph.D

Note: (F) stands for Female

NOBEL PRIZE WINNERS IN PHYSICS: 1901-2000
[CONTINUED]

Year	Name/Contribution	Born	Place	Prize Age	Death	Nat.	Country Credited	Univ. Credited	Degree
1976	Richter, Burton	1931	USA	45	----	American	USA	Stanford	Ph.D
	Ting, Samuel Chao Chang	1936	USA	40	----	American	USA	M.I.T.	Ph.D
	Heavy elementary subatomic particle								
1977	Anderson, Philip Warren	1923	USA	54	----	American	USA	Bell Lab	Ph.D
	Mott, Sir Nevill Francis	1905	UK	72	1996	British	UK	Cambridge	M.A.
	Van Vleck, John Hasbrouck	1899	USA	78	1980	American	USA	Harvard	Ph.D
	Electronic structure of magnetic and disordered systems								
1978	Kapitsa, Pyotr Leonidovich	1894	Russia	84	1984	Russian	Russia	Acad Sci	Ph.D
	Low-temperature physics								
	Penzias, Arno Allen	1923	German	55	----	Ger/Am	USA	Bell Lab.	Ph.D
	Wilson, Robert Woodrow	1936	USA	42	----	American	USA	Bell Lab.	Ph.D
	Cosmic microwave background radiation								
1979	Glashow, Sheldon Lee	1932	USA	47	----	American	USA	Harvard	Ph.D
	Salam, Abdus	1926	Pakistan	53	1996	Pak/Br	Pakistan	InCen/Imp Col	Ph.D
	Weinberg, Steven	1933	USA	46	----	American	USA	Harvard	Ph.D
	Unified weak and electromagnetic interaction								
1980	Cronin, James Watson	1931	USA	49	----	American	USA	Chicago	Ph.D
	Fitch, Val Logsdon	1923	USA	57	----	American	USA	Princeton	Ph.D
	Fundamental symmetry principles in decay of neutral K-mesons								
1981	Bloembergen, Nicholaas	1920	Neth	61	----	Dutch/Am	USA	Harvard	Ph.D
	Schawalow, Arthur Leonard	1921	USA	60	1999	American	USA	Stanford	Ph.D
	Laser spectroscopy								
	Siegbahn, Kai Manne Boerje	1918	Sweden	63	----	Swedish	Sweden	Uppsala	Ph.D
	High resolution electron spectroscopy								
1982	Wilson, Kenneth Geddes	1936	USA	46	----	American	USA	Cornell	Ph.D
	Critical phenomena in connection with phase transitions								
1983	Chandrasekhar, Subrahmanyan	1910	India	73	1995	Indian/Am	USA	Chicago	Ph.D
	Structure & evolution of stars (black holes)								
	Fowler, William Alfred	1911	USA	72	1995	American	USA	Cal Tech.	Ph.D
	Nuclear reactions of chemical elements in the universe								
1984	Rubbia, Carlo	1934	Italy	50	----	Italian	Italy	CERN	Ph.D
	van der Meer, Simon	1925	Neth	59	----	Dutch	Neth	CERN	M.Sc.
	Field particles W & Z—weak interaction (radioactivity)								
1985	Klitzing, Klaus von	1943	Germany	42	----	German	Germany	Max-Plank-Inst/ Stut	Ph.D
	Discovery of quantized Hall effect								
1986	Binnig, Gerd Karl	1947	Germany	39	----	German	Germany	IBM/Zurich	Ph.D
	Rohrer, Heinrich	1933	Switz	53	----	Swiss	Switz	IBM/Zurich	Ph.D
	Ruska, Ernst	1906	Germany	80	1988	German	Germany	Max-Planck-Co.	Ph.D
	Design of the scanning tunneling microscope								
1987	Bednorz, Johannes Georg	1950	Germany	37	----	German	Germany	IBM/Zurich	Ph.D
	Müller, Karl Alexander	1927	Switz	60	----	Swiss	Switz	IBM/Zurich	Ph.D
	Superconductivity in ceramic materials								
1988	Lederman, Leon Max	1922	USA	66	----	American	USA	Fermi Lab.	Ph.D
	Schwartz, Melvin	1932	USA	56	----	American	USA	Digital Pathway	Ph.D
	Steinberger, Jack	1921	Germany	67	----	Ger/Am	USA	CERN	Ph.D
	Neutrino beam method; structure of leptons with muon neutrino								

NOBEL PRIZE WINNERS IN PHYSICS: 1901-2000
[CONTINUED]

Year	Name/Contribution	Born	Place	Prize Age	Death	Nat.	Country Credited	Univ. Credited	Degree
1989	Dehmelt, Hans Georg	1922	Germany	67	----	Ger/Am	USA	Washington	Ph.D
	Paul, Wolfgang	1913	Germany	76	1993	German	Germany	Bonn	Ph.D
	Ion trap technique								
	Ramsey, Norman Foster, Jr	1915	USA	74	----	American	USA	Harvard	Ph.D
	For inventing a method to measure time (atomic clocks)								
1990	Friedman, Jerome Isaac	1930	USA	60	----	American	USA	M.I.T.	Ph.D
	Kendall, Henry Way	1926	USA	64	1999	American	USA	M.I.T.	Ph.D
	Taylor, Richard E.	1929	Canada	61	----	Can/Am	Canada	Stanford	Ph.D
	Inelastic scattering of electrons on protons and bound neutrons for quark model								
1991	Gennes, Pierre-Gilles de	1932	France	59	----	French	France	Col de France	Ph.D
	Generalizing simple systems to complex matter such as liquids								
1992	Charpak, Georges	1924	Poland	68	----	Pol/Fr	France	Physique/CERN	Ph.D
	Development of particle detectors; multiwire proportional chamber								
1993	Hulse, Russel Alan	1950	USA	43	----	American	USA	Princeton	Ph.D
	Taylor, Joseph Hooton	1941	USA	52	----	American	USA	Princeton	Ph.D
	New type of pulsar for study of gravitation								
1994	Brockhouse, Bertram Neville	1918	Canada	76	----	Canadian	Canada	McMaster	Ph.D
	Neutron spectroscopy to study condensed matter								
	Shull, Clifford Glenwood	1915	USA	79	----	American	USA	M.I.T.	Ph.D
	Neutron diffraction technique								
1995	Perl, Martin L.	1927	USA	68	----	American	USA	Stanford	Ph.D
	Discovery of tau lepton								
	Reines, Frederick	1918	USA	77	1998	American	USA	UC/Irvine	Ph.D
	Detection of the neutrino								
1996	Lee, David M.	1931	USA	65	----	American	USA	Cornell	Ph.D
	Osheroff, Douglas D.	1945	USA	51	----	American	USA	Stanford	Ph.D
	Richardson, Robert C.	1937	USA	59	----	American	USA	Cornell	Ph.D
	Superfluidity in helium-3								
1997	Chu, Steven	1948	USA	49	----	American	USA	Stanford	Ph.D
	Cohen-Tannoudji, Claude	1933	Alger	64	----	French	France	Col de France/Ecole	Ph.D
	Philips, William D.	1948	USA	49	----	American	USA	Nat.Inst.Stan.&Tech	Ph.D
	Cooling and trapping atoms with laser light								
1998	Laughlin, Robert B.	1950	USA	48	----	American	USA	Stanford	Ph.D
	Störmer, Horst L.	1949	Germany	49	----	Ger/Am	German	Columbia	Ph.D
	Tsui, Daniel C.	1939	China	59	----	American	USA	Princeton	Ph.D
	Quantum fluid with fractionally charged excitations								
1999	Hooft, Gerardus 't	1946	Neth	53	----	Dutch	Neth/USA	Utrecht	Ph.D/ D.Sc.
	Veltman, Martinus	1931	Neth	68	----	Dutch	Neth	Michigan	Ph.D
	Quantum structure of electroweak interaction								
2000	Alferov, Zhores I.	1930	Russia	70	----	Russian	Russia	PhisicoTec. Inst	Dr.
	Kroemer, Herbert	1928	German	72	----	Ger/Am	USA	UC/Sta Barbara	Dr.
	Semiconductor heterostructures for high-speed, opto-electronics								
	Kilby, Jack S.	1923	USA	77	----	American	USA	Texas Instruments	Ph.D
	Invention of the integrated circuit (used in Internet)								

NOBEL PRIZE WINNERS IN ECONOMICS: 1969-2000

Year	Name/ Contribution	Born	Place	Prize Age	Death	Nat.	Country Credited	Univ. Credited	Degree
1969	Frisch, Ragnar Kittil Anton	1895	Norway	74	1973	Norweg.	Norway	Oslo	Ph.D.
	Tinbergen, Jan	1903	Neth.	66	1994	Dutch	Neth.	Leiden	Ph.D.
	Developed dynamic models for the analysis of economic processes								
1970	Samuelson, Paul Anthony	1915	USA	55	----	American	USA	Harvard	Ph.D.
	Static & dynamic economic theory								
1971	Kuznets, Simon Smith	1901	Russia	70	1985	Russian USA	USA	Harvard	Ph.D.
	Insights into the economic and social structure								
1972	Arrow, Kenneth Joseph	1921	USA	51	----	American	USA	Harvard	Ph.D.
	Hicks, Sir John Richard	1904	UK	68	1989	British	UK	Oxford	M.A.
	Economic equilibrium and welfare theories								
1973	Leontief, Wassily W.	1906	Russia	67	1999	Russian American	USA	Harvard	Ph.D.
	Input-output method and its application to economics								
1974	Hayek, Friedrich A. Von	1899	Austria	75	1992	Austrian/ Brit/Amer.	UK	London(?)	Ph.D.
	Myrdal, Karl Gunnar	1898	Sweden	76	1987	Swedish	Sweden	Stockholm(?)	Dr.
	Theory of money & economic fluctuations								
1975	Kantorovich, Leonid V.	1912	Russia	63	1986	Russian	Russia	Acad Science	Ph.D.
	Koopmans, Tjulling Charles	1910	Neth.	65	1986	Dutch American	USA	Yale	Ph.D.
	Theory of optimum allocation of resources								
1976	Friedman, Milton	1912	USA	64	----	American	USA	Chicago	Ph.D.
	Consumption, analysis of monetary and complexity of stabilization								
1977	Meade, James Edward	1907	UK	70	1995	British	UK	Cambridge	B.A.
	Ohlin, Bertil Gotthard	1899	Sweden	78	1979	Swedish	Sweden	Sch. Econ.	Ph.D.
	International trade & international capital movements								
1978	Simon, Herbert Alexander	1916	USA	62	----	American	USA	Carnegie-Mellon	Ph.D.
	Decision-making processes within economic organizations								
1979	Lewis, Sir William A.	1915	St.Lucia	64	1991	St.Lucian Brit./Amer.	UK	Princeton	Ph.D.
1979	Schultz, Theodore William	1902	USA	77	----	USA	USA	Chicago	Ph.D.
	Economic development of developing countries								
1980	Klein, Lawrence Robert	1920	USA	60	----	USA	USA	Pennsylvania	Ph.D.
	Econometric models and analysis of economic fluctuations & policies								
1981	Tobin, James	1918	USA	63	----	USA	USA	Yale	Ph.D.
	Analysis of financial markets/ relation to economic decisions								
1982	Stigler, George Joseph	1911	USA	71	1991	USA	USA	Chicago	Ph.D.
	Industrial structures, functioning of markets, and impact of regulations								
1983	Debreu, Gerard	1921	France	62	----	French American	USA	Univ. of Cal. Berkeley	Dr.
	Reformulation of theory of equilibrium								
1984	Stone, Sir John R. N.	1913	UK	71	1991	British	UK	Cambridge	D.Sc.
	Systems of national accounts to improve economic analysis								
1985	Modigliani, Franco	1918	Italy	67	----	Italian American	USA	MIT	Ph.D.
	Analyses of saving and financial markets								

NOBEL PRIZE WINNERS IN ECONOMICS: 1969-2000
[CONTINUED]

Year	Name/Contribution	Born	Place	Prize Age	Death	Nat.	Country Credited	Univ. Credited	Degree
1986	Buchanan, James McGill, Jr. Bases for the theory of economics and political decision	1919	USA	67	----	American	USA	Cen. Study Public Choice	Ph.D.
1987	Solow, Robert Merton Theory of economic growth	1924	USA	63	----	American	USA	MIT.	Ph.D.
1988	Allais, Maurice Theory of markets and efficient utilization of resources	1911	France	77	----	French	France	Ec. Nat. Sup. des Mines	Ph.D.
1989	Haavelmo, Trygve Probability foundation for econometrics	1911	Norway	78	----	Norweg	Norway	Oslo	Ph.D.
1990	Markowitz, Harry M.	1927	USA	63	----	American	USA	City Univ. New York	Ph.D.
	Miller, Merton Howard	1923	USA	67	----	American	USA	Chicago	Ph.D.
	Sharpe, William F. Theory of financial economics	1934	USA	56	----	American	USA	Stanford	Ph.D.
1991	Coase, Ronald Harry Discovery of the significance of transaction costs & property rights	1910	UK	81	----	British	UK	Chicago	D.Sc.
1992	Becker, Gary Stanley Extension of micro economic analysis to human behavior	1930	USA	62	----	American	USA	Chicago	Ph.D.
1993	Fogel, Robert William	1926	USA	67	----	American	USA	Chicago	Ph.D.
	North, Douglass Cecil Historical research to explain economic & institutional changes	1920	USA	73	----	American	USA	Wash. Univ.	Ph.D.
1994	Harsanyi, John Charles	1920	Hungary	74	----	Hungarian American	USA	Univ. of Cal Berkeley	Ph.D.
	Nash, John F.	1928	USA	66	----	American	USA	Princeton	Ph.D.
	Selten, Reinhard Analysis of equilibria in theory of non-cooperative games	1930	Germany	64	----	German	Germany	Rein. Friedrich-Wilhelms	Ph.D.
1995	Lucas, Robert E., Jr. Hypothesis of rational expectations/macroeconomics analysis	1937	USA	58	----	American	USA	Chicago	Ph.D.
1996	Mirrlees, James A.	1936	UK	60	----	British	UK	Cambridge	Ph.D.
	Vickrey, William Theory of incentives under asymmetric information	1914	Canada	82	1996	Canadian	USA	Columbia	Ph.D.
1997	Merton, Robert C.	1944	USA	53	----	American	USA	Boston	Ph.D.
	Scholes, Myron S. New method to determine the value of derivatives	1941	Canada	56	----	Can/Amer	USA	Long Term Capital Mgmt	Ph.D.
1998	Sen, Amartya Contributions to welfare economics	1933	India	65	----	Indian	India	Trinity	Ph.D.
1999	Mundell, Robert A. Monetary analysis and fiscal policy involving exchange rates	1932	Canada	67	----	Canadian	Canada	Columbia	Ph.D.
2000	Heckman James J.	1944	USA	56	----	American	USA	Chicago	Ph.D.
	McFadden, Daniel L. Theory & methods for analysing discrete choice	1937	USA	63	----	American	USA	Univ. Cal. Berkeley	Ph.D.

NOBEL PRIZE WINNERS IN LITERATURE: 1901-2000

Year	Name/ Contribution	Born	Place	Prize Age	Death	Nat.	Country Credited	Career	Degree
1901	Sully Prudhomme Poetic composition featuring qualities of heart and intellect	1839	France	62	1907	French	France	Poet	B.Sc.
1902	Mommsen, Christian M. T. Greatest living master of historical writing (History of Rome)	1817	Germany	85	1903	German	Germany	Author/Prof.	Dr. Law
1903	Björnson, Björnstjerne M. Tribute to his noble, magnificent and versatile poetry	1832	Norway	71	1910	Norweg	Norway	Poet/Author	None
1904	Echegaray Y Eizaguirre, José Numerous and brilliant compositions of Spanish drama	1832	Spain	72	1916	Spanish	Spain	Playwite/Prof	Eng
	Mistral, Frederic Recognition of the originality and true artistic genius of his poetry	1830	France	74	1914	French	France	Poet	B.A.(?)
1905	Sienkiewicz, Henryk For historical novels about his country (Quo Vadis)	1846	Poland	59	1916	Polish	Poland	Author	None
1906	Carducci, Giosue Creative energy, freshness, and lyrical force of his masterpieces	1835	Italy	71	1907	Italian	Italy	Poet/Prof.	Ph.D.
1907	Kipling, Joseph Rudyard For observations, imagination, and talent (The Jungle Book)	1865	India	42	1936	British	UK	Author	None
1908	Eucken, Rudolph Christoph Search for truth, range of vision, and idealistic philosophy of life	1846	Germany	62	1926	German	Germany	Author	D.Phil.
1909	Lagerlof, Selma Ottilia Lovisa (F) Educator, writer, poet, dramatist, of romantic Swedish literature	1858	Sweden	51	1940	Swedish	Sweden	Author/Teach	Grad.
1910	Heyse, Paul Johann Ludwig von Lyric poet, novelist, dramatist, short story writer	1830	Germany	80	1914	German	Germany	Poet	Dr.
1911	Maeterlinck, Count Maurice Dramatic works distinguished by wealth of imagination	1862	Belgium	49	1949	Belgian	Belgium	Wrriter	Law
1912	Hauptmann, Gerhart J. R. Fruitful, varied, and outstanding production of dramatic art	1862	Germany	50	1946	German	Germany	Author/Sculpt	None
1913	Tagore, Sir Rabindranath Fresh and beautiful poetic verse in his own English	1861	India	52	1941	Indian	India	Poet/Author	None
1915	Rollald, Romain Biographical material (Handel, Gandhi) and Jean Chritophe	1866	France	49	1944	French	France	Author/Prof.	Dr.
1916	Von Heidenstam, Carl Gustaf V. Leading representative of a new era of literature	1859	Sweden	57	1940	Swedish	Sweden	Poet	None
1917	Gjellerup, Karl Adolph (Epigonos) Trying to describe meaning of life without Christianity	1857	Denmark	60	1919	Danish	Denmark	Author	B.D.
	Pontoppidan, Henrik Authentic descriptions of every day life in Denmark	1857	Denmark	60	1943	Danish	Denmark	Author/Teach	None
1918	Karlfeldt, Erik Axel (Refused. See 1931)	----	----	----	----	----	----	----	----
1919	Spittiler, Carl Friedrich Georg Appreciation for an epic: Olympian Spring	1845	Switz	74	1924	Swiss	Switz	Poet	Theo
1920	Hamsun, Knut Pedersen For his monumental work: "Growth of the Soil"	1859	Norway	61	1952	Norweg	Norway	Author/Farmer	None

Note: (F) stands for Female

NOBEL PRIZE WINNERS IN LITERATURE: 1901-2000
[CONTINUED]

Year	Name/Contribution	Born	Place	Prize Age	Death	Nat.	Country Credited	Career	Degree
1921	France, Anatole *Recognition of brilliant literary achievements*	1844	France	77	1924	French	France	Author	B.A.
1922	Benavente y Martinez, Jacinto *For continuation of the tradition of Spanish drama*	1866	Spain	56	1954	Spanish	Spain	Author	None
1923	Yeats, William Butler *Inspired poetry*	1865	Ireland	58	1939	Irish	Ireland	Poet/Ed	None
1924	Reymont, Wladyslaw Stanislaw *For a national epic:* The Peasants	1867	Poland	57	1925	Polish	Poland	Author	None
1925	Shaw, George Bernard *For plays marked both by idealism and humanity*	1856	Ireland	69	1950	Irish	Ireland	Author	None
1926	Deledda, Grazia (F) *For idealistic inspired writing*	1871	Italy	55	1936	Italian	Italy	Author	None
1927	Bergson, Henri Louis *For rich & vitalizing ideas and the skill in which they were written*	1859	France	68	1941	French	France	Author/Prof.	Dr.
1928	Undset, Sigrid (F) *Descriptions of Scandinavian life in the Middle Ages*	1882	Denmark	46	1949	Danish Norweg.	Norway	Author	None
1929	Mann, Paul Thomas *For the novel:* Boodenbrooks	1875	German	54	1955	Ger/Czech American	German	Author	None
1930	Lewis, Harry Sinclair *Vigorous & graphic art of description*	1885	USA	45	1951	American	USA	Author	A.B.
1931	Karlfeldt, Erik Axel *Poetry with singular power and exquisite charm*	1864	Sweden	67	1931	Swedish	Sweden	Poet	Licentiate
1932	Galsworthy, John *For his distinguished art at its highest form:* The Forsyte Saga	1867	UK	65	1933	UK	UK	Author	BA/Law
1933	Bunin, Ivan Alexeievich *Writing in the tradition of classical Russian prose*	1870	Russia	63	1953	Russia	Russia	Author/Prof	None
1934	Pirandello, Luigi *Revival of dramatic & scenic art*	1867	Italy	67	1936	Italian	Italy	Playwrite/Prof	D.Phil.
1936	O'Neill, Eugene Gladstone *For the power, honesty, and emotions of his dramatic works*	1888	USA	48	1953	American	USA	Playwrite	None
1937	Martin du Gard, Roger *For series of novels:* Les Tibault	1881	France	56	1958	French	France	Author	B.A.
1938	Buck, Pearl (F) *Epic pictures of Chinese life and for her masterly biographies*	1892	USA	46	1973	American	USA	Author	M.A.
1939	Sillanpää, France Eemil *Understanding of peasant way of life and its relationship with Nature*	1888	Finland	51	1964	Finish	Finland	Author	None
1944	Jensen, Johannes Vilhelm *Noted for his epic historical and imaginative prose*	1873	Denmark	71	1950	Danish	Denmark	Author	M.A.
1945	Mistral, Gabriela (F) *Lyric poetry representing the aspirations of Latin America*	1889	Chile	56	1957	Chilean	Chile	Poet/Dip	Diploma
1946	Hesse, Herman *Inspired writing with classical humanitarian ideals*	1877	Germany	69	1962	Ger/Swiss	Switz	Author	None
1947	Gide, André Paul Guillaume *Significant writings and keen psychological insight*	1869	France	78	1951	French	France	Author/Critic	B.A.

Note: (F) stands for Female

129

NOBEL PRIZE WINNERS IN LITERATURE: 1901-2000
[CONTINUED]

Year	Name/ Contribution	Born	Place	Prize Age	Death	Nat.	Country Credited	Career	Degree
1948	Eliot, Thomas Stearns *Outstanding contribution to present-day poetry*	1888	USA	60	1965	American	USA	Poet	M.A.
1949	Faulkner, William Cuthbert *Unique contribution to the modern American novel*	1897	USA	52	1962	American	USA	Author	None
1950	Russell, Earl Bertrand A.W. *Writings praising humanitarian ideals of love, knowledge, pity.*	1872	UK	78	1970	British	UK	Philosopher	M.A.
1951	Lagerkvist, Par Fabian *Poetry searching for answers to eternal questions of mankind*	1891	Sweden	60	1974	Swedish	Sweden	Poet	None
1952	Mauriac, Francois *The spiritual insight in his novels penetrate the drama of life*	1885	France	67	1970	French	France	Author	B.A.
1953	Churchill, Sir Winston *Mastery of historical and biographical description; oratory*	1874	UK	79	1965	British	UK	Hist./PM	B.A.
1954	Hemingway, Ernest Miller *Mastery of narrative as in: The Old Man and the Sea*	1899	USA	55	1961	American	USA	Author	None
1955	Laxness, Halldor Kiljan *Epic power that renews the great narrative art of Iceland*	1902	Iceland	53	1998	Iceland	Iceland	Author	None
1956	Jimenez, Joan Ramón *Spanish lyrical poetry of high spirit & artistic purity*	1881	Spain	75	1958	Spanish	Spain	Poet	B.A.
1957	Camus, Albert *Illuminating the problems of the human conscience in our times*	1913	Algeria	44	1960	French	France	Author	B.A.
1958	Pasternak, Boris Leonidovich *Achievements in poetry and Russian epic tradition: Dr. Zhivago*	1890	Russia	68	1960	Russian	Russia	Poet/Author	B.A.
1959	Quasimodo, Salvatore *Poetry expressing the tragic experience of life in our times*	1901	Italy	58	1968	Italian	Italy	Poet	None
1960	Saint-John, Perse *For his poetry*: Anabasis	1887	France	73	1975	French	France	Poet	Law
1961	Andric, Ivo *Writing about human destinies from the history of Serbia, Bosnia*	1892	Yugo	69	1975	Yugo	Yugo	Author	Ph.D.
1962	Steinbeck, John Ernst *Realistic writings combined with humor*: Of Mice and Men	1902	USA	60	1968	American	USA	Author	None
1963	Seferis, Giorgos *Poetry inspired by feelings for the Hellenic world of culture*	1900	Turkey	63	1971	Greek	Greece	Poet/Dipl	Law
1964	Sartre, Jean-Paul *(Declined)*	1905	France	59	1980	French	France	Philosopher	M.A.
1965	Sholokov, Mikhail Alek. *Expressing the history of the Russian people: The Quiet Don*	1905	Russia	60	1984	Russian	Russia	Author	None
1966	Agnon, Shmuel Yosef *Narrative art with motifs from the life of the Jewish people*	1888	Austria	78	1970	Austri/Isr.	Israel	Poet	None
	Sachs, Leonie Nelly (F) *Writing about the Holocaust with interpretations of Israel's destiny*	1891	Germany	75	1970	Ger/Swed	Sweden	Author	None

Note: (F) stands for Female

NOBEL PRIZE WINNERS IN LITERATURE: 1901-2000
[CONTINUED]

Year	Name/Contribution	Born	Place	Prize	Death	Nat.	Country Credited	Career	Degree
1967	Asturias, Miguel Angel *Literary achievement, rooted in Indian peoples of Latin America*	1899	Guate	68	1974	Guate	Guate	Author	Law
1968	Kawabata, Yasunari *Narrative mastery of the Japanese mind*	1899	Japan	69	1972	Japanese	Japan	Author	B.A.
1969	Beckett, Samuel Barclay *Introducing new forms for the novel and drama*	1906	Ireland	63	1989	Irish	Ireland	Auth/Play	M.A.
1970	Solzhenitisyn, Alexander *For the ethical force in pursuing the tradition of Russian literature*	1918	Russia	52	----	Rus/Am	Russia	Author	B.A.
1971	Neruda, Pablo *Poetry that brings alive a continent's destiny and dreams*	1904	Chile	67	1973	Chile	Chile	Poet/Dipl	None
1972	Böll, Heinrich *Contributions to the renewal of German literature*	1917	Germany	55	1985	German	Germany	Author	None
1973	White, Patrick V. M. *Introduced a new continent (Australia) into literature*	1912	UK	61	1990	Austra	Australia	Author	B.A.
1974	Johnson, Eyvind Olof Verner *A narrative art in the service of freedom*	1900	Sweden	74	1976	Swedish	Sweden	Author	None
	Martinson, Harry Edmund *Writings that catch the dewdrop and reflect the cosmos*	1904	Sweden	70	1978	Swedish	Sweden	Poet/Auth	None
1975	Montale, Engenio *Poetry of great artistic sensitivity and with no illusions on life*	1896	Italy	79	1981	Italian	Italy	Poet	None
1976	Bellow, Saul *Understanding and analysis of contemporary culture*	1915	Canada	61	----	Can/AM	USA	Auth/Prof.	B.S.
1977	Aleixandre, Vicente *Renewal of Spanish poetry that illuminates the cosmos*	1898	Spain	79	1984	Spanish	Spain	Poet/Prof.	Law/ Bus
1978	Singer, Isaac Bashevis *Polish-Jewish cultural tradition to illustrate the human conditions*	1904	Poland	74	1991	Pol/Am	USA	Author	None
1979	Elytis, Odysseus (Alepoudelis) *Poetry describing man's struggle for freedom and creativeness*	1911	Greece	68	1996	Greek	Greece	Poet	None
1980	Milosz, Czelaw *Voices man's exposed condition in a world of conflicts*	1911	Lith	69	----	Pol/Am	USA/Pol	Poet	M.A.
1981	Canetti, Elias *Powerful writings in Spanish, Ladino, German, and English*	1905	Bulgaria	76	1994	Bul/Au/Br	UK	Author	D.Sc.
1982	García Márquez, Gabriel José *The fantastic and realistic join in a richly composed world*	1928	Colombia	54	----	Colombia	Colombia	Author	None
1983	Golding, William Gerald *Man himself is the cause of evil: Lord of the Flies*	1911	UK	72	1993	British	UK	Author	M.A.
1984	Seifert, Jaroslav *Poetry about indomitable human spirit*	1901	Czech	83	1986	Czech	Czech	Poet	None
1985	Simon, Claude Eugene Henri *Combines the poet's and the painter's creativeness*	1913	Madagas	72	----	French	France	Author	None

Note: (F) stands for Female

NOBEL PRIZE WINNERS IN LITERATURE: 1901-2000
[CONTINUED]

Year	Name/ Contribution	Born	Place	Prize Age	Death	Nat.	Country Credited	Career	Degree
1986	Soyinka, Wole *Wide cultural perspective fashions the drama of existence*	1934	Nigeria	52	----	Niger	Nigeria	Playwrite/Prof.	B.A.
1987	Brodsky, Joseph Alexandrovich *Authorship with clarity of thought and poetic intensity*	1940	Russia	47	1996	Rus/Am	USA	Poet/Prof.	None
1988	Mahfouz, Naguib *Arabian narrative art that applies to all mankind*	1911	Egypt	77	----	Egypt	Egypt	Author	None
1989	Cela, Camilo José *Prose that forms a challanging vision of man's vulnerability*	1916	Spain	73	----	Span	Spain	Author	None
1990	Paz, Octavio *Impassioned writing with wide horizons and humanistic integrity*	1914	Mexico	76	1998	Mexico	Mexico	Poet	None
1991	Gordimer, Nadine (F) *Literature, free speech opposing censorship in police state*	1923	SoAfr	68	----	SoAfr	SoAfr	Author	None
1992	Walcott, Derek Alton *West Indian culture found its great poet*	1930	SntLucia	62	----	StLucia	SoAfr	Poet	B.A.
1993	Morrison, Toni (F) *Novels give life to the American reality of racism*	1931	USA	62	----	American	USA	Author	M.A.
1994	Oe, Kenzaburo *The dignity of the human being*	1935	Japan	59	----	Japanese	Japan	Author	B.A.
1995	Heaney, Seamus Justin *Guardian spirit of Irish poetry*	1939	No Ire	56	----	Irish	Ireland	Poet/Prof.	B.A.
1996	Szymborska, Wislawa (F) *Poetry that allows historical and biological factors to come to light*	1923	Poland	73	----	Polish	Poland	Poet	B.A.
1997	Fo, Dario *Sensitive and powerful writings about the Middle Ages*	1926	Italy	71	----	Italian	Italy	Auth/Direct	Architect
1998	Saramago, José *Writings of imagination, compassion and irony*: Baltasar & Blimunda	1922	Portugal	76	----	Port	Portugal	Auth/Journ	None
1999	Grass, Günter (Wilhelm) *Black fables portray a forgotten face of history*: The Tin Drum	1927	Germany	72	----	German	Germany	Author	None
2000	Gao Xingjian *A refugee, opened new paths for Chinese novels and drama*	1940	China	60	----	Chin/Fren	France	Author	B.A.

Note: (F) stands for Female

NOBEL PRIZE WINNERS IN PEACE: 1901-2000

Year	Name/Contribution	Born	Place	Prize Age	Death	Nat.	Country Credited	Position	Degree
1901	Dunant, Jean Henry Founder, International Committee of the Red Cross, Geneva	1828	Switz	73	1910	Switz	Switz	President	None
	Passy, Frédéric Founder and president of first French peace society	1822	France	79	1912	France	France	President	Legal
1902	Ducommun, Elie	1833	Switz	69	1906	Switz	Switz	Director	None
	Gobat, Charles Albert Honorary Secretaries, Permanent International Peace Bureau, Bern	1843	Switz	59	1914	Switz	Switz	Professor	Dr. Law
1903	Cremer, Sir William Randal Secretary, International Arbitration League	1828	UK	75	1908	British	UK	MP	None
1904	Institute of International Law The legal conscience of the civilized world								
1905	von Suttner, Bertha F.S. Kinsky (F) Honorary Secretary, Permanent International Peace Bureau, Bern	1843	Austria	62	1914	Austrian	Austria	Editor, writer	None
1906	Roosevelt, Theodore Collaboration on various peace treaties (on natural resources, etc.)	1858	USA	48	1919	American	USA	President	A.B.
1907	Moneta, Ernesco Teodoro President, League of Peace	1833	Italy	74	1918	Italian	Italy	Publisher	None
	Renault, Louis Helped establish the Hague Permanent Court of Arbitration	1843	France	64	1918	French	France	Professor	Dr. Law
1908	Arnoldson, Klas Pontus Founder, Swedish Peace and Arbitration League	1844	Sweden	64	1916	Sweish	Sweden	Writer	None
	Bajer, Fredrik Honorary Secretary, Permanent International Peace Bureau, Bern	1837	Denmark	71	1922	Danish	Denmark	Polit/Writer	None
1909	Beernaert, Auguste M. F. Member, Hague Permanent Court of Arbitration	1829	Belgium	80	1912	Belgian	Belgium	ex-Prime Min	Dr. Law
1909	d'Estournelles, Baron Paul Henry Founder and president, French group for voluntary arbitration	1852	France	57	1924	French	France	Diplomat	A.B./law
1910	The Permanent International Peace Bureau Bureau of arbitration and disarmament								
1911	Asser, Tobias Michael Carel Originator, international conferences of private law at the Hague	1838	Neth	73	1913	Dutch	Netherlands	Prime Min	Dr. Law
	Fried, Alfred Hermann Founder "Die Friedenswarte" (peace publication)	1864	Austria	47	1921	Austrian	Austria	Journ./Pub	None
1912	Root, Elihu Originator, arbitration treaties	1845	USA	67	1937	American	USA	ex-Sec State	A.B./ law
1913	La Fontaine, Henri Marie International cooperation of united states of the world	1854	Belgium	59	1943	Belgian	Belgium	Prof.,Senator	Dr. Law
1917	The International Committee of the Red Cross Help given to prisoners of war								
1919	Wilson, Thomas Woodrow Founder, League of Nations	1856	USA	63	1924	American	USA	Prof./Pres	Ph.D.
1920	Bourgeois, Léon-Victor Auguste Spiritual father, League of Nations	1851	France	69	1925	French	France	Pub Official	Dr.

Note: (F) stands for Female

NOBEL PRIZE WINNERS IN PEACE: 1901-2000
[CONTINUED]

Year	Name/Contribution	Born	Place	Prize Age	Death	Nat.	Country Credited	Career	Degree
1921	Branting, Karl Hjalmar Geneva protocol for international security	1860	Sweden	61	1925	Swedish	Sweden	Astro./PM	B.A.
	Lange, Christian Lous Secretary General, Inter-Parliamentary Union	1869	Norway	52	1938	Norweg	Norway	Writer/Activist	Ph.D.
1922	Nansen, Fridtjof Norwegian delegate, League of Nations for Refugees	1861	Norway	61	1930	Norweg	Norway	Scientist/Prof.	Dr. Phil.
1925	Chamberlain, Sir Joseph A UK Foreign secretary, co-creator Locarno Pact	1863	UK	62	1937	British	UK	MP	B.A.
	Dawes, Charles Gates Chairman, Allied reparation commission ("Dawes Plan")	1865	USA	60	1951	American	USA	Vice President	M.A.
1926	Briand, Aristide Co-creator Locarno Pact, Briand-Kellogg Pact	1862	France	64	1932	Frnche	France	Foreign Min	Law
	Stresemann, Gustav Co-creator Locarno Pact	1878	Germany	48	1929	German	Germany	Foreign Min	Ph.D.
1927	Buisson, Ferdinand Edouard Founder and President, League of Human Rights	1841	France	86	1932	French	France	Professor	Ph.D.
1927	Quidde, Ludwig Participant in various peace conferences	1858	German	69	1941	Germany	Germany	Prof., PM	Ph.D.
1929	Kellogg, Frank Billings Co-creator, Briand-Kellogg Pact	1856	USA	73	1937	American	USA	ex-Sec State	None
1930	Söderblom, Lars O. N. (Jonathan) Leader of ecumenical movement	1866	Sweden	64	1931	Swedish	Sweden	Archbishop	Dr. Th.
1931	Addams, Laura Jane (F) International President, Women's International League for Peace and Freedom	1860	USA	71	1935	American	USA	Sociologist	A.B.
	Butler, Nicholas Murray Supporter, Briand-Kellogg Pact	1862	USA	69	1947	American	USA	President. Columbia U	Ph.D.
1933	Angell (Ralph Lane), Sir Norman Member, executive committee League of Nations (peace council)	1874	UK	59	1967	British	UK	Writer Activist	None
1934	Henderson, Arthur President 1932 disarnament conference	1863	UK (Scotland)	71	1935	UK	UK	ex-For Sec	None
1935	Ossietzky, Carl von Symbol of struggle for peace (leader of German Peace Society)	1889	Germany	46	1938	German	Germany	Journalist	None
1936	Saavedra Lamas, Carlos President, League of Nations; mediated Paraguay and Bolivia dispute	1878	Argent	58	1959	Argent	Argent	SecState	Dr. Laws
1937	Cecil, Sir Edgar Algernon R. G. Founder and president international peace campaign	1864	UK	73	1958	British	UK	ex-Lord, MP	B.A Law
1938	The Nansen International Office of Refugees International relief organization								
1944	The International Committee of the Red Cross Second Peace Prize for its humanitarian activities								

Note: (F) stands for Female

NOBEL PRIZE WINNERS IN PEACE: 1901-2000
[CONTINUED]

Year	Name/Contribution	Born	Place	Prize Age	Death	Nat.	Country Credited	Career	Degree
1945	Hull, Cordell *Prominent participant in organizing the United Nations*	1871	USA	74	1955	American	USA	ex-SecState	Law
1946	Balch, Emily Greene (F) *Honorary President, Women's International League for Peace and Freedom*	1857	USA	79	1961	USA	USA	Prof.	A.B.
	Mott, John Raleigh *Chairman, International Missionary Council; President, World Alliance of YMCAs*	1865	USA	81	1955	American	USA	Administrator	Ph.B.
1947	Am. Friends Service Comm. *Quaker organization*								
	The Friends Service Council *Volunteers administer food, clothing, and medical care*								
1949	Lord Boyd Orr of Brechin *President, National Peace Council and World Union of Peace*	1880	UK (Scotland)	69	1971	British	UK	Univ Rector Director/FAO	M.D., D.Sc.
1950	Bunche, Ralph Johnson *UN Director of Trustees; mediator in Palestine in 1948*	1904	USA	46	1971	American	USA	Professor Pub. Official	Ph.D.
1951	Jouhaux, Leon *President, Committee of European Council; U.N. representative for the struggle of working class*	1879	France	72	1954	French	France	Union Official	None
1952	Schweitzer, Albert *Founder and director of the Schweitzer hospital in Gabon*	1875	Germany	77	1965	Ger/Fra	France	Preacher Surgeon	M.D., Ph.D.
1953	Marshall, George C., Gen. *Created "Marshall Plan" for European Relief*	1880	USA	73	1959	American	USA	General	BA
1954	Office of U.N. High Commissioner for Refugees *Work for and among refugees*								
1957	Pearson, Lester Bowels *President, U.N. General Assembly; resolved Suez Canal crisis*	1897	Canada	60	1972	Canadian	Canada	PM/SecState	M.A.
1958	Pire, Georges Dominique, Rev. *Leader of refugee relief group*	1910	Belgium	48	1969	Belgian	Belgium	Priest	Dr. Theo
1959	Noel-Baker, Philip John *Ardent worker for international peace and cooperation*	1889	UK	70	1982	British	UK	Prof., MP	M.A.
1960	Luthuli, Albert John *President of the African National Congress in South Africa*	1898	So.Afr	62	1967	So African	So Afr	Teacher, Chief	None
1961	Hammarskjold, Dag Hjalmar *Mediator in Congo, Middle East, and USA-China disputes*	1905	Sweden	56	1961	Swedish	Sweden	UN Sec Gen	Ph.D.
1962	Pauling, Linus Carl *Campaign against radioactive fall-out in weapons testing and war*	1901	USA	61	1994	American	USA	Scientist	Ph.D.
1963	Int. Committee of the Red Cross League of Red Cross Societies *On 100th anniversary of founding*								
1964	King, Martin Luther, Jr. *Leader, Southern Christian Leadership Conference*	1929	USA	35	1968	American	USA	Pastor	Ph.D.
1965	United Nations Children's Fund *Providing for needs of children*								

Note:*(F) stands for Female

NOBEL PRIZE WINNERS IN PEACE: 1901-2000
[CONTINUED]

Year	Name/Contribution	Born	Place	Prize Age	Death	Nat.	Country Credited	Career	Degree
1968	Cassin, Rene-Samuel President, European Court for Human Rights	1887	France	81	1976	France	France	Atty/Prof.	Dr.
1969	Int. Labour Organization 50th Anniversary of effort to improve conditions of workers								
1970	Borlaug, Norman Ernest International Maize & Wheat Improvement Center, Mexico	1914	USA	56	----	American	USA	Scientist/.Administ	Ph.D.
1971	Brandt, Willy Fought for peace in Europe	1913	Germany	58	1992	German	Germany	Chancellor	None
1973	Kissinger, Henry Alfred Negotiations to end Vietnam War	1923	German	50	----	Ger/Am	USA	SecState	Ph.D.
	Le Duc Tho Declined	1910	Vietnam	63	1990	Vietnam	Vietnam	Communist Party Official	None
1974	MacBride, Sean President, Int Peace Bureau & Commission of Namibia	1904	France	70	1988	Irish	Ireland	Journ/Atty	Law
	Sato, Eisaku Reconciliation policy contributing peace for the Pacific area	1901	Japan	73	1975	Japanese	Japan	PM	Law
1975	Sakharov, Andrei Dmitrievich For human uman rights and true democratic socialism in USSR	1921	Russia	54	1989	Russian	Russia	Physicist	Ph.D.
1976	Corrigan, Mairead (F) Founder and Administration of No. Ireland's Peace People	1944	No.Ire	32	----	No.Ire	NI/UK	Secretary	None
	Williams, Betty Elizabeth (F) Leader of Peace People	1943	No.Ire	33	----	No.Ire	NI/UK	ClerkWaitress	None
1977	Amnesty International Protecting prisoners from treatment ignoring human rights								
1978	Begin Menachem, Wolfovitch El-Sadat, Muhammed Anwar Framework for MiddleEast peace and Israel/Egypt treaty	1913 1918	Poland Egypt	65 60	1992 1981	Israel Egypt	Israeli Egyptian	PM Gen/Pres	Master B.A.
1979	Mother Teresa (F) Mother Superior, Missionaries of Charities, Calcutta	1910	Turkey	69	1997	Yugo/Indian	India	Teacher/Prin	None
1980	Esquivel, Adolfo Perez Human rights leader	1931	Argent	49	----	Argent	Argent	Arch/Prof.	Art
1981	Office of U.N. High Commissioner for Refugees 30th Anniversary								
1982	Garciá Robles, Alfonso Contribution to treaty banning nuclear weapons in Latin America	1911	Mexico	71	1991	Mexican	Mexico	Dipl/U.N. Delegate	Law
	Myrdal, Alva Reimer (F) Pursuit of disarmament	1902	Sweden	80	1986	Swedish	Sweden	Minister/Dipl Writer	M.A.
1983	Walesa, Lech Leader for freedom of Polish workers to organize	1943	Poland	40	----	Polish	Poland	Union Official	None
1984	Tutu, Desmond Mpilo For fight against apartheid	1931	So Afr	53	---	So Afr	So Afr	Bishop	M.Th
1985	Inter. Physicians for Prevention of Nuclear War Information on catastrophic consequences of US/USSR atomic war								

Note: (F) stands for Female

NOBEL PRIZE WINNERS IN PEACE: 1901-2000
[CONTINUED]

Year	Name/Contribution	Born	Place	Prize Age	Death	Nat.	Country Credited	Career	Degree
1986	Wiesel, Elie Chairman, US Commission on the Holocaust	1928	Romania	58	----	Ro/Fr/Am	USA	Writer/Lect	None
1987	Arias Sanches, Oscar As President of Costa Rica, sought Central American peace	1941	CostaRica	46	----	Costa Rica	Costa Rica	Prof./Polit	Law
1988	The U.N. Peace-Keeping Forces For "the manifest will of...nations to achieve peace"								
1989	Dalai Lama, XIV Nonviolent campaign to end China's domination of Tibet	1935	Tibet	54	----	Tibet	Tibet	Rel. Leader	None
1990	Gorbachev, Mikahail S. Changes in relationship between East & West	1931	USSR	59	----	Russian	Russia	Pres USSR	Law
1991	Aung San, Suu Kyi (F) Leader of the democratic, non-violent opposition in Burma	1945	Burma	46	----	Burmese	Burma	Researcher	B.A.
1992	Menchu Tum, Rigoberta (F) Work in Guatamala and the world for peace	1959	Guate	33	----	Guate	Guate	Activist	None
1993	de Klerk, Frederik Willem Mandela, Nelson Policy of peace and reconciliation as a model for others	1936 1918	So Afr So Afr	57 75	---- ----	So Afr So Afr	So Afr So Afr	Lawyer/PM, Lawyer/Pres	LLB. LLB.
1994	Arafat, Yasser Peres, Shimon Rabin, Yitzhak Contribution to process of peace to end Israel/Palestinian conflict	1929 1923 1922	Egypt Poland Israel	65 71 72	---- ---- 1995	Palestine Israeli Israeli	Palestine Israel Israel	Revolutionary For Min Gen/PM	Eng None None
1995	Pugwash Conferences Science and World Affairs Gathering scientists and politicians to reduce nuclear threat Rotblat, Joseph Head of Pugwash conferences for science and world affairs	 1908	 Poland	 87	 ----	 Pol/Br	 UK	 Professor	 Ph.D.
1996	Belo, Carlos Filipe Ximenes Ramos-Horta, José Non-violent dialog for self-determination of East Timor	1948 1949	E. Timor E Timor	48 47	----- ----	E Timor E Timor	E Timor E Timor	Bishop Journalist	None M.A.
1997	Int. Campaign to Ban Land Mines Williams, Jody (F) Coordinator of ICBL effort	 1950	 USA	 47	 ----	 American	 USA	 Administrator	 M.A.
1998	Hume, John Trimble, David Search for a peaceful solution to conflict in Northern Ireland	1938 1944	No Ire No Ire	60 54	---- ----	Irish Irish	No Ire No Ire	MP MP	M.A. Law
1999	Doctors Without Borders Medical help to victims of famine, war, and genocide								
2000	Dae-Jung, Kim For peace and reconciliation with North Korea	1925	Korea	75	----	So Korea	So Korea	President	Ph.D.

Note:(F) stands for Female

SELECTED BIBLIOGRAPHY

-----, *International Biographical Centre Cambridge 2000*, Melrose Press Ltd., England, 2000.

-----, *Nobel Foundation Directory 1999-2000*, Nobel Foundation, NobelPriset Tryckindustri, Solna, Sweden, 2000.

-----, "The Century's Greatest Minds," *Time Magazine*, March 29, 1999, pp. 30-133.

-----, *Who's Who in the World 2000: Millennium Edition*, Marquis Who'sWho, New Providence, 2000.

Abraham, Irwin, Ed., *Nobel Lectures in Peace 1991-1995*, River Edge, N.J., World Scientific, 1999.

Allen, Garland, *Life Science in the Twentieth Century*, New York, Wiley,1975.

Allen, Sture, Ed., *Nobel Lectures in Literature 1991-1995*, River Edge, N.J., World Scientific, 1999

Clark, Ronald W., *The Life and Times of Einstein*, New York, Harry N. Abrams, Inc., 1984.

Crick, Francis, *What Mad Pursuit: A Personal View of Scientific Discovery*, New York, Basic Books, 1988.

DeWitt, Lisa F., *Nobel Prize Winners: Biographical Sketches for Listening and Reading*. Pro Lingua Associates, Vermont, 1991.

Ekspong, Gosta, Ed., *Nobel Lectures in Physics 1991-1995*. River Edge, N.J., World Scientific, 1997.

Feldman, Burton, *The Nobel Prize – A History of Genius, Controversy and Prestige*, Arcade Publishing, New York, 2000.

Larsson, Ulf, Ed., *Cultures of Creativity*, Science History Publications/USA and The Nobel Museum, 2001.

Malmstrom, Bo G, Ed., *Nobel Lectures in Chemistry 1991-1995*, River Edge, N.J., World Scientific, 1997.

McKown, Robin, *She Lived for Science: Irene Joliot-Curie*, New York: Julian Messner, Inc., 1961.

Nobel Foundation, (Schubert, E., translator), *The Legacy of Alfred Nobel*,The Bodley Head, London, 1983.

Persson, Torsten, Ed., *Nobel Lectures in Economics Sciences 1991-1995*,River Edge, N.J., World Scientific, 1999.

Ringertz, Nils, Ed., *Nobel Lectures in Physiology and Medicine 1991-1995*,River Edge, N.J., World Scientific, 1999.

Schlessinger, Bernard and Schlessinger, June, Eds., *The Who's Who of Nobel Prize Winners 1901-1995*. The Oryx Press, Phoenix, 1996.

Tore, Frangsmyr, *Alfred Nobel*, Svenska Institute, Stockholm, 1998.

Watson, James, *The Double Helix*, New York, Atheneum, 1968.

INDEX

INDEX

A

A Beautiful Mind — 43, 70
Abraham, Irwin — 138
Abrikosov, Alexei A. — vii
Academia Nazionale Delle Scienze — 80
Academy Awards —43, 70
Academy of Science — 37
Accelerator — 51
Acids — 76
Addams, Laura Jane — 134
Adrian, Baron Edgar Douglas — 115
Advertisements — iv
Aerosols — 75
Africa — 89
African National Congress — 91
Age — 9, 41, 44-45, 46, 47-48, 102
Agnon, Shmuel Yosef — 61, 130
Agnostics — 57
Agre, Peter— vii
Agriculture — 94, 97
Airplane— 92, 95
Akerlof, George A. — iv, viii
Alder, Kurt — 110
Aleixandre, Vicente — 131
Alfa-Helix — 70
Alferov, Zhores I. — 75, 125
Alfven, Hannes Olof Gosta — 123
Allais, Maurice — 127
Allen, Garland — 138
Allen, Sture — 138
Altman, Sidney — 61, 113
Alvarez, Luis Walter — 123
American Friends Service Committee — 135
Americans (See United States)
Ammonia — 97
Amnesty International — 136
Anderson, Carl David — 18, 121
Anderson, Philip Warren — 124
Andric, Ivo — 130
Anfinsen, Christian Boemer — 111
Angell (Ralph Lane), Sir Norman — 134
Annan, Kofi — iv, viii
Antartica — 69
Anthropology — 95
Antibacterial — 67
Antigravity — 42
Antineutron — 80
Antiprotons — 79
Anti-Semitism — 81, 85, 88, 89
"Anybody" — 79
Appleton, Sir Edward Victor — 122
Arafat, Yasser — 61, 72,89, 93, 97, 98, 137
Arber, Werner — 118
Arias Sanches, Oscar — 98, 137
Arnoldson, Klas Pontus — 133

Arrest — 92
Arrhenius, Svante August — 108
Arrow, Kenneth Joseph — 61, 126
Asser, Tobias Michael Carel — 61, 133
Aston, Francis William — 108
Astrology — 62-64, 103
Astrophysics — vii
Asturias, Miguel Angel — 131
Asymmetric information — viii
Atheists — 57
Atlantic Alliance — i
Atom bomb — 47, 71, 91
Atomic nucleus — iv
Atoms — 67, 76, 79
Aung San, Suu Kyi — 66, 92, 137
Auschwitz — ii
Australia — 21, 67
Austria — 81
Autumn — 61
Aviation — 95
Awards (other) — 53
Axel, Richard — vii
Axelrod, Julius — 61, 117

B

B12 — 43
Bacteria — 67
Bacteriology — 26
Bajer, Fredrik — 133
Balch, Emily Greene — 135
Baltimore, David — 61, 118
Bank of Sweden — 7, 87
Banks — 70
Banting, Sir Frederick Grant — 114
Bárány, Robert — 61, 114
Bardeen, John — 74, 75, 78, 122, 123
Barkla, Charles Glover — 120
Barton, Derek Harold Richard — 111
Basov, Nikolai Gennadievich — 75, 123
Beadle, George Wells — 116
Becker, Gary Stanley — 61, 127
Beckett, Samuel Barclay — 131
Becquerel, Antoine Henri — 120
Bednorz, Johannes Georg — 124
Beernaert, Auguste Marie Francois — 133
Begin Menachem, Wolfovitch — ii, vi 61, 89, 136
Belgium — 21
Bell, Jocelyn — 46-47, 97
Bell Laboratories — 39
Bellow, Saul — 61, 131
Belo, Carlos Filipe Ximenes — 98, 137
Benacerraf, Baruj — 61, 118
Benavente y Martinez, Jacinto — 129
Berg, Paul — 112
Bergius, Friedrich Karl Rodolph — 109
Bergson, Henri Louis — 129
Bergstrom, Sune — 118

Berns-Lee, Tim — 95
Best, C. H. — 97
Bethe, Hans Albrecht — 123
Big Bang — 95
Binnig, Gerd Karl — 124
Biochemistry — iv, 26
Births — 62, 103
Bishop, John Michael — 119
Björnson, Björnstjerne Martinius — 128
Black — i
Black holes — 42
Black, Sir James W. — 119
Blackett, Patrick Maynard Stuart — 122
Blair, Prime Minister Tony — 97
Blobel, Günter — vi, 119
Bloch, Felix — 61, 122
Bloch, Konrad E. — 117
Bloembergen, Nicholaas — 124
Blood — 73
Blumberg, Baruch Samuel — 118
Bohr, Aage Niels — 123
Bohr, Niels Henrik David — 120
Böll, Heinrich — 131
Bordet, Jules Vincent — 114
Borlaug, Norman Ernest — iv, 34, 75, 94, 136
Born, Max — 28, 61, 122
Bosch, Carl — 109
Bothe, Walther Wilhelm Georg — 122
Boundaries — iv
Bourgeois, Léon-Victor — 73, 133
Bovet, Daniel — 116
Bower Award — v
Boyd Orr of Brechin, Lord — 135
Boyer, Paul D. — 113
Bragg William Lawrence — 44, 77, 120
Bragg, Sir William Henry — 44, 77, 120
Brain migration — 24, 26, 28, 58, 81-89, 101
Brainstorming — 71
Brandt, Willy — 136
Branting, Karl Hjalmar — 134
Brattain, Walter Houser — 74, 122
Braun, Carl Ferdinand — 120
Brecht, Bertolt — 97
Brenner, Sydney — iii, iv
Briand, Aristide — 134
Bridgman, Percy Williams — 121
Brink, Lars — iv
British (See United Kingdom)
Brockhouse, Bertram Neville — 125
Brodsky, Joseph Alexandrovich — 61, 88, 132

Broglie, Louis-Victor de — 121
Brown, Herbert Charles — 61, 112
Brown, Michael Stuart — 61, 118
Buchanan, Jr., James McGill — 127
Buchenwald — ii
Buchner, Eduard — 108
Buck, Linda B. — vii
Buck, Pearl — 129
Buddists — 46
Buisson, Ferdinand Edouard — 134
Bunche, Ralph Johnson — 135
Bunin, Ivan Alexeievich — 129
Berger Precision Camera — 39
Burma — 66, 92
Burnet, Sir Frank MacFarlane — 116
Business cycles — iv, viii
Butenandt, Adolf F. J. — 109
Butler, Nicholas Murray — 134

C
Calculators — 71
Calvin, Melvin — 111
Cambridge University — 10, 27, 39
Camera — 39
Camus, Albert — 61, 72, 130
Canada — 21
Cancer — iv, 47, 69, 96
Canetti, Elias — 61, 88, 131
Capricorn — 62
Carducci, Giosue — 128
Carlsson, Arvid — 119
Carrel, Alexis — 114
Carson, Rachel — 46, 95
Carter Center — vi
Carter, Earl James (Jimmy), Jr. — ii, vi, viii
Cassin, Rene-Samuel — 61, 136
CDs — 148
Cech, Thomas Robert — 113
Cecil, Sir Edgar Algernon Robert — 134
Cela, Camilo José — 132
Celebacy — 90
Cells — iv, vii
Central America — v
CERN (See European Organization for Nuclear Research)
Chadwick, Sir James — 121
Chain, Sir Ernst Boris — 61, 67, 74, 115
Chamberlain, Owen — 79, 122
Chamberlain, Sir Joseph A. — 134
Chandrasekhar, Raman V. — 77, 121
Chandrasekhar, Subrahmanyan — 42, 77, 124
Chain, Ernest B. — iv
Charities — v
Charpak, Georges — 125
Chemical bonds — 78
Chemistry — i, 24-25, 42, 46, 47, 81-82
Cherenkov, Pavel Alekseyevich — 122

Chickens — 42
Chiechanover, A — ii, iii, iv, vii
Children — 47-48, 90
China — 15, 32
Chlorofluorocarbons (CFCs) — 69, 75
Chlorophyll — 73, 78
Cholesterol — 78
Chlorine — 69
Christianity — 46, 57
Chu, Steven — 76, 125
Churchill, Sir Winston — 32, 130
Civil rights — 92
Clark, Ronald W. — 138
Claude, Albert — 118
Clinton, President Bill — 97
Cloning — 76
Cloud chamber — 72
Coase, Ronald Harry — 127
Cockcroft, Sir John Douglas — 122
Coetzee, Maxwell John — viii
Cohen, Stanley — 61, 118
Cohen-Tannoudji, Claude — 76, 125
Collaboration — 50-52
Commerce — 57
Committees — 51, 96
Communism — 20, 79
Competition —104-105
Compton, Arthur Holly — 121
Computers — 71, 76, 95
Condensates— vii
Congo — 92
Consulting — 148
Cooper, Leon Neil — 75, 123
Correlations — 101
Corey, Elias James — 61, 113
Cori, Carl Ferdinand — 77, 115
Cori, Gerty Theresa Radnitz — 77, 115
Cormack, Allan Macleod — 118
Cornell, Eric A. — i, ii, vii
Cornell University — 70
Cornforth, Sir John Warcap — 111
Corrigan, Mairead — 136
Cortisone — 78
Costa Rica — 98
Country credits — 81, 83, 85, 101
Cournand, Andre F. — 116
Cram, Donald James — 112
Creativity — 8, 20, 66
Cremer, Sir William Randal — 133
Crick, Francis — 51, 117, 133, 138
Crick, Francis Harry Compton — iii, 5, 69, 74
Criminal activities — 92
Cronin, James Watson — 124
Crutzen, Paul — 75, 113
Crystal structures — 44
Curie, Marie — 46, 47, 66, 77, 78, 81, 96, 108, 120
Curie, Pierre — 66, 77, 120
Curiosity — 66

Curl Jr., Robert F. — 112
Cyclatron — 74
Cystic fibrosis — iv

D
D.Phil. (Doctorate in Philosophy) — 55
d'Estournelles, Baron Paul Henry — 133
Dae-Jung, Kim — 92, 137
Dalai Lama, XIV — 90, 137
Dale, Sir Henry Hallet — 115
Dalén, Niels Gustaf — 120
Dam, Carl Peter Henrik — 115
Damadian, Raymond V. — iv
Darwin, Charles — 58
Dausset, Jean Baptiste Johachim — 118
Davis, Raymond, Jr. — vii
Davisson, Clinton Joseph — 121
Dawes, Charles Gates — 134
Day care — 48
de Duve, Christian — 118
de Klerk, Frederik Willem — 137
Debreu, Gerard — 126
Debye, Peter J. W. — 109
Degrees (Academic) — 32, 34, 46, 47, 55-56, 101
Dehmelt, Hans Georg — 125
Deisenhofer, Johann — 112
Delbrück, Max — 117
Deledda, Grazia — 129
Democracies — ii, iii, viii, 20-21, 92, 101
Denmark — 21, 81
Destiny — ii
Developed countries — 99
Development — viii
DeWitt, Lisa F. — 138
Diagnostic technology — iii
Diels, Otto Paul Hermann — 110
Digital — 71, 74
Dirac, Paul Adrien Maurice — 121
Disease — iv
Dishwashers — 7
Distribution (countries, years) — 22-36
Divorce —90, 103
DNA — iii, 26, 69, 74
Doctors (See Physicians)
Doctors Without Borders — 76, 137
Doherty, Peter C. — 75, 119
Doisy, Edward Adelbert — 115
Domagk, Gerhard — 115
Donations — vi
Double Helix (See Helix)
Dr. (General doctorate) — 55
Dr. Zhivago — 79
Drama — 32 (See also Plays)
Dresden — vi
Du Vigneaud, Vincent — 110
Ducommun, Elie — 133
Dulbecco, Renato — 118
Dunant, Jean Henry — 133

141

Dynamite — 7
E
East Germany — vi
East Timor — 34, 98
Ebadi, Shirin — vi
Eccles, Sir John Carew — 117
Echegaray y Eizaguirre, José — 128
Ecology — ii, iv
Economics — ii, viii, 30-31, 43, 54, 87, 96
Edelman, Gerard Maurice — 61, 117
Edison, Thomas Alva — 95
Education — 9, 57, 81
Egas Muniz, Antonio Caetano — 96, 116
Egypt — ii, 34, 81, 93
Ehrlich, Paul — 114
Eigen, Manfred — 111
Eijkman, Christiaan — 115
Einstein, Albert — vi, 6, 28, 41-42, 61, 70-71, 73, 85, 120
Einthoven, Willem — 73, 114
Ekspong, Gosta — 138
Electric light — 95
Electricity — 68
Electrocardiagram — 73
Electron microscope — 42, 74
Electrons — 51, 71
Elements — 97
Elion, Gertrude Belle — 61, 119
Eliot, Thomas Stearns — 130
El-Sadat, Muhammed Anwar — ii, 61, 93, 136
Elytis, Odysseus (Alepoudelis) — 131
Emotional Quotient (EQ) — 52
Enders, John Franklin — 74, 116
Engineer — 71, 76
Engle, Robert E. III — viii
England (See United Kingdom)
Environment — iv, v, 46, 71-72, 95
Erlanger, Joseph — 61, 115
Erlich, Paul — 61, 114
Ernst, Richard Robert — 113
Esaki, Leo — 123
Esquivel, Adolfo Perez — 136
Eucken, Rudolph Christoph — 128
Europe — i, 24, 34, 57, 66, 75, 94
European Organization for Nuclear Research — 51, 85
Evolution — 6, 58
Experiments — 66, 67
Ekspong, Gosta— 138

F
Fallout — 34
Family life — 47, 55, 72
Famine —76, 94, 99
Farmers — 57
Faarnswold, Philo — 95
Faulkner, William Cuthbert — 130
Feldman, Burton — 138

Female — (See Women)
Fenn, John B. — iv
Fermi, Enrico — 28, 79, 85, 121
Fertilization — 97
Feynman, Richard Philllips — 61, 70, 123
Fibiger, Johannes Andreas Grib — 96, 114
Fiction — 32
Finland — 21
Finsen, Niels Ryberg — 114
Fischer, Edmond Henry — 119
Fischer, Emil Herman — 108
Fischer, Ernst Otto — 111
Fischer, Hans — 109
Fitch, Val Logsdon — 124
Fleming, Sir Alexander — iv, 67, 74, 115
Florey, Sir Howard Walter — iv, 67, 74, 115
Flory, Paul John — 111
Fo, Dario — 132
Fogel, Robert William — 127
Food — 15, 94
Food and Agriculture Organization — 148
Forssmann, Werner Theodor Otto — 66, 116
Foundation, Nobel Prize — 7-8
Fowler, William Alfred — 124
Fragl, Fritz — 108
France — 12, 15, 32 34, 36, 39, 46, 47
France, Anatole —129
Franck, James — 61, 121
Frank, Ilya Mikaylovich — 122
Franklin, Rosalind — v, 51, 69
Franklin Institute — v
Freethinkers — 46, 57
Freud, Sigmund — 95
Fried, Alfred Hermann — 61, 133
Friedman, Jerome Isaac — 61, 125
Friedman, Milton — 61, 126
Friends Service Council — 135
Frisch, Karl von — 117
Frisch, Ragnar Kittil Anton — 126
Fukui, Fenichi — 112
Furchgott, Robert Francis — 119

G
Gabor, Dennis — 61, 74, 123
Gajdusek, Daniel Carleton — 92, 118
Galsworthy, John — 129
Gao Xingjian — 32, 88, 132
García Márquez, Gabriel José — 131
García Robles, Alfonso — 136
Gasser, Herbert Spencer — 61, 115
Geese — 148
Gell-Mann, Murray — 61, 123
Gemini — 62
Gender — 9 (See also Women)
General Electric — v
Genetics — iii, 24, 58, 72, 74, 76, 148
Genius — 66, 67, 70-71, 100

Gennes, Pierre-Gilles de — 125
Genocide — 76 (See also Holocaust)
Georgia — i
German Peace Society — 91
Germany — 12, 15, 19, 21, 24, 26, 28, 32, 36, 39, 81, 82, 88, 91, 97
Ghandi, Mohatma — 98
Giacconi, Riccardo — vii
Giaever, Ivar — 123
Giauque, William Francis — 110
Gide, André Paul Guillaume — 129
Gilbert, Walter — 61, 76, 112
Gilman, Aifred Goodman —61, 119
Ginzburg, Vitaly L. — iii, vii
Gjellerup, Karl Adolph (Epigonos) — 128
Glaser, Donald Arthur — 61, 122
Glashow, Sheldon Lee — 124
Global warming — 94
Globular proteins — 39
Gobat, Charles Albert — 133
God — vi
Goeppert-Mayer, Maria — 123
Golding, William Gerald — 131
Goldman's Egg City — 148
Goldstein, Joseph Leonard — 61, 118
Golgi, Camillo — 114
Gorbachev, Mikahail Sergryevich — 76, 137
Gordimer, Nadine — 61, 132
Governments — iv
Granger, Clive W.J. — viii
Granit, Ragnar Arthur — 117
Grass, Günter (Wilhelm) — 132
Gratia , D. A. — 67
Greece — 21
Green Belt Movement — iv, vi
Green revolution — v, 34, 75
Greengard, Paul — 119
Grignard, Francois Auguste Victor — 108
Gross, David J. — iii, iv, viii
Gross National Product — 15, 18, 36, 103
Guillaume, Charles Édouard — 120
Guillemin, Roger — 118
The Gulag Archipelago — 92
Gullstrand, Allvar — 114

H
Haavelmo, Trygve — 127
Haber, Fritz — 97, 108
Hagen, Carl — v
Hahn, Otto — 47, 91, 109
Hammarskjold, Dag — 92, 135
Hamsun, Knut Pedersen — 128
Harden, Sir Arthur — 109
Harris, Godfrey — 6
Harsanyi, John Charles — 127
Hartline, Halden Keffer — 117
Hartwell, Leland H. — vii

100 YEARS OF NOBEL PRIZES

Harvard University — ii-iii, 3
Hassel, Odd — 111
Hauptman, Herbert Aaron — 61, 112
Hauptmann, Gerhart Johann — 128
Haworth, Sir Walter Norman — 74, 109
Hayek, Friedrich August Von — 126
Health care — 15
Heaney, Seamus Justin — 132
Hebrew University, The — ii, 148
Heckman James J. — 127
Heeger, Alan J. — 61, 76, 113
Heisenberg, Werner Karl — 91, 121
Helen, Ava — 46
Helix — 51, 69, 70, 74
Hemingway, Ernest Miller — 130
Hemoglobins — 39
Hench, Philip Showalter — 116
Henderson, Arthur — 134
Herschbach, Dudley Robert — 61, 112
Hershey, Alfred Day — 117
Hershko, Avram — iii, iv, vii
Hertz, Gustav Ludwig — 61, 121
Herzberg, Gerhard — 111
Hess, Victor Franz — 121
Hess, Walter Rudolph — 116
Hesse, Herman — 129
Hevesy, George de (von) — 24, 61, 81, 109
Hewish, Antony — 46, 123
Heymans, Corneille Jean Francois — 115
Heyrovsky, Jaroslav — 110
Heyse, Paul Johann Ludwig von — 61, 128
Hicks, Sir John Richard — 126
High-tech — 58
Hill, Archibald Vivian — 114
Hinshelwood, Sir Norman Cyril — 110
Historical writing — 32
History — viii
History of Rome — 32, 44
Hitchings, George Herbert — 119
Hitler, Adolf — v, 96
HIV — 94
Hodgkin, Dorothy Crowfoot — 43, 111
Hodgkin, Sir Alan Lloyd — 117
Hoffman, Roald — 61, 112
Hofstadter, Robert — 61, 122
Holley, Robert William — 117
Holocaust — ii, 43, 57, 58
Holography — 74
Hooft, Gerardus — 125
Hopkins,Sir Frederick Gowl2and — 115
Hormones — 76
Horvitz, Robert — iii, vii
Hounsfield, Sir Godfrey Newbold — 118
House arrest — 92
Houssay, Bernardo Alberto — 116
Hubble, Edwin — 95
Hubble telescope — 42
Hubel, David Hunter — 118
Huber, Robert — 61, 112

Huggins, Charles Brentom — 117
Hull, Cordell — 135
Hulse, Russel Alan — 125
Human Development Index — 15, 18, 20
Human genome — 52, 97
Human resources — 52
Human rights — i, viii
Hume, John — 98, 137
Hungary — ii, 81
Hunger — 99, 106
Hunt, Timothy R. — vii
Husband — 92
Huxley, Sir Andrew Fielding — 117
Hyundai — v

I
IBM — 39
Iceland — 21
Ignarro, Louis J. — 119
Imagination — 6
Immunology — 75
Imprisonment — 91-92
India — 15, 89
Indicies — 15, 108-137
Inflation — iv, 8
Innovations — 73-76
Inspiration — 67, 70
Institute of International Law — 133
Insulin — 73, 97
Integrated circuits — 75
Intelligent Quotient (IQ) — 52
Interferon — 76
International Campaign to Ban Land Mines — 137
International Committee of the Red Cross — 133, 134, 135
International Labour Organization — 136
International Peace Bureau — 104
International Physicians for the Prevention of Nuclear War — 136
Internet — 71, 95
Inventions — 95, 96
Irabn — iii
Ireland — 21
Israel — ii, iii, iv, v, 21, 34, 58, 93
Italy — 24, 26, 85

J
Jacob, Francois — 61, 117
Jelinek, Elfriede — i, iii, v, viii
Jensen, Johannes Hans Daniel — 123
Jensen, Johannes Vilhelm — 129
Jerne, Niels Kaj — 118
Jerusalem — ii, 148
Jewish physics — 42
Jews — iii, 24, 28, 36, 46, 57, 58, 61, 81, 83, 85, 87, 88, 89, 93
Jewish — vi
Jimenez, Joan Ramón — 130

John Paul II — v
Johnson, Eyvind Olof Verner — 131
Joliot-Curie, Frederic — 77, 109
Joliot-Curie, Irene — 77, 109
Josephson, Brian David — 61, 123
Jouhaux, Leon — 135
Journalism — 91
Joyce, James — 91
Judging — 48

K
Kahneman, Daniel — iii, viii
Kamerlingh-Onnes, Heike — 73, 120
Kandel, Eric — 119
Kantorovich, Leonid Vitaliyevich — 61, 126
Kapitsa, Pyotr Leonidovich — 20, 37, 61, 91, 124
Karle, Jerome — 61, 112
Karlfeldt, Erik Axel — 45, 79, 128, 129
Karolinska Institute — 8
Karrer, Paul — 109
Kastler, Alfred — 123
Katz, Sir Bernard — 61, 117
Kawabata, Yasunari — 72, 131
Kellogg, Frank Billings — 134
Kendall, Edward Calvin — 116
Kendall, Henry Way — 125
Kendrew, Sir John Cowdery — 39, 111
Kenya — iv
Kertész, Imre — ii, iii, viii
Ketterle, Wolfgang — vii
Khorana, Har Gobind — 117
Kilby, Jack S. — 71, 75, 125
Kim Dae Jung — v
Kim Jong II — v
King, Martin Luther, Jr. — 92, 135
Kipling, Joseph Rudyard — 128
Kissinger, Henry Alfred — 61, 79, 89, 98, 136
Klein, Lawrence Robert — 61, 126
Klitzing, Klaus von — 124
Klug, Aaron — 61, 112
Knowledge — 6
Knowles, William S. — vii
Koch, Heinrich Hermann Robert — 114
Kocher, Emil Theodor — 114
Köhler, Georges J.F. — 118
Kohn, Walter — 113
Koopmans, Tjulling Charles — 126
Kornberg, Arthur — 61, 116
Koshiba, Masatoshi — vii
Kossel, Karl Martin — 114
Krebs, Edwin Gerhard — 61, 119
Krebs, Sir Hans Adolf — 61, 116
Kroemer, Herbert — 75, 125
Krogh, Schack August — 114
Kroto, Sir Harold W. — 113
Krutzen, Paul — 69
Kuhn, Richard — 109

143

Kusch, Polycarp — 122
Kuznets, Simon Smith — 61, 126
Kydland, Finn E. — iv, viii

L
La Fontaine, Henri Marie — 133
Laboratories — 37
Lagerkvist, Par Fabian — 130
Lagerlof, Selma Ottilia Lovisa — 128
Lamb, Willis Eugene, Jr. — 122
Landau, Lev Davidovich — 61, 91, 123
Landsteiner, Karl — 61, 115
Lange, Christian Lous — 134
Langmuir, Irving — 109
Larsson, Ulf — 138
Lasers — 75, 76
Laue, Max von — 91, 120
Laughlin, Robert B — 125
Lauterbur, Paul C. — iii, vii
Laveran, Charles Luis Alphonse — 114
Law suit — 80
Lawrence, Ernest Orlando — 74, 121
Laxness, Halldor Kiljan — 130
Le Duc Tho — 78, 98, 136
League of Nations — 73
League of Red Cross Societies — 135
Learning — 95
Lederberg, Josua — 61, 116
Lederman, Leon Max — 61, 124
Lee, David M. — 125
Lee, Tsung-dau — 122
Lee, Yuan Tseh — 112
Leggett, Anthony J.— vii
Lehn, Jean-Marie Pierre — 112
Leloir, Luis Federico — 111
Lenard, Phillipp Eduard von — 120
Leontief, Wassily W. — 126
Levi-Montalcini, Rita — 61, 118
Lewis, Edward B. — iii, 61, 119
Lewis, Harry Sinclair — 129
Lewis, Sir William Arthur — 126
Libby, Willard Frank — 110
Libraries — 37
Life expectancy — iii, 94, 105
Light — 72
Linda, B. — i
Lindgren, Astrid — 47
Lipmann, Fritz Albert — 61, 116
Lippmann, Gabriel Jonas — 61, 120
Lipscomb, William Nun — 112
Literature — i, ii, 32-33, 43, 46, 47, 52, 88, 96
Lobotomies — 96
Loewi, Otto — 115
Longevity — 15, 103, 105 (See also Life expectancy)
Longstocking, Pippi —47
Lord Boyd Orr (See Boyd Orr of ...)
Lord Rayleight (See Strutt, John W.)
Lorentz, Hendrich Antoon — 120

Lorenz, Konrad Zacharias — 76, 117
Lottery — 78
Lucas, Robert E., Jr. — 127
Luck — ii, 8, 66-70
Lundestad, Geir — ii
Luria, Salvador Edward — 61, 117
Luthuli, Albert John — 135
Lwoff, André Michael — 61, 117
Lynen, Feodor Felix Konrad — 117

M
M.D. (Medical doctorate) — 55
Maathai, Wangari — i, iv, vi, viii
MacBride, Sean — 89, 136
MacDiarmid, Alan G. — 76. 113
MacKinnon, Roderick— vii
Macleod, John James Richard — 114
Macromolecules— vii
Maeterlinck, Count Maurice — 128
Magnetics — 95
Mahfouz, Naguib — 61, 132
Mail — 79
Malaria — 96
Male — (See Men)
Malmstrom, Bo G — 138
Mandela, Nelson — 91, 137
Mann, Paul Thomas — 32, 88, 129
Mansfield, Sir Peter— iii, vii
Marconi, Guglielmo — 120
Marcus, Rudolph Arthur — 61, 113
Market fluctuations — iv
Markowitz, Harry M. — 61, 127
Marriage — 90
Marshall, George Catlett — 34, 75, 135
Mathematical theory — iv
Martin du Gard, Roger — 129
Martin, Archer John Porter — 110
Martinson, Harry Edmund — 131
Matter — 72
Maturation — ii, 103, 148
Mauriac, Francois — 130
Max-Planck Institutes — 39
McClintock, Barbara — 118
McFadden, Daniel L. — 127
McKown, Robin — 138
McMillan, Edwin Mattison — 110
Meade, James Edward — 126
Mechnikov, Ilya Ilyich — 61, 114
Medawar, Sir Peter Brian — 61, 116
Medicine — i, 26-27, 42, 46, 54, 83-84
Meitner, Lise — 47
Men — 11, 46
Mendeleev, Dimitri — 97
Menchu Tum, Rigoberta — 137
Merrifield, Robert Bruce — 112
Merton, Robert C. — 127
Mesotron — 79
Meyerhof, Otto Fritz — 61, 114
Mice — 67
Michel, Hartmut — 112

Michaeli, David — iv
Michelson, Albert Abraham — 61, 120
Microphone — 95
Middle East — 89
Migration — 9, 32, 34, 36 (See also Brain migration)
Military — 34, 91, 93
Miller, Merton Howard — 61, 127
Millikam, Robert Andrews — 121
Milosz, Czelaw — iii, 88, 131
Milstein, César — 61, 118
Minority — 57
Minot, George Richards — 115
Mirrlees, James A. — 127
Mistral, Frederic — 128
Mistral, Gabriela — 129
M.I.T. — 39
Mitchell, Peter Denis — 112
Modigliani, Franco — 61, 126
Moissan, Ferdinand Frederick — 61, 108
Mold — 67
Molina, Mario — 69, 75, 113
Mommsen, Christian M. — 32, 44, 128
Moneta, Ernesco Teodoro — 133
Mong-hun, Chung — v
Monod, Jacques Lucien — 117
Montale, Engenio — 131
Moore, Stanford — 111
Morensen, Penelope — 6
Morgan, Thomas Hunt — 115
Morrison, Toni — 132
Mössbauer, Rudolf Ludwig — 122
Mother Tereza — v, 89, 90, 136
Mott, John Raleigh — 135
Mott, Sir Nevill Francis — 124
Mottelson, Benjamin Roy — 61, 123
M.R.I. — iii, iv, v, vii
Mucus — 67
Müller, Hermann Joseph — 61, 115
Müller, Karl Alexander — 124
Müller, Paul Hermann — 116
Mulliken, Robert Sanderson — 111
Mullis, Kary Banks — 113
Mundell, Robert A. — 127
Murad, Ferid — 61, 119
Murphy, William Parry — 115
Murray, Joseph E. — 119
Muslims — i, iii, 57, 93, 105, 106
Myanmar (See Burma)
Myoglobins — 39
Myrdal, Alva Reimer — 77, 136
Myrdal, Karl Gunnar — 77, 126

N
Naipaul, Sir Surajprasad V. — viii
Namibia — 89
Nansen International Office of Refugees — 134
Nansen, Fridtjof — 134
Nash, John F. — 43, 70, 127

Nathans, Daniel — 61, 118
Natta, Giulio — 111
Nazis — 32, 68, 91
Neel, Louis Eugene Felix — 123
Negative effects — iv
Neher, Erwin — 119
Nernst, Walther Hermann — 108
Neruda, Pablo — 131
Netherlands — 21, 69
Neutrinos — vii
Nicaragua — 98
Nicolle, Charles Jules Henri — 115
Nigeria — 91
Nirenberg, Marshall Warren — 61, 117
Nitrogen — 97
Nitrogen oxides — 69
Nixon, President Richard — 79
Nobel, Alfred — iii, 7, 87, 94-98, 105
Nobel Foundation — i
Noel-Baker, Philip John — 135
Nominations — ii, 8, 96
Non-equilibrium thermodynamics — 42
Nonviolence — 97
Norrish, Ronald George Wreyford — 111
North, Douglass Cecil — 127
North Korea — v, 92
North South Pacific — 92
North Vietnam — 34, 98
Northern Ireland — 34, 89. 98
Northrop, John Howard — 110
Norway — 7, 8, 21
Noyori, Ryoji — vii
Nuclei — 79
Nucleic acids — 76, 78
Number (of Laureates) — i
Number (of Prizes) — 11, 12, 13, 14, 16, 17, 18, 20, 22-36, 50, 99, 100-101, 104
Nurse, Sir Paul — vii
Nüsselien-Volhard, Christiane — 119

O
O'Neill, Eugene Gladstone — 129
Obesity — 94
Ochoa, Severo — 116
Oe, Kenzaburo — 132
Office of U.N. High Commissioner (See United Nations...Refugees)
Ohlin, Bertil Gotthard — 126
Olah, George Andrew — 113
Onsager, Lars — 42, 111
Oratory — 32
Organic synthesis — 78-79
Organizations — 34, 43, 92, 96, 104
Orr, John Boyd (See Boyd Orr of...)
Oscars — 70
Osheroff, Douglas D. — 125
Organ development— vii
Ossietzky, Carl von — v, 91, 134
Oswald, Friedrich Wilhelm — 108
Oxford University — 67

Ozone — 69

P
Pacemakers — 71
Palade, George Emil — 118
Palestine — 89, 93
Particles — iv, 80
Passy, Frédéric — 133
Pasternak, Boris Leonidovich — 61, 79, 130
Pasternak, Hanoch — 6
Pasteur, Louis — 66, 94
Patents — v, 7, 71
Paul, Wolfgang — 125
Pauli, Wolfgang Ernst — 121
Pauling, Linus Carl — 34, 43, 46, 70, 74, 78, 110, 135
Pavlov, Ivan Petrovich — 114
Paz, Octavio — 132
Peace — v, 7, 34-35, 43, 46, 52, 54, 89, 96
Pearson, Lester Bowels — 135
Pedersen, Charles John — 112
Penicillin — iv, 67, 68, 74
Penzias, Arno Allen — 61, 124
Peres, Shimon — vi, 61, 89, 98, 137
Perl, Martin L. — 61, 125
Permanent International Peace Bureau — 133
Perrin, Jean Baptiste — 121
Persson, Torsten — 138
Perutz, Max Ferdinand — 39, 61, 111
Ph.D. (Doctor of Philosophy) — 55
Philips, William D. — 76, 125
Philosophy — 32
Phonograph — 95
Photography — v, 51, 69, 74
Photoelectric — vi, 42, 71
Physics — i, 28-29, 41, 46, 47, 54, 84-85, 96
Physicians — 57
Physiology — 26
Piaget, Jean — 95
Piccioni, Oreste — 79-80
Pictures — (See Movies, Photography)
Pirandello, Luigi — 129
Pire, Rev. Georges Dominique — 135
Planck, Max Karl Ernst — 43, 73, 120
Plastics — 68
Plays — 7, 32
Poetry — iii, 7, 32, 91
Pogroms — 58
Poland — iii, 47, 66, 88
Polanyi, John Charles — 112
Polio — 74, 97
Politzer, David H. — iii, iv, viii
Pollution — 94, 106
Polonium — 67, 78
Polymerase Chain Reaction — 70
Polymers — 76

Pontoppidan, Henrik — 128
Pope — v
Pople, John A. — 113
Population — 15, 18, 20, 57, 62, 94
Porter, George — 111
Porter, Rodney Robert — 117
Positrons — 51, 68
Posthumous — ii, 45
Poultry — 148
Poverty — 72
Powell, Cecil Frank — 122
Prelog, Vladimir — 112
Prescott, Edward C. — iv, viii
Preservation — iv
Prigogine, Ilya — 61, 112
Prison (See Imprisonment)
Prize Distribution — i
Prokhorov, Alexander M. — 75, 123
Protestants — 57
Proteins — iv, vii
Prusiner, Stanley B. — 119
Psychiatry — 26
Psychology — ii, viii, 95
Publications — 41-42
Pugwash Conferences — 137
Pulsar — 46, 97
Purcell, Edward Mills — 122

Q
Quakers — (See American Friends...)
Quantum matters — 43, 73, 74, 75
Quasimodo, Salvatore — 130
Quidde, Ludwig — 134
Quinine — 78

R
Rabi, Isidor Isaac — 61, 121
Rabin, Yitzhak — vi, 61, 93, 98, 137
Race — 96
Radar — 73
Radiation — 46, 67, 75, 78
Radio waves — 73
Radioactivity — 34
Radium — 67, 78
Rainwater, Leo James — 123
Ramón y Cajal, Santiago — 114
Rahmos-Horta, José — 98, 137
Ramsay, Sir William — 108
Ramsey, Norman Foster, Jr. — 125
Rayleigh, Lord — (See Strutt, John W.)
Red Cross — (See Int. Committee...)
Refugees — (See United Nations...)
Reichstein, Tadeus — 116
Reines, Frederick — 125
Relatives — 77-78, 104
Relativity — 42, 71
Religion — 9, 46, 57-61, 90, 105
Renault, Louis — 133
Research — 15, 37, 51, 58, 67, 72, 99
Resistance — 75

145

Reverse migration — 85
Reymont, Wladyslaw Stanislaw — 129
Rice — 34
Richards, Dickinson Woodruff — 116
Richards, Theodore William — 108
Richardson, Robert C. — 125
Richardson, Sir Owen Willians — 121
Richet, Charles Robert — 114
Richter, Burton — 61, 124
Ringertz, Nils — 138
Robbins, Frederick Chapman — 74, 116
Roberts, Richard John — 61, 119
Robinson, Sir Robert — 110
Rockefeller University — 39
Rodbell, Martin — 61, 119
Roentgen, Wilhelm Conrad — 120
Rohrer, Heinrich — 124
Rollald, Romain — 128
Roman Catholic — 57
Roosevelt, President Theodore — 34, 133
Root, Elihu — 133
Rose, Irvin — iii, iv, vii
Ross, Sir Ronald — 114
Rotblat, Joseph — 44, 89, 137
Rous, Francic Peyton — 42, 44, 66, 117
Rowland, Frank Sherwood — 69, 75, 113
Rubbia, Carlo — 124
Ruska, Ernst — 42, 74, 124
Russell, Earl Bertrand — 130
Russia — 12, 15, 76, 88, 91, 92, 97
Rutherford, Sir Ernest — 108
Ruzicka, Leopold Stephen — 109
Ryle, Sir Martin — 46, 123

S
Saavedra Lamas, Carlos — 134
Sabatier, Paul — 108
Sachs, Leonie Nelly — 61, 130
Saint-John Perse — 130
Sakharov, Andrei Dmitrievich — 136
Sakmann, Bert — 61, 119
Salam, Abdus — 61, 124
Salk, Jonas — 97
Samuelson, Paul A. — 61, 126
Samuelsson, Bengt Ingemar — i, 118
Sandanistas — 98
Sanger, Frederick — 76, 78, 110, 112
Saramago, José — 132
Sartre, Jean-Paul — 72, 79, 130
Satellites — 74
Sato, Eisaku — 136
Schally, Andrew Victor — 118
Schawalow, Arthur Leonard — 124
Schizophrenia — 70
Schlessinger, Bernard — 138
Schlessinger, June — 138
Scholes, Myron S. — 127
Schrieffer, John Robert — 75, 123
Schrödinger, Erwin — 70, 121
Schultz, Theodore William — 126

Schwartz, Melvin — 61, 124
Schweitzer, Albert — 89, 135
Schwinger, Julian Seymour — 61, 123
Science — ii
Scotland — 67
Seaborg, Glenn T. — 110
Seasons — 62
Security — 15, 58
Seferis, Giorgos — 130
Segré, Emilio Gino — 28, 61, 79, 122
Seifert, Jaroslav — 131
Selten, Reinhard — 127
Semenov, Nikolay Nikolaevich — 110
Semiconductors — 74, 75
Sen, Amartya — 15, 127
Shalev, Baruch Aba — 148
Shalev, Rina — 6
Sharp, Philip Allen — 61, 119
Sharpe, William F. — 127
Sharpless, Barry K. — vii
Shaw, George Bernard — 129
Sherrington, Sir Charles Scott — 115
Shirakawa, Hideki — 68, 76, 113
Shirin, Ebadi — i, iii, viii
Shockley, William Bradford — 74, 122
Sholokov, Mikhail A. — 130
Shull, Clifford Glenwood — 125
Siegbahn, Kai Manne Boerje — 77, 124
Siegbahn, Karl Mann Georg — 77, 121
Signature — 98
Sienkiewicz, Henryk — 128
Silicon — 71, 74
Sillanpää, France Emil — 129
Simon, Claude Eugene Henri — 88, 131
Simon, Herbert Alexander — 61, 126
Singer, Isaac Bashevis — 61, 88, 131
Skou, Jens C. — 113
Smalley, Richard — 113
Smell — vii
Smith, Hamilton Othanel — 118
Smith, Michael — 113
Smith, Vernon L. — viii
Snell, George Davis — 118
Societies — iii
Soddy, Frederick — 108
Söderblom, Lars Olof Nathan — 134
Solar cells — 68
Solow, Robert Merton — 61, 127
Solvay Conference — 71
Solzhenitisyn, Alexander — 88, 92, 131
Sorbonne — 47, 66
South Africa — 34, 91
South Korea — 34, 92
Southern Christian Leadership
  Conference — 92
Soviet Union (See Russia)
Soyinka, Wole — 91, 132
Space — 71
Spemann, Hans — 115
Spence, Michael A. — viii

Sperry, Roger Wolcott — 118
Spittiler, Carl Friedrich Georg — 128
Spring — 62
Spying — 91
Stalin, Joseph — 91, 92, 96
Stanford University — 39
Stanley, Wendell Meredith — 110
Staphylolococcus — 67
Stark, Johannes — 120
Statistics — 62, 83
Staudinger, Hermann — 110
Stein, William Howard — 61, 111
Steinbeck, John Ernst — 130
Steinberger, Jack — 61, 124
Stern, Otto — 61, 121
Stigler, George Joseph — 126
Stiglitz, Joseph E. — viii
Stockholm — iii (See also Sweden)
Stone, Sir John Richard N. — 126
Störmer, Horst L. — 125
Storting — 8, 97
Stresemann, Gustav — 134
Stress — ii, 103, 148
Strutt, John William — 120
Strychnine — 78
Subconscious — 95
Sully, Prudhomme — 128
Sulston, Sir John E. — vii
Summer, James Batcheller — 110
Superconductivity — vii, 73, 78
Sutherland, Earl Wilbur, Jr. — 117
Svedberg, The (Theodor) — 109
Sweden — 7, 12, 21, 46, 81
Swedish Academy — 7, 45, 47, 79
Swedish Acad. of Sciences, Royal — 8
Switzerland — 12, 15, 21, 51, 71, 85
Synge, Richard Laurence M. — 110
Synthesis — (See Organic synthesis)
Szent-Györgyi, Albert von
  Nagyrapolt — 115
Szymborska, Wislawa — 132

T
Tagore, Sir Rabindranath — 128
Talent — 55
Tamm, Igor Evgenevich — 61,122
Tanaka, Koichi — ii, vii
Tatum, Edward Lowrie — 116
Taube, Henry — 112
Taylor, Joseph Hooto — 125
Taylor, Richard E. — 125
Teaching — 148
Teams — iv, 51, 103
Telephone — 68, 76
Telescope — 42, 74
Television — 95
Telsa, Nikola — 95
Temin, Howard Martin — 61, 118
Tennis — 51
Texas Instruments — 71

Theiler, Max — 116
Theorell, Axel Hugo Theodor — 116
Third world — 100
Thomas, Edward Donnall — 7, 119
Thomson, Sir George Paget — 77, 121
Thomson, Sir Joseph John — 77, 120
Three dimentional — 69
Tibet — 34
Timeliness — ii
Tinbergen, Jan — 126
Tinbergen, Nikolaas — 117
Ting, Samuel Chao Chang — 124
Tiselius, Arne Wilhelm Kaurin — 110
Tobin, James — 126
Todd, Sir Alexander Robertus — 110
Tolstoy, Leo — 97
Tomonaga, Shinichiro — 123
Tonegawa, Susumu — 119
Tore, Frangsmyr — 138
Totalitarianism — ii
Townes, Charles Hard — 75, 123
Tradition — iii
Transistors — 74, 75
Treaties — 43, 98
Trees — iv
Trimble, David — 98, 137
Tsui, Daniel C. — 125
Tuberecolosis — 94
Turing, Alan — 95
Tutu, Desmond Mpilo — 90, 136
Tversky, Amos — ii

U
UA1 — 51
Undeveloped — 72, 99
Undset, Sigrid — 129
United Kingdom — i, 12, 15, 21,
  24-26, 28-29, 30, 34, 36, 39, 46, 66, 81,
  91, 92
United States — i, v, 12, 15, 19, 21,
  24-26, 28-29, 30, 32, 34, 36, 37, 39, 46,
  81-82, 83, 87, 91, 92-93
United Nations — iv, 92
  Children's Funds — 135
  Peace-Keeping Forces — 137
  Refugees — 135, 136
Universities — 39-40, 99
University of California — 39, 148
University of Chicago — 37, 39
University of Copenhagen — 37
University of Reading — 148
Unworthiness — v
Urey, Harold Clayton — 109
USSR (See Russia)

V
Value (of Nobel Prize) — 8
van der Meer, Simon — 124
Van der Waals, Johness Diderik — 120
Van Vleck, John Hasbrouck — 124

Van't Hoff, Jacobus Henricus — 108
Vane, John Robert — 118
Varmus, Harold Eliot — 61, 119
Veltman, Martinus — 125
Vickrey, William — 44, 127
Vidal, Desiree — 6
Vietnam — v (See also North Vietnam)
Virgo — 62
Virtanen, Artturi Ilmari — 109
Virus — 92
Vitamins — 24, 26, 74
Von Baeyer, Adolf Johann F. — 61, 108
Von Behring, Emil Adolph — 114
Von Békésy, Georg — 117
Von Euler, Ulf Svante — 77, 117
Von Euler-Chelpin, Hans Karl von — 109
Von Heidenstam, Carl Gustaf — 128
Von Suttner, Bertha F. Kinsky — 133

W
W particles — 51, 85
Wagner von Jauregg, Julius — 96, 115
Waksman, Selman Abraham — 116
Walcott, Derek Alton — 132
Wald, George — 61, 117
Walesa, Lech — 136
Walker, John E. — 113
Wallace, Otto — 61, 108
Walton, Ernest Thomas Sinton — 122
War — v, 34, 58, 76, 78, 94, 106
Warburg, Otto Heinrich — 61, 115
Watches — 71
Water channels — vii
Watson, James — iii, 51, 69, 74, 117,
  138
Watson, James Dewey — 117
Weapons — 46
Weather — 72
Weinberg, Steven — 61, 124
Weller, Thomas Huckle — 74, 116
Werner, Alfred — 108
Wheat — 34, 75
Whipple, George Hoyt — 115
White, Patrick Victor Martindale — 131
Wieland, Heinrich Otto — 109
Wieman, Carl E. — vii
Wien, Wilhelm — 120
Wieschaus, Eric F. — 119
Wiesel, Elie — 43, 61, 89, 137
Wiesel, Torsten N. — 118
Wigner, Eugene Paul — 123
Wilczek, Frank — iv, viii
Wilkins, Maurice Hugh Frederick — v,
  51, 69, 74, 117
Wilkinson, Geoffrey — 111
Will (Nobel) — 7, 41, 102
Williams, Betty Elizabeth — 136
Williams, Jody — 137
Willstätter, Richard Martin — 61,73, 108
Wilson, Charles Thomson Rees — 72, 121

Wilson, Kenneth Geddes — 124
Wilson, Robert Woodrow — 124
Wilson, President Woodrow — 34, 73, 133
Windaus, Adolf Otto Reinhold — 109
Windows — 68
Winter — 62
Wittig, Georg Fridriech Karl —
Wives — 28, 85
Women — i, vii, viii, 11, 30, 46-49, 96,
  100
Woodward, Robert Burns — 78, 111
Woolf, Virginia — 97
World War I — 97
World War II — 19, 34, 57, 91
Wright brothers — 95
Wüthrich, Kurt — vii

X
X-Rays — v, vii, 51, 69

Y
Yalow, Rosalyn Sussman — 61, 118
Yang, Chen Ning — 122
Year differentials — 102
Yeats, William Butler — 129
Yukawa, Hideki — 122

Z
Z particles — 51, 85
Zeeman, Pieter — 120
Zernike, Frits (Frederik) — 122
Zewail, Ahmed Hassan — 61, 81, 113
Ziegler, Karl — 111
Zinkernagel, Rolf M. — 75, 119
ZIP codes — vi
Zsigmondy, Richard Adolf — 109

147

ABOUT THE AUTHOR

BARUCH ABA SHALEV is an Israeli geneticist. Like many of the Nobel Laureates profiled in this book, he has been involved in multi-national study, research, teaching, and consulting during his distinguished career. After graduation from The Hebrew University in Jerusalem, he earned a Master's Degree at the University of California, Davis, and a Ph.D. at the University of Reading in England. He has published more than 200 scientific papers, most of them dealing with genetic selection in animals. In developing a method of selection under stress to force early maturation, he has been able to better evaluate the genetic capability of the animals. That began a process of wondering whether humans under stress also produce improved genetic products. He chose Nobel laureates as his target population to consider the question and this book is the result of his considerations. Dr. Shalev is married, has three children, and lives in Herzliya, Israel.

Dr. Shalev was born in Jerusalem in 1936 and served in the Israeli military between 1954 and 1957. During his years in the United States, he became a Senior Supervisor at Goldman's Egg City in the Los Angeles area—a facility with 3 million laying hens. When he returned to Israel, he became a senior geneticist at the Ministry of Agriculture in Tel Aviv. While in government service and beyond his scientific investigations, Dr. Shalev was in charge of his Division's first centralized computer unit. He also served as a principal investigator in a US/Israeli Bi-National Agricultural Research and Development project involved with the breeding, nutrition, reproduction, and management of geese; as Israel's delegate to the European Breeding and Genetics Working Group; as a Food and Agriculture Organization advisor in Rome and Africa; and as a senior advisor to Israel's poultry industry. He was awarded the Prize of Excellence for outstanding achievements during his government service. As a private consultant, he is currently advising China on waterfowl genetics and production.

NOTE

A CD-ROM containing all the data in the book is available for separate purchase for $21.95. It allows users to sort Nobel information by name, year, sex, country, institution, nationality, religion, and so on. In addition, users can obtain full information on each laureate and country if desired. For information on acquiring the CD-ROM, please communicate with the publisher as follows:

Nobel Prizes/CD
c/o The Americas Group
9200 Sunset Blvd., Suite 404
Los Angeles, CA 90069-3506 USA

Tel: (1) 310 278 8037
Fax: (1) 310 271 3649
EM: hrmg@aol.com
www.americasgroup.com